MY THREE YEARS IN AMERICA

MY THREE YEARS IN AMERICA

BY

COUNT BERNSTORFF

NEW YORK
CHARLES SCRIBNER'S SONS
1920

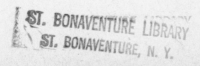

THE SCRIBNER PRESS

CONTENTS

CONTENTS

MY THREE YEARS IN AMERICA

MY THREE YEARS IN AMERICA

INTRODUCTION

MY FUNDAMENTAL POLITICAL VIEWS BEFORE AND DURING THE WAR

It was in my own home, the German Embassy in London, where the atmosphere was entirely political, that I learned my first steps in politics. My father did not belong to that class of diplomats, so prevalent to-day, who treat politics as an occupation to be pursued only in their spare time. His whole life was consecrated to the cause of the German nation, and from my earliest childhood my mind was filled with the same idea, to the exclusion of all others.

Owing to my father's share in the negotiations which brought about the marriage of the Emperor Frederick with the Princess Royal of England, the Imperial couple became closely connected with my parents, and, as Crown Prince and Princess, frequently resided at the Embassy in London. It was the entourage of the Emperor Frederick that first inspired in me those political views, which, during a long diplomatic career, gradually crystallized into the deep-rooted convictions of my political outlook. I believed Germany's salvation to lie in the direction of a liberal development of Unification and Parliamentary Government, as also in an attitude of consistent friendliness towards England and the United States of America. Thus, to use a modern phrase, I

1

was an avowed supporter of the Western Policy. At the present moment, while we are standing as mourners at the grave of our national hopes, I am more than ever convinced, that had this policy been steadily pursued, we should have been spared the catastrophe that has overtaken us.

On the other hand, I will not deny, that even the Oriental Policy would have proved a feasible political scheme, if only we had decided to pursue it in good time. Albeit, I am of opinion that even Bismarck had already started us in the direction of the Western Policy, when in 1879 he decided in favor of Austria-Hungary and not Russia. Despite all that the careworn recluse of Friedrichsruhe may have written against Caprivi's policy, which was decidedly Western in tendency, he was himself the founder of the Triple Alliance, which, without the good-will of England, could not have come into existence. Had we pursued an Eastern Policy, though it would ultimately have led to the sacrifice and partition of Austria-Hungary, it would not have secured us those advantages in the Orient of which Marschall speaks. Nevertheless, I have always regretted that we sent such a first-rate man to Constantinople, for him ultimately to become the able director of the false policy which we pursued there. There is an Oriental proverb which says: "Never lay your load on a dead camel's back."

If, as I always used to hope, we had resolved to adopt the Western Policy, we should in any case have had to be prepared, in certain circumstances, to venture with England's help upon a war against Russia. And the experiences of the Five-Years War have taught us that we should have won such a conflict with ease. I never wanted a war with Russia, and was never an enemy of that country; but I believed that our position among the nations of the world would compel us to decide one way or the other, and I felt, just as Caprivi did, that we should not very well be able to avoid war. Even if, in the event of a war between the Triple Alliance and Russia and France, England had only maintained an attitude of friendly neutrality, this would have proved very much more favorable for us than the situation which developed out of the Encirclement Policy (*Einkreisungspolitik*). Furthermore, had we pursued the Western Policy, we should have had to reckon with the possibility of England's wishing to moderate, even in a perfectly friendly manner, our somewhat explosive economic development. I should not, however, have regarded this altogether as a disadvantage. For, truth to tell, we grew a little too rapidly. We ought, as "junior partners" in Britain's world-empire, to have gathered our strength more slowly. As an example of what I mean, take the policy which France and Japan have pursued since the beginning of the present century. If we had done the same, we should, at all events, have been saved from so seriously overheating the boilers of our industrial development, we should not have outstripped England as quickly as we undoubtedly could have done if we had been left to develop freely, but we should also have escaped the mortal danger which we drew upon ourselves by provoking universal hostility.

It is impossible now for me to demonstrate retrospectively that we should have been able to conclude an alliance with England. Prince Bülow denies that this was ever the case. Maybe that during his tenure of office this possibility did not offer a sufficient guarantee of future security to warrant our incurring the hostility of Russia. I am convinced, however, that an alliance with England would have been within our power, if we had pursued Caprivi's policy consistently, and the Kruger telegram had never been dispatched. Unfortu-

nately we have always had statesmen at the helm in
Germany,—Bismarck not excepted,—the bulk of whose
views and knowledge were essentially continental, and
who never felt quite at home with English ways of
thinking. I feel perfectly satisfied on this point, however, that English commercial jealousy, with which we
naturally had to reckon, would not have proved an insuperable obstacle to a good understanding with England, provided that we had declared ourselves ready, if
necessary, to fight Russia.

The policy of the free hand, which we pursued until
the outbreak of war, aimed at the highest possible results. Prince Bülow, who was the inaugurator of this
policy, might possibly have known how to steer us
through the "Danger-Zone" without provoking war.
And then in a few years to come, we should have become
so strong and should have left the Danger-Zone so very
far behind us, that, as far as human judgment could
tell, we should no longer have had any need to fear war.
German naval construction from the beginning of the
present century certainly made our relationship to
England very much worse, while it also materially increased the danger of our position from the standpoint
of world-politics. The Bülow-Tirpitz notion of a *Risiko-
flotte,** may, however, only have been practicable on
condition that our diplomacy were sufficiently skilful to
avoid war, as long as the "risk" idea in England was
not able, of itself, to maintain peace.

German foreign policy had been ably conducted by
Bismarck; but, in keeping with the times, it had been
almost exclusively Continental and European. At the
very moment when Bismarck withdrew from the arena,
Germany's era of world-politics began. It was not the

---

*Literally: a fleet for risks or for taking risks; a fleet to be used at a
venture.

free bloom of our statesmen's own creative powers; but a bitter necessity, born of the imperative need of providing Germany's increasing population with sufficient foodstuffs. But it was not our world-politics, as such, that brought about our downfall; but the way we set to work in prosecuting our policy. The Triple Alliance, with its excellent Reinsurance Treaty, did not constitute a sufficiently powerful springboard from which to take our plunge into world-politics. The Reinsurance contract could not be anything but a makeshift, which merely deferred the inevitable choice which had to be made between Russia and Austria-Hungary. In the course of time, we should either have had to decide entirely in favor of Russia, in the manner outlined above, or we should have had to try to come to an understanding with England, upon terms which, at all events, we should not have been at liberty to choose for ourselves. Unfortunately, however, it was an axiom of post-Bismarckian German politics, that the differences between Russia and England were irreconcilable, and that the Triple Alliance would have to constitute the needle-index of the scales between these two hostile Powers. This proposition was incessantly contested both verbally and in writing by Herr von Holstein, who was then the leading spirit at the Foreign Office. He perceived that its chief flaw was the weak point in the Triple Alliance itself,— that is to say, the differences between Austria-Hungary and Italy on the one hand, and Italy's dependence upon England's superior power in the Mediterranean on the other. Furthermore, he recognized the prodigious possibility, which was not beyond the art of English statesmanship, of a compromise between England and Russia. He did not see, however, how the hostility of the French to ourselves would serve as a medium for this universal coalition against us.

In the last Entente Note of the Five-Years War there is the following passage:

"For many years the rulers of Germany, true to the Prussian tradition, strove for a position of dominance in Europe. They required that they should be able to dictate and tyrannize to a subservient Europe, as they dictated and tyrannized over subservient Germany."

We Germans know that this indictment is a lie; but unfortunately all unprejudiced Germans must acknowledge that for years this lie has been believed outside Germany. We, for our part, cherished similar views about our enemies, nor did we make a sufficient effort to dissipate their prejudices. On the contrary we constantly lent color to them by means of the extravagant and high-flown speeches, which formed the accompaniment to our world and naval policy, and by means of our opposition to pacifism, disarmament, and arbitration schemes, etc., etc. The extent to which our attitude at the Hague Conference damaged us in the eyes of the whole world is no longer a secret to anybody. As Heinrich Friedjung rightly observes:

"At the Hague Conference German diplomacy delivered itself up to the vengeance of the pacifists, like a culprit."

During my tenure of office in Washington I succeeded on three occasions in coming to an agreement with the Government there regarding the terms of an arbitration treaty. All three treaties were, however, rejected in Berlin, and consequently in America I never ceased from being questioned reproachfully as to the reason why the United States had been able to conclude arbitration treaties with every other State in the world, but not with Germany.

The Entente Note, already quoted above, contained this further statement:

"As soon as their preparations were complete, they encouraged a subservient ally to declare war against Serbia at forty-eight hours' notice, knowing full well that a conflict involving the control of the Balkans could not be localized and almost certainly meant a general war. In order to make doubly sure, they refused every attempt at conciliation and conference until it was too late, and the world war was inevitable for which they had plotted, and for which alone among the nations they were fully equipped and prepared."

The leaders of the Entente Powers would like to exalt this distortion of history into a dogma, in order that their various peoples may not bring any unpleasant charges against them. And yet the historical truth is already pretty clear to all who look for it honestly and without prejudice. The German Government believed that the Serbian propaganda would annihilate Austria-Hungary, and hoped, moreover, that her last faithful ally would experience a political renaissance as the result of her chastisement of Serbia. That is why they gave Count Berchtold a free hand, in the belief that Count Bülow's success over the Bosnian crisis could be repeated. Meanwhile, however, the situation had changed. Russia and France, relying upon England's help, wanted to risk a war. When the German Government saw this they tried, like a driver of a car about to collide with another vehicle, to jam on all breaks, and to drive backwards. But it was then too late. The mistake our Government made was to consent to Austria-Hungary's making so daring an experiment, at a moment of such critical tension.

It is not true either that we were thoroughly equipped and prepared for war. We had neither sufficient supplies of munitions, foodstuffs and raw materials, nor any plan of campaign for a war with England. Be this as it may, we should not have been defeated if we had abided firmly by our defensive policy. The heroic spirit displayed by the German people surpassed all bounds, and they believed quite honestly that they were fighting a war of defence. If our policy had been conducted with corresponding consistency we should have saved our position in the world. We ought always to have borne in mind the analogy of the Seven Years War, in order to have been ready at any moment to extricate ourselves from the hopeless business with the least possible amount of loss.

After the first battle of the Marne, President Wilson consistently maintained that a decision was no longer possible by force of arms. This view, which I also shared, gave us some common ground, upon which, despite our other differences, we were able to some extent to work together.

Regarding Dr. Wilson's personality certain doubts have been and are still entertained by many people. He is the most brilliant and most eloquent exponent of the American point of view. But he does not devote the same energy and consistency to the execution of his various programmes as he does to their formation. There can be no question that, as a result both of his origin and his training, the President is very much under the sway of English thought and ideals. Nevertheless, his ambition to be a Peacemaker and an *Arbiter Mundi* certainly suggested the chance of our winning him over to our side, in the event of our being unable to achieve a decisive victory with the forces at our disposal. In this case, Wilson, as the democratic leader of the strongest neutral Power, was the most suitable person to propose and to bring about a Peace by arrangement.

After the opening of the U-boat campaign, two alternatives remained open to us, one of which we were compelled to choose. If the prospects of a U-boat war promised to secure a victory, it was naturally incumbent upon us to prosecute it with all possible speed and energy. If, as I personally believed, the U-boat war did not guarantee a victory, it ought, owing to the enormous amount of friction to which it could not help giving rise, under all circumstances to have been abandoned; for, by creating American hostility, it did us more harm than good.

I, as the German Ambassador, in the greatest neutral State, with the evidences of American power all about me, could not help feeling it my duty to maintain our diplomatic relations with the United States. I was convinced that we should most certainly lose the war if America stepped in against us. And thus I realized ever more and more the supreme importance of preventing this from taking place.

My communications to the Central Government were framed with a view to inducing them also to adopt this attitude; but they, of course, had to form their conclusions, not from one source, but from all the sources of information they possessed. At all events, isolated as I was at Washington, I could not confine myself merely to the task of furnishing my Government with information; but was compelled on occasion to act on my own initiative, in order to prevent any premature development in the diplomatic situation from becoming utterly hopeless.

The policy for which I stood not only promised the negative success of keeping America out of the war, but it also offered the only prospect there was of obtaining, with neutral help, a Peace by arrangement. My belief that such a peace could have been obtained through Dr. Wilson is, of course, no longer susceptible of proof to-day. It may perhaps sound improbable in view of the President's behavior at Versailles. It is my opinion, however, that, previous to the 31st of January, 1917, Dr. Wilson's attitude towards us was radically different. I base my assumption that Wilson might in those days have assisted us in obtaining a Peace by negotiation upon the following points:

(1) A Peace by mediation was the only way in which the United States could avoid becoming involved in the war, and this is what the American public opinion of the day wished above all to prevent.

(2) It is true that even if he had wished to do so, Wilson could not have declared war on England, neither could he by any exercise of force have prevented the delivery of munitions to the Allies, or have compelled England to observe the rights of nations. He could, however, have obliged England to conclude a Peace by arrangement with us; not only because in so doing he would have had the support of American public opinion, but also because such a policy was in keeping with the best political interests of the United States.

I therefore pursued the policy of Peace with undeviating consistency, and to this day I still believe it to have been the only right policy. A thorough prosecution of the U-boat campaign was also a feasible scheme. But the worst thing that we could possibly do, was to steer the zigzag course; for by so doing we were certain not only to cause constant vexations to America, but, by our half measures and partial pliancy, also to drive Mr.

Wilson even further and further into the inflexible attitude of a policy of prestige. Unfortunately, however,
it was precisely this zigzag course that we adopted; and
thus, in addition to destroying the prospects which
my policy had offered, according to the view of the
Naval people, we also crippled the effects of the U-boat
campaign.

My policy might best be described as that of "a silent
resolve to obtain Peace." It was utterly wrong to publish our readiness for Peace broadcast. We should have
presented a strong front to the outside world, and we
should have increased the powers of resistance which
we actually possessed by emphasizing our strength both
to our people at home and to other States. According
to my view, we ought, after the first battle of the Marne,
to have recognized in our heart of hearts that victory
was out of the question, and consequently we should
have striven to conclude a Peace, the relatively unfavorable terms of which might perhaps have temporarily
staggered public opinion in Germany and created some
indignation. It was not right, however, to allow defer-
ence to public opinion to outweigh other considerations,
as it did in our case. The political leaders of the Empire ought to have kept the High Military Command,
which from its point of view naturally demanded firmer
"assurances" than the general situation warranted, more
thoroughly within bounds, just as Bismarck did. Presumably the High Military Command would have been
able to perform its duties quite as efficiently if it had
been prevented from exercising too much influence on
the policy which aimed at a conclusion of peace.

As a politician I consider that the ultimate cause of
our misfortune was our lack of a uniform policy both
before and during the war. If, at the time of Bismarck's
retirement, we had made a timely and resolute decision

either in favor of the Western Policy that he advocated, or in favor of the Eastern Policy, we should have prevented the development of a situation in the politics of the world which ultimately led to our own undoing. If, during the war, however, we had completely abandoned the U-boat campaign, and had made every possible effort to come to an understanding with America, we should, in my opinion, have been able to extricate ourselves from it satisfactorily. Be this as it may, it is also possible that if the U-boat campaign had been prosecuted resolutely, and without any shilly-shallying—a thing I never wished—we should not have suffered so complete a collapse from the military, economic, political and moral point of view, as we must otherwise have done. According to my view it is the hesitating zigzag course that we pursued which is chiefly to blame for the fact that of all possible results of the epoch of German world-politics, the unhappiest for ourselves has come to pass. The Wilhelminian Age perished owing to the fact that no definite objects were either selected or pursued in good time, and, above all, because both before and during the war, two systems in the Government of the country were constantly at variance with each other and mutually corroding.

CHAPTER I

GERMANY AND THE UNITED STATES BEFORE THE WAR

ANYONE who has lived some time in the United States will feel with Goethe that "America is better off than our own Continent." Owing to the almost perfect autarchy existing there, grave economic problems never really arise. Nowhere else, during the whole course of my various diplomatic wanderings, have I ever seen a happier people, who looked more cheerfully into the future. In view of the comparatively sparse population of the country, intensive agricultural production has only become necessary in a few isolated districts; there are always purchasers in plenty for the rich surplus of raw materials available, and industry has not yet been directed solely towards export. As a result of these happy conditions, the American citizen feels but little interest for what goes on in other countries. In the period preceding the Five-Years War, if the political interests of the United States ever happened to cross those of Europe, it was almost exclusively in regard to American questions. As a proof of this we have only to think of the Spanish-American War, and of the various incidents relating to Venezuela; whereas it was only with difficulty that the German Government succeeded in inducing President Roosevelt's Administration to take part in the Algeciras Conference, at which the presence of the United States representative in no way alleviated our task.

13

Up to the time of the Five-Years War, the Foreign
Policy conducted from Washington was almost entirely
Pan-American, and the Monroe Doctrine was the beginning and end of it; for even if that versatile man, President Roosevelt, was fond of extending his activities to
other spheres, as, for instance, when he brought the
Russo-Japanese War to an end by the Peace of Portsmouth, the Panama Canal scheme remained his favorite
child. But in the case of the Russo-Japanese War, it
was home politics, which in America are chiefly responsible for turning the scales in regard to Foreign Policy,
that again played the principal part. Mr. Roosevelt
wished to win over to his side the very strong pacifist
element in America; whereas the Imperialists—particularly later on—deprecated these successful attempts at
mediation, because they prevented a further weakening
of both of the belligerent parties. Even Roosevelt's Secretary of State, John Hay, concerned himself actively
with the Far East, and was known in America as the
spiritual founder of the policy of the "Open Door." In
this particular matter, the German Government frequently acted hand in hand with the American, and it
was owing to this circumstance that the Foreign Office
at Berlin very much wished to have the United States
represented at the Algeciras Conference. The German
Government believed that the Americans would also declare themselves in favor of the "Open Door" even in
Morocco. This assumption, however, turned out to be
a false one, owing to the fact that the political and economic interest shown by the United States for countries
on the other side of the Atlantic Ocean was not sufficiently
keen. The Algeciras Conference was a fairly trustworthy forecast of all that subsequently happened at the
Peace Conference at Versailles. Equally lacking in foundation was also the assumption, so prevalent in Ger-

many, that, as the result of their energetic Far-Eastern policy, the Americans would plunge themselves into a serious conflict with Japan.

The question of the Philippines, which arose out of the Spanish-American War and the Cuban affair, constitutes a certain contrast to the customary Pan-American Foreign Policy of the United States. A large number of Americans—possibly the majority—would like to relinquish the Philippines as soon as the inhabitants of these islands are in a position to rule themselves. At its inception, the question of the Philippines brought us into a conflict with the United States, which was remembered by Americans for years. Heinrich Friedjung, referring to this incident, says:

"Quite superfluously it occurred to the German Government to make our East-Asiatic Squadron, under Admiral Diederichs, appear before Manila precisely at the moment when, in 1898, the decision was made regarding the Philippines. This was done simply out of a pointless consciousness of power, without any intention to cause offence."

This criticism is partly justified. And yet the affair was somewhat different from the version of it which the American Ambassador, Andrew White, allowed to filter through; for, seeing that, as the United States did not intend to retain the Philippines, they could raise no objection to Germany's wishing to acquire them. Thanks to his friendly attitude towards Germany, Andrew White had, on his own initiative, exceeded his instructions and was duly censured by his Government for his zeal. Nevertheless, a misunderstanding had occurred, as the result of which the Berlin Foreign Office had acted in perfect good faith. In the public mind in the United States, however, the feeling still rankled that Germany had wished to make a demonstration against their Government; and the English Press, which at that time was hostile to us, applied the bellows enthusiastically to the glowing embers of American ill-humor.

The Venezuela affair, in the year 1902, which was a matter of lodging certain complaints against the Venezuelan Government, ended in a similar manner. Germany and England together sent their ultimatum to Venezuela, and when no heed was paid to it, they instituted a blockade of a number of Venezuelan ports. It was at this time that I was appointed Secretary to the Embassy in London, where I had to conduct a good deal of the negotiations regarding the Venezuela question, with the Foreign Office. The whole affair, as initiated by ourselves, was, in proportion to the German claims, much too elaborate. The first suggestion which led to the common action on the part of the British and ourselves, came from the English side; but we should have been wiser, from the point of view of our own advantage, if we had not listened to the suggestion. It was absolutely clear from the start that the American Government would raise objections to this sort of procedure, on the part of European powers, in South America, and that England, true to her usual custom, would climb down before the United States the moment she recognized plainly the latter's displeasure. And when public opinion in America raised a violent protest, and, incidentally, resolutely assumed that Germany wished to obtain a footing in Venezuela, the English Press attacked us in the rear by asserting that the whole affair had been engineered by Germany, in order to embroil England with the United States. At President Roosevelt's wish the matter was finally settled with America's help; but in the United States it left behind the widely prevalent impression that Germany would infringe the Monroe Doctrine the moment she had the power to do so.

President Taft, who in the year 1909 took President Roosevelt's place, endeavored, with his Secretary of State, Philander Knox, to develop still further the policy of the "Open Door," inaugurated by John Hay. Both gentlemen felt the keenest interest in the Far East. The former had been Governor of the Philippines, the latter had been closely connected with the Pittsburgh iron industry, and knew the need of extending its sphere of activities. Mr. Knox suggested the proposal of internationalizing the railways of Manchuria. When, however, this American notion met with response in Germany, and apart from its general rejection elsewhere, had the further effect of drawing Japan and Russia together again, Mr. Knox abandoned his active Far-Eastern policy, and confined himself to stimulating the large banks of America into becoming interested in the building of railways and other economic means of development in China. This policy was described as "Dollar Diplomacy" by the Democratic Opposition, and violently opposed. When, therefore, the votes went against the Republican Party, and President Wilson came to the helm, he let the Far-Eastern policy drop. High Finance immediately seized this opportunity in order to extricate itself from Chinese undertakings. It had only embarked upon "Dollar Diplomacy" at the request of the Government, and the venture had yielded but little profit, owing to the fact that Americans are not inclined to invest in foreign securities.

Secretary of State Knox's policy, which was always supported by us, accounted for the fact that the official relations between the German and American Governments were never more cordial than during the years 1909-13, in spite of a short disturbance resulting from a dispute over our potash exports to the United States. The best proof of how friendly the official relations of the two Governments were is shown by the ease with which this quarrel was settled. We were also successful in concluding a commercial agreement which was satisfactory to both sides, and overcame the danger of a customs war as the result of America's new customs tariffs; whereas Taft's economic plans, which aimed at reciprocity and union with Canada, came to grief for political reasons, as the result of Canadian Opposition, and left behind a bitter after-taste both in the United States, Canada and England.

Official diplomatic communications excepted, however, it must unfortunately be admitted, that mutual misunderstanding has been the principal feature of German-American relations. In Germany there was no understanding for the curious mixture of political sagacity, commercial acumen, tenacity and sentimentality, which goes to make up the character of the American people. The power of the Union was therefore underestimated by us, and the high-spirited utterances of American youthful strength were more disapproved of than was necessary, because they were interpreted as mere "bluff" and arrogance. We never sufficiently allowed for the fact that the Americans are very "emotional"—that is to say, that they are easily carried away by their feelings and then become uncertain. Political surprises in the United States are almost the rule.

On the other hand, Americans never give themselves time to learn to understand a foreign nation. A knowledge of foreign languages is by no means general in the United States. The Americans unconsciously borrow their thoughts and ideas from England, because it is the only nation whose literature and Press are accessible to them in the original tongue. Naturally this fact contributed very considerably, before the Five-Years War, towards making the comprehension of Germany difficult; because in those days German-English relations were growing more and more unfavorable every day, and this decline in friendliness found a powerful echo in the English Press and other literature. The English language exercises more absolute power in the United States than even in England itself. For example, it would never occur to any diplomat in Washington to transact his business in any other language than English. Whereas, in London, I never once heard the French Ambassador pronounce one word of English—even in an after-dinner speech—M. Jusserand in Washington always spoke English. But, in spite of the claim that the French make, that their language prevails in diplomatic circles, he could not have done otherwise; because I have never, during the whole of the eight years of my official activities in Washington, met one Secretary of State who had mastered any other language than English. It is obvious that this state of affairs opens all doors and avenues to English political and cultural influences.

Thus, before the outbreak of the Five-Years War, the majority of Americans already looked upon the Germans, however unconsciously, through the optics of the English Press and English literary publications. A large number of people in the United States honestly believed, moreover, in the rumored German scheme to seize the empire of the world. Our enormous successes in the economic field provoked unbounded admiration and led, on the one hand, to an over-estimation of our power, which did not prove favorable to us politically, while, on the other hand, the Americans who frequently indulged in generalizations about Germany were prone to judge us according to the German-American Beer-Philistine, whom they disdainfully called a "Dutchman." The Americans' view of the German people wavered between these two extremes; but every year opinion tended to incline more and more in the direction of the former. The phantom of a German world-empire, extending from Hamburg to Bagdad, had already taken possession of the American mind long before the war; and in the United States it was feared that the next step would be that this world-empire would infringe the Monroe Doctrine and found colonies in South America. Professor Baumgarten, in an entertaining book, has pointed out to what extent the publications of the Pan-German party contributed towards promoting such conceptions in America.

Our Press was a little too fond of making attacks on the Monroe Doctrine in particular. I was always of the opinion that we ought, openly and officially, to have recognized this American article of faith. As regards the Monroe Doctrine, the question is not one of Right, but one of Power. We certainly had not the power to infringe the Monroe Doctrine, even if we had had the intention, which was never the case. It would, therefore, have been more wise to acknowledge it, and thus to improve the political attitude, towards ourselves, of a country on which we were so very much dependent for a number of our raw-material supplies. I have often wondered whether the Imperial Government would not have regarded it as its duty to avoid war at all costs, if our economic dependence upon foreign countries had been more clearly recognized. German prosperity was based to a great extent on the Germans overseas, who had settled down in every corner of the earth, just as in former days the Greeks had settled all over the Roman Empire. The Germans overseas constituted a colonial empire, which was a far more precious source of wealth than many a foreign possession belonging to other Powers. In my opinion not sufficient allowance was made for this state of affairs.

Finally, a further cause of misunderstandings, as I have already mentioned in the Introduction, was to be found in the general disfavor with which American pacifist tendencies were regarded in Germany. Nine-tenths of the American nation are pacifists, either through their education and sentimental prepossession in favor of the principle, or out of a sense of commercial expediency. People in the United States did not understand that the German people, owing to their tragic history, are compelled to cultivate and to uphold the martial spirit of their ancestors. The types of the German officer of the reserve and of the members of the student corps are particularly unsympathetic to the American, and, for certain German foibles, all sign of that understanding that readily forgives, is entirely absent in the United States, owing to the fact that our historical development is not realized over there.

Although the Americans are largely and unconsciously swayed by the influence of English ideas, we must be careful to avoid falling into the error, so common in Germany, of regarding them as Anglo-Saxons. The Americans themselves, in their own country, scarcely ever call themselves Anglo-Saxons. This term is used by the English when they are anxious to claim their American cousins as their own. Occasionally, too, an American may use the expression when making an after-dinner speech at some fraternizing function. As a rule, however, the Americans insist on being Americans, and nothing else. On the 11th May, 1914, at a memorial service for the men who fell at Vera Cruz, President Wilson, in one of his finest speeches, said:

"Notice how truly these men were of our blood. I mean of our American blood, which is not drawn from any one country, which is not drawn from any one stock, which is not drawn from any one language of the modern world; but free men everywhere have sent their sons and their brothers and their daughters to this country in order to make that great compounded nation which consists of all the sturdy elements and of all the best elements of the whole globe. I listened again to this list of the dead with a profound interest, because of the mixture of the names, for the names bear the marks of the several national stocks from which these men came. But they are not Irishmen or Germans or Frenchmen or Hebrews or Italians any more. They were not when they went to Vera Cruz; they were Americans; every one of them, with no difference in their Americanism because of the stock from which they came. They were in a peculiar sense of our blood, and they proved it by showing that they were of our spirit, that no matter what their derivation, no matter where their people came from, they thought and wished and did the things that were American; and the flag under which they served was a flag in which all the blood of mankind is united to make a free nation.''

The above words of President Wilson are the key to the attitude of the Americans who are of German origin. True, these people, almost without exception, still cling to their old home with heartfelt affection; but they are Americans, like the rest of the nation. "Germania is our mother, and Columbia is our bride," said Carl Schurz, and with these words he described the situation in a nutshell. Just as a man shall "leave his father and his mother, and shall cleave unto his wife," so the man who is generally styled the German-American decides in favor of his new home-land, when a conflict arises between America and Germany. He will, however, do anything in his power to avoid such a conflict. Even before the war, we in Germany entirely failed to understand the difficult and delicate position of the American of German origin. And during the war this was more than ever the case. The question of the "German-Americans" has never been dealt with tactfully in Germany. Our greatest mistake was to expect too much from them. The Americans of German origin have retained in their new home all the failings and virtues of the German people. *We* could not, therefore, blame them if they showed less interest and less understanding in regard to political questions than the rest of America; for did they not, on the other hand, distinguish themselves by their respect for the established order of things, and by the fidelity and industry with which they pursued their various callings? The inevitable consequence of these national qualities was that they did not exercise the political influence which would have been only in keeping with their numerical superiority. For instance, I might mention that, on the occasion when I first visited Milwaukee, I was welcomed by an Irish mayor, a circumstance which somewhat surprised me, seeing that at the time the town contained from 300,000 to 400,000 Germans.

In consequence of the state of affairs described above, the principal object of German policy in the United States before the war was to try to bring about a more satisfactory understanding between the two peoples. Prince Henry's journey to America, the exchange of University professors and school teachers, which took place on this occasion, the visits of the two fleets, the American Institute in Berlin, and similar more or less successful undertakings served the same purpose. German diplomatic representatives were instructed to promote this policy with all their power. When I was appointed Ambassador in Washington, the Kaiser's and the Chancellor's principal injunction, in taking leave of me, was that I should enlighten public opinion in the United States regarding the peaceful and friendly intentions of German policy. Prince Bülow also said to me that I must without fail bring the negotiations about an Arbitration Treaty with the United States, which had been left unfinished owing to the death of my predecessor, to a satisfactory conclusion. Despite these definite instructions, the German Government, as I have already pointed out, ultimately blundered and stumbled over legal quibbles. In any case, however, Prince Bülow had meanwhile vacated his office. The effect upon the American mind of our obstruction of this matter should not be under-estimated. It helped not a little to convince public opinion in the United States of the alleged warlike intentions of the German people.

In accordance with American custom, the semi-official and semi-private activities concerned with fostering a better understanding between the two States had to be published to the whole world, and this had the inevitable disadvantage of provoking opposition, both in Germany and in the United States, among all those who had reasons for being hostile. Unfortunately, the official representatives of Germany in Washington were always a thorn in the side of a certain section of the German Press, whenever they tried, in consideration of the American attitude of mind and social customs, to introduce a warmer feeling into the relations between the two sides. Even in the time of my predecessor, Speck von Sternburg, the German Embassy was on such occasions charged with softness and an excessive desire to become adapted to American ways; and this remained the case during my tenure of office.

Our Press in general, moreover, never revealed a sufficient amount of interest or understanding in regard to

American affairs. There were only a very few German newspaper correspondents in the United States, and those that did happen to be there were too poorly paid to be able to keep properly in touch with American social life. About twelve months before the war, the well-known wealthy German-American, Hermann Sielcken, offered to help me out of this difficulty by undertaking to pay the salary of a first-rate American journalist, of German origin, who was to reside in Washington, and act as the representative there of Wolff's telegraphic bureau. I immediately took steps to organize this telegraphic service. Very shortly afterwards, however, I was informed by Berlin, that the telegrams would be too expensive, as the subject was not of enough interest, and in this case the Wolff Bureau would only have had to defray the cost of the actual telegrams. This was the way the supply of news was organized in a country that imagined it was practising world-politics.

Mr. Wilson took up his quarters in the White House, Washington, about a year before the war, and opened his period of office with several internal reforms. Then came the American-Mexican crisis, and relations with Europe in general, and Germany in particular, therefore, fell somewhat into the background.

Woodrow Wilson was a University don and an historian. His works are distinguished by their brilliant style and the masterly manner in which he wields the English language—a power which was also manifested in his political speeches and proclamations. Mr. Wilson sprang into political and general fame when he was President of the University of Princeton, and was elected as Governor of the State of New Jersey. Even in those days he displayed, side by side, on the one hand, his democratic bias which led him violently to oppose the aristocratic student-clubs, and on the other, his egocentric and autocratic leanings which made him inaccessible to any advice from outside, and constantly embroiled him with the governing council of the University. As Governor of New Jersey, The Holy Land of "Trusts," Mr. Wilson opened an extraordinarily sharp campaign against their dominion. Mr. Roosevelt, it is true, had spoken a good deal against the trusts, but he had done little. He could not, however, have achieved much real success, because the Republican Party was too much bound up with the trusts, and dependent on them. At the time when Mr. Roosevelt wanted to take action, he also succeeded in splitting up his party, so that real reform could only be expected from the Democratic side. The conviction that this was so was the cause of Mr. Wilson's success in the Presidential election of 1912.

In regard to external politics, Mr. Wilson was pacifistic, as was also his party; whereas the Imperialists belonged almost without exception to the Republican Party. In spite of "Wall Street," and the influence of English ideas and opinions upon American society, Pacifist tendencies largely prevailed in the United States before the outbreak of the Five-Years War; how much more was this the case, therefore, when Mr. Wilson, in accordance with American custom, gave the post of Secretary of State to the politician to whose influence he owed his nomination as candidate for the Presidency by the Democratic Party. Thus did Mr. William Jennings Bryan attain to the dignity of Secretary of State after he had thrice stood as a candidate for the Presidency without success.

In all political questions, Mr. Bryan followed a much more radical tendency than Mr. Wilson. His opponents call him a dishonest demagogue. I, on the contrary, would prefer to call Mr. Bryan an honest visionary and fanatic, whose passionate enthusiasm may go to make an exemplary speechmaker at large meetings, but not a statesman whose concern is the world of realities. He who in his enthusiasm believes he will be able to see his ideal realized in this world next Thursday week is not necessarily dishonest on that account, even if he overlooks the fact that things are going very badly indeed.

It was believed in a large number of circles that Mr. Bryan would not accept the post of Secretary of State, for even at that time everybody who was in the know was already aware that Mr. Wilson could only tolerate subordinates and not men with opinions of their own. Mr. Bryan, however, felt the moral obligation, at least to attempt to give his radical views a chance of succeeding, and declared, as he took over the post, that so long as he was Secretary of State the United States would never go to war. He even wanted this principle to be generally accepted by the rest of the world, and with this end in view, submitted to all foreign Governments the draft of an Arbitration and Peace-Treaty, which was to make war utterly impossible in the future. As is well known, the German Government, unlike all the others, refused to fall in with Mr. Bryan's wishes. The Secretary of State was a little mortified by this, even though he still hoped that we should ultimately follow the example of the other Powers. Every time we met, he used to remind me of his draft Arbitration Treaty, which I had forwarded to Berlin. Later on I often regretted that we did not fall in with Mr. Bryan's wishes; who, by the by, during the war, again returned to the question, but in vain. If the treaty had been signed by us, it would most probably have facilitated the negotiations about the U-boat campaign.

The diplomatic corps in Washington thus found itself confronted by an entirely new situation. The Republican Party had been at the helm for sixteen years, and had now to vacate every one of the administrative posts. Even our personal intercourse with the President was governed by different formalities from those which existed in the days of his predecessors. Mr. Roosevelt liked to maintain friendly relations with those diplomats whose company pleased him. He disregarded the old traditional etiquette, according to which the President was not allowed to visit the Ambassadors or any private houses in Washington. The friendly relations that existed between Mr. Roosevelt and Baron Speck von Sternburg are well known. When in the year 1908, after this gentleman's decease, I assumed his post at Washington, Mr. Roosevelt invited me to the White House on the evening after my first audience, to a private interview, in which every topic of the day was discussed. Invitations of this kind were of frequent occurrence during the last two months of Roosevelt's administration, which, at the time of my entering office, was already drawing to its close. For instance, Mr. Roosevelt showed me the draft of the speech which after his retirement he delivered at the University of Berlin.

My dealings with President Taft were on the same footing; for he also was in favor of an amicable and unconventional relationship. On one occasion he invited me to join him in his private Pullman on a journey to his home in Cincinnati, where we attended the musical festival together. On another occasion, he suddenly appeared, without formal notice, at the Embassy, while we were holding a ball in honor of his daughter, and later on he accepted an invitation to my daughter's wedding.

President Wilson, who by inclination and habit is a recluse and a lonely worker, does not like company. He re-introduced the old etiquette and confined himself only to visiting the houses of Cabinet members, which had been the customary tradition. He also kept himself aloof

from the banquets, which are such a favorite feature of
social life in America, and severely limited the company
at the White House. Thus the New Year Reception was
discontinued entirely. This attitude on the part of the
President was the outcome of his tastes and inclinations.
But I certainly do not believe that he simply developed
a theory out of his own peculiar tastes, as so often happens in life. I am more inclined to believe that Mr. Wilson regarded the old American tradition as more expe-
dient, on the grounds that it enabled the President to
remain free from all intimacy, and thus to safeguard
the complete impartiality which his high office demanded.
The peculiar friendship which unites Mr. Wilson with
Mr. House is no objection to this theory, for the latter
has to some extent always been in the position of a minister without portfolio. An adviser of this sort, who
incurs no responsibility by the advice he gives, is more
readily accepted by American opinion than by any other,
because the President of the United States is known to
be alone and exclusively responsible, whereas his ministers are only looked upon as his assistants.

Generally speaking, the political situation in the
United States before the Five-Years War was as follows: On the one hand, owing to the influence of English ideas, which I have already mentioned, it was to
be expected that a feeling of sympathy with the Entente
would probably preponderate in the public mind; while
on the other hand, owing to the general indifference that
prevailed with regard to all that happened in Europe,
and to the strong pacifist tendencies, no interference in
the war was to be expected from America, unless unfore-
seen circumstances provoked it. At all events it was
to be feared that the inflammability of the Americans'
feelings would once again be under-estimated in Germany, as it had been already. It has never been prop-

erly understood in our country, despite the fact that the Manila and Venezuela affairs might have taught us a lesson in this respect. The juxtaposition in the American people's character of Pacifism and an impulsive lust of war should have been known to us, if more sedulous attention had been paid in Germany to American conditions and characteristics. The American judges affairs in Europe, partly from the standpoint of his own private sentiment of justice, and partly under the guidance of merely emotional values; but not, as was generally supposed in Germany, simply from a cold and business-like point of view. If this had been reckoned with in Germany, the terrible effect upon public opinion in America of the invasion of Belgium and of the sinking of the *Lusitania*—particularly in view of the influence of English propaganda—would have been adequately valued from the start.

On May 17th, 1915, in a report addressed to the Imperial Chancellor, I wrote as follows:

"It is not a bit of good glossing over things. Our best plan, therefore, is frankly to acknowledge that our propaganda in this country has, as the result of the *Lusitania* incident, completely collapsed. To everyone who is familiar with the American character this could have been foreseen. I therefore beg leave to point out in time, that another event like the present one would certainly mean war with the United States. Side by side in the American character there lie two apparently completely contradictory traits. The cool, calculating man of business is not recognizable when he is deeply moved and excited —that is to say, when he is actuated by what is here called 'emotion.' At such moments he can be compared only to an hysterical woman, to whom talking is of no avail. The only hope is to gain time while the attack passes over. At present it is impossible to foresee what will be the outcome of the *Lusitania* incident. I can only hope that we shall survive it without war. Be this as it may, however, we can only resume our propaganda when the storm has subsided."

Here I should like to intrude a few of my own views regarding the importance of public opinion in the United States.

In Europe, where people are constantly hearing about the truly extraordinary and far-reaching authority of the American President—the London *Times* once said that, after the overthrow of the Russian Czar, the President of the United States was the last remaining autocrat—it is difficult to form a correct estimate of the power of public opinion in the Union. In America, just as no mayor can with impunity ignore the public opinion of his city, and no governor the public opinion of his state, so the President of the Republic, despite his far-reaching authority, cannot for long run counter to the public opinion of his country. The fact has often been emphasized by Mr. Wilson himself, among others, that the American President must "keep his ear to the ground"—that is to say, must pay strict attention to public opinion and act in harmony with it. For the American statesman, whose highest ambition consists either in being re-elected, or at least in seeing his party returned to power, any other course would amount to political suicide; for any attempt at swimming against the tide will certainly be avenged at the next elections.

It must be remembered that public opinion in the United States is seldom so homogeneous and unanimous a thing as, for example, in England. Particularly in questions of foreign politics, public opinion in the Union, stretching, as it does, over a whole continent, reacts in widely varying ways in different localities, and to a very different degree. Thus, in the States bordering on the Atlantic coast, which are more closely in touch with the Old World, there is, as a rule, a very definite public opinion on European questions, while the West remains more or less indifferent. On the other hand, in the Gulf States a very lively interest is taken by the public in the Mexican problem, and the Pacific States are closely concerned with the Japanese question, matters which arouse hardly more than academic interest in other localities. This is also reflected in the American Daily Press, which does not produce papers exerting equal influence over the whole nation, but rather, in accordance with the customary geographical division of the Union into seven economic spheres of interest—namely, New York, New England, Middle Atlantic States, Southern States, Middle West, Western and Pacific States, comprises seven different daily presses, each of which gives first place to quite a different problem from the rest. It is true that the New York Press is certainly the most important mirror of American public opinion on European questions. Nevertheless, this importance should not lead to the erroneous assumption that the American Press and the New York Press are synonymous terms. The perusal of the latter does not suffice for the formation of a reliable judgment of American public opinion, with regard to certain questions which concern the whole nation; rather it is necessary also to study the leading papers of New England, the Middle Atlantic States, and particularly the West. The reports of German and English correspondents on feeling in America, which, as so often happens, are based purely on the New York Press, frequently play one false, if one relies on them for an estimate of the public opinion of the whole nation. The "Associated Press," therefore, makes it a rule with all questions of national importance, not only to reproduce extracts from the New York Press, but also to publish précis of the opinions of at least fifty leading journals from all parts of the Union.

The American daily papers are more important as a medium for influencing public opinion than as a mirror for reflecting it. The United States is the land of propaganda *par excellence!* Every important enterprise, of no matter what nature, has its Press agent; the greatest of all is the propaganda lasting for months, which is carried on before the biennial elections, and of the magnitude of which it is difficult for the average European to gain any conception. It is therefore not surprising that the political leaders of the country make very wide use of the Press in important questions of foreign politics, to influence public opinion in favor of the Government policy. Not only the great news agencies, but also all leading newspapers of the Union maintain their permanent special correspondents in Washington, and these are received almost daily by the Secretary of State, and as a rule once a week by the President. The information that they receive at these interviews they communicate to their papers in the greatest detail, without naming the high officials from whom it has emanated, and in this way they naturally act as megaphones through which the views of the Government are spread throughout the whole country. In foreign questions it was often striking how newspapers would hold back their comments until they had received in this way a *mot d'ordre* from Washington.

Of course this possibility for the Government to create opinion on concrete questions only applies so long as a firm public opinion has not already set in. As soon as the process of "crystallization," as it is called, is complete, there is nothing left for the Government but to follow the preponderating public opinion. Even a man like Mr. Wilson, who possesses an unusually high degree of self-will, has always followed public opinion, for the correct interpretation of which—apart from his own proverbial instinct—he commands the services of his secretary, Mr. Tumulty, and a large staff, as well as the organization of the Democratic party, which spreads through the length and breadth of the country. If, in a few exceptional cases, the President has set himself in opposition to public opinion, we might be sure that it would not be long before he again set his course on theirs.

CHAPTER II

THE GERMAN PROPAGANDA IN THE UNITED STATES

WHEN I received the news of the murder of Archduke Francis Ferdinand, I was dining with the Spanish Ambassador at the Metropolitan Club in Washington. Signor Riano and I were not for a moment in doubt as to the very serious, peace-menacing character of the incident, but we found little interest in the matter among the Americans in the club, who, as always, regarded European affairs with indifference. As to the results of the murder, I received in Washington no information, either officially or through the Press.

I therefore, on the 7th July, began my usual summer leave, which had been granted a few weeks before. For the last time I crossed the ocean on one of the proud German liners, and, indeed, on the finest of our whole merchant fleet, the *Vaterland*. For the last time I saw, on my arrival, the port of Hamburg and the lower Elbe in all their glory. Germans who live at home can hardly imagine with what love and what pride we foreign ambassadors and exiled Germans regarded the German shipping-lines.

A few days after I had arrived in my home at Starnberg there began strong public excitement and uneasiness over the political situation. However, of late years so many crises had been successfully averted at the eleventh hour, that this time, too, I hoped up to the last minute that a change for the better would set in. It seemed as though the responsibility for a war was too great to be

35

borne by any one man—whoever he might be—who would have to make the final decision.

On the wonderful, still summer evening of the 1st August, we heard across the Starnberger Lake, in all the surrounding villages, the muffled beat of drums announcing mobilization. The dark forebodings with which the sound of the drums filled me have fixed that hour indelibly in my memory.

The following day was devoted to preparations for the journey to Berlin, where I had to receive instructions before returning with all possible speed to Washington. The journey from Munich to Berlin, which could only be made in military trains, occupied forty-eight hours.

In the Wilhelmstrasse I had interviews with the authorities, the substance of which was instructions to enlighten the Government and people of the United States on the German standpoint. In doing so I was to avoid any appearance of aggression towards England, because an understanding with Great Britain had to be concluded as soon as possible. The Berlin view on the question of guilt was even then very much the same as has been set down in the memorandum of the commission of four of the 27th May, 1919, at Versailles, namely, that Russia was the originator of the war.

Further, I was informed at the Foreign Office, that in addition to some other additions to the staff of the Washington Embassy, the former Secretary of State of the Colonial Office, Dr. Dernburg, and Privy Councillor Albert, of the Ministry of the Interior, were to accompany me; the former as representative of the German Red Cross, the latter as agent of the "Central Purchasing Company." Dr. Dernburg's chief task, however, was to raise a loan in the United States, the proceeds of which were to pay for Herr Albert's purchases for the aforesaid company. For this purpose the Imperial Treasury supplied us with Treasury notes, which could only be made negotiable by my signature. This gave rise later to the legend that Dr. Dernburg was armed with millions for propaganda purposes.

Our journey was wearisome but passed off without incident. In forty-eight hours we reached Rotterdam, where we boarded the Dutch steamer *Noordam*. As we went aboard we were all in high spirits, for we had seen everywhere in Germany a wonderful, self-sacrificing and noble enthusiasm. On the steamer, however, which incidentally was badly overloaded, the picture changed. We suddenly found ourselves surrounded by hostile feeling, and among our fellow-passengers there were only a few friendly to the German cause. The bitter daily struggle toward which we were travelling was to begin on the ship. We plunged straight into it, and tried as far as possible to influence our fellow passengers.

At Dover the ship was inspected by a British officer; the inspection, however, passed off without any inconvenience to us, as in those first days of the war the regulations of international law were still to some extent respected. We had already made all preparations to throw the Treasury notes overboard, in case we were searched. As a curiosity I mention a comic interlude that occurred after we had left Dover Harbor. A friendly German-American from a Western State, who did not know who I was, but had recognized me as a German, accosted me with the remark: "Take care that you don't expose yourself to annoyance; the people on board think you are the German Ambassador in Washington." The excellent man was overcome with amazement when I admitted my identity. We had not had our names entered on the passengers' list, but apart from this made no secret of our journey, as it was already known in Rotterdam.

After an eleven days' voyage, we landed in New York

on the 23rd August. Our arrival was a relief, as during the journey we had been overwhelmed exclusively with enemy wireless reports of French victories. Every day we had received news of the annihilation of a fresh German Army Corps. In comparison with this mental torture, the cross-fire of questions from countless American Pressmen, not altogether friendly towards Germany, was comparatively easy to bear.

As is known, American public opinion at that time had been given a one-sided view of the causes and course of the war, for England, who, immediately after the declaration of war, had cut our Transatlantic cable, held the whole of the Transatlantic news apparatus in her hands. Apart from this, however, our enemies found from the beginning very important Allies in a number of leading American newspapers, which, in their daily issue of from three to six editions, did all they could to spread anti-German feeling. In New York the bitterest attacks on Germany were made by the *Herald* and the *Evening Telegram,* which were in close touch with France, as well as the *Tribune* and *Times,* which followed in England's wake; somewhat more moderate were the *Sun* and the *Globe;* the only neutrals were the *Evening Post* and the *American.* Outside New York the Press raged against us, particularly in New England and the Middle-Atlantic States. In the South and West we were also baited by the Press, but with considerably less intensity. The only papers which could be called neutral were those of the Hearst Press, which took up an outspoken National-American standpoint, and, in addition, the *Chicago Tribune,* the *Washington Post,* and a few minor newspapers. It was already very significant that papers like the *Boston Transcript,* the *Brooklyn Eagle,* the *Baltimore Sun,* and a few others opened their letter-boxes to anti-German articles, which, it is true, they condemned with fair regularity in their leading articles or editorial notes. Against this campaign, fed systematically and daily with British propaganda information—especially on the subject of German atrocities in Belgium—the small number of papers in the German language, which, moreover, were little heeded by public opinion, and at the head of which stood the old *New Yorker Staatszeitung* and the courageous weekly *Fatherland,* founded shortly after the outbreak of war by the young German-American, G. S. Vierick, could make but little headway.

On my arrival in New York, and during the next few weeks, I made an honest effort by daily interviews of the representatives of the leading daily newspapers to explain the German standpoint to the American public. I soon noticed, however, that these efforts were not only practically fruitless but that they were even fraught with certain dangers for me. The daily struggle with the Press was threatening to undermine my official position and to compromise my relations with the Washington Government so seriously that I should not have been in a position to carry through with success the diplomatic negotiations which were likely to be called for. I therefore considered it as my duty to the German people to give up, as far as I personally was concerned, all propaganda in favor of the German cause. Certainly I have had a good deal further to do with American journalists until the final rupture; but I categorically refused to grant interviews or to receive newspaper correspondents who were not prepared to treat my statements purely as confidential, private information.

I should like to take this opportunity to remark that the American journalist is far better than the reputation he enjoys in Europe. In spite of the hostile atmosphere which surrounded me in America I have never had to complain of an indiscretion. True, many minor New

York reporters whom I did not receive invented statements which I had never made; but such experiences are common to all politicians in America. Moreover, the results of these journalistic tricks were almost always local and were easily contradicted. In Washington such things never occurred. The journalists there were quite extraordinarily capable and trustworthy men, who always behaved like "gentlemen." My relations with them remained very friendly to the last. In so far as I was not forced to keep silence for political reasons I have always told them the real truth. Of course, I was as little capable as the American journalists of foreseeing that the policy I was representing was doomed to ultimate failure.

Just at the time when I gave up personal propaganda in order to devote myself to my political and diplomatic activities in Washington, the financial mission of Secretary of State Dr. Dernburg had failed. President Wilson had stated clearly that it would be an unneutral act for loans to be raised in the Union by the combatant States. Our friends in high financial circles in New York regarded this decision as favorable to Germany, for they foresaw—what actually happened—that for every million received by us, our enemies would raise a hundred millions. As a result of this decision of the President, Privy Councillor Albert had to finance his purchases as far as possible privately, while Dr. Dernburg, whose time was not fully occupied by his duties as delegate of the Red Cross, which had meanwhile been organized by Geheim Oberregierungrat Meyer Gerhardt and Rittmeister Hecker, would have left America if there had remained any possibility of doing so. There was not, however, as the English inspected all neutral ships shortly after they left the American ports and—in flagrant contravention of international law, which only allows the arrest of persons who are already enrolled in the fighting forces—summarily arrested and interned every German capable of bearing arms. As Dr. Dernburg was thus an unwilling prisoner in New York he began to write articles on the world-war for the daily Press. He had a gift for explaining the causes of the war in a quiet, interesting manner, and particularly for setting out the German standpoint in a conciliatory form. His propaganda work therefore met with extraordinary success. The editors of newspapers and periodicals pressed him to contribute to their columns, and the whole New York Press readily printed all the articles he sent in to contradict the statements of the anti-Germans.

Out of this activity developed, in co-operation with the Foreign Office, Dr. Dernburg's New York Press Bureau, a solution of the propaganda question which was exceedingly welcome to me. As a private person Dr. Dernburg could say and write much that could not be said officially and therefore could not come from me. Consequently I took it for granted that—in spite of certain suggestions to the contrary—Dr. Dernburg would not be attached to the Embassy, which would only hamper his work, and also that the Press Bureau would retain its independent and unofficial character. I may take it as a well-known fact that Washington is the political, and New York the economic, capital of the United States, which has always resulted in a certain geographical division of the corresponding diplomatic duties. It naturally had its disadvantages that there should be, apart from the Consulate-General, four other independent German establishments in New York, namely, the offices of Dr. Dernburg, Privy Councillor Albert, the military attaché Captain von Papen and the naval attaché Commander Boy-Ed. In order to keep, to some extent, in touch with these gentlemen, I occasionally travelled to New York and inter-

viewed them together in the Ritz-Carlton Hotel, where
I usually stayed and in which Dr. Dernburg lived; for
their offices, scattered as they were over the lower town,
and which, moreover, I never entered, were unsuitable
for the purpose. Our mutual personal relations were
always of the best. On the other hand, it was naturally
difficult to make any headway with our official business,
since each received independent instructions from Berlin.
This was least the case with Dr. Dernburg, because his
responsible authority as far as propaganda was concerned was partly the Foreign Office itself and partly
the semi-official "Central Office for Foreign Service."
The other three gentlemen, however, were all responsible
to home departments other than mine. Captain von
Papen and Commander Boy-Ed frequently held back
from me the instructions they had received from Berlin
in order not to embarrass the Embassy by passing on
military or naval information. Financially, too, the four
officials were completely independent and had their own
banking accounts, for which they had to account individ-
ually to their respective departments at home. Only
Privy Councillor Albert had, for the purchase on a large
scale of raw material, definite funds which were in any
event under my control. Concerning the activities of
these four gentlemen, countless legends have been spread
in America and in part have found their way to Germany.
In spite of all the reproaches levelled against them, and
indirectly against myself, with regard to propaganda—
I shall speak of the so-called conspiracies in Chapter V.
—nothing has reached my ears of which these gentlemen
need in any way be ashamed. Individual mistakes we
have, of course, all made; in view of the ferocity and
protraction of the struggle they were inevitable. But
in general the German propaganda in America in no way
deserves the abuse with which it has been covered, in

part, too, at home. If it had really been so clumsy or ineffective as the enemy Press afterwards claimed, the Entente and their American partisans would not have set in motion such gigantic machinery to combat it. One need only read G. Lechartier's book, "Intrigues et Diplomaties à Washington," to see what importance was attached to our propaganda by the enemy. In spite of all the bitterness which the author infuses into his fictitious narration, admiration for the German activity in the United States shines through the whole book. Further, at the end of 1918 a Commission of the Senate appointed to investigate German propaganda, as a result of the publication of protocols on this subject, repeatedly stated that its work had in no way been in vain, but rather its after effects had made themselves strongly felt "like poison gas" long after America's entry into the war. One may well venture to say that, had it not been for the serious crisis caused by the submarine war, it would probably in time have succeeded in completely neutralizing the anti-German campaign.

As regards our justification for openly championing the German cause before the people of the United States by written and spoken word, this is self-evident in a country which recognizes the principles of freedom of the Press and free speech. Apart from this, however, the American Government have themselves provided a precedent in this connection during the civil war, when President Lincoln in 1863 sent to England the famous preacher, Henry Ward Beecher, whose sympathies were strongly on the side of the Federals. Through his speeches, afterwards published as "Patriotic Addresses," he did much towards swaying public opinion in favor of the Northern States. In this war, too, America, after abandoning her neutrality, has carried out vigorous propaganda in neutral countries, as is shown by the mission of the well-known New York supporter of woman suffrage, Mrs. Norman Whitehouse, under the auspices of the official Press Bureau and with the special approval of Secretary of State Lansing. Moreover our justification has been expressly upheld by a statement of Commissioner Bruce Bielaski of the American Law Department, who appeared as chief witness against us before the above mentioned Commission of Inquiry. He declared that there was no law in the United States which, before her entry into the war, rendered illegal German or any other foreign propaganda. Why all this noise then?—it is reasonable to ask. Why, then, has the suggestion persisted at home and abroad, almost from the appearance of Dr. Dernburg until the present day, that we had, with our propaganda campaign, made ourselves guilty of treachery to the United States?

From the moral point of view, too, no exception can be taken to the German propaganda. The United States was neutral and wished to remain so. The German propaganda was working for the same end. I have never heard of a single case of bribery by our representatives. If money was spent on our side, it was purely for the purpose of spreading articles and pamphlets pleading United States neutrality. Applications were frequently made to us by writers and editors who from inner conviction were ready to write and circulate articles of this kind, but were not financially in a position to do so. The leaders of German propaganda would surely have been neglectful of their duty if in such cases they had not provided the necessary funds. All Governments in the world have always proceeded in a similar way, and in particular· that of the United States since their entry into the war, as is shown by the case of the *Freie Zeitung* of Bern—therefore equally in a neutral country. These facts must throw a strange light on the inquiry of the

American Senate into German propaganda, delayed as it was until last winter and carried through with such elaborate machinery. It is obvious that beneath it all there lay—what irony!—a purely propagandist purpose, namely, that of humiliating Germany in the person of her late official representative accredited to the United States, and to make her appear contemptible in the eyes of the uncritical public!

Whereas in the first months of the war no one in America had thought of connecting "German Propaganda" with anything shocking, our opponents afterwards succeeded in disseminating the idea that a few offences against the law committed by Imperial and American Germans represented an important, even the most important, part of the German propaganda work. So it was brought about that even in the time before America's entry into the war, everyone who openly stood up for Germany's cause was stamped by the expression "German Propagandist" as a person of doubtful integrity. The gradual official perpetuation of this admittedly misleading identification of our absolutely unexceptionable propaganda with a few regrettable offences against the American penal code—this and no other was the object of that inquiry by the Senate. The prejudicial headlines under which the published articles were printed, such as "Brewery and Brandy Interests" and "German-Bolshevist Propaganda," themselves sufficed to indicate that our propaganda was to be crucified between two "malefactors"; for to the average American citizen there is nothing more horrifying than the distillery on the one hand and Bolshevism on the other. In this connection I must not omit to mention that the great majority of the documents laid before the Commission had been secured by means of bribery or theft. It is also worth while to remind the reader of the significant words of Senator Reed, a member of the Commission, who said at one point in the examination: "I am interested in trying to distil some truth from a mass of statements which are so manifestly unfair and distorted that it is hard to characterize them in parliamentary language."

As for the fantastic figures with which the Americans have undertaken to estimate the cost of our propaganda, they rest—in so far as they are not simply the fruit of a malicious imagination—on the, to say the least of it, superficial hypothesis that all the money paid out by the different German offices from the outbreak of war until the breaking off of diplomatic relations between Germany and America, the amount of which has been arrived at on the strength of a minute scrutiny of the books of all the banks with which these offices have done business, were used for purposes of propaganda. As a matter of fact, of course, far the greater part of this outlay went to finance the very extensive purchases of Privy Councillor Albert as well as certain business transactions concluded by Captain von Papen, which will be discussed later. In comparison with this the sum we devoted to propaganda work was quite small. The Press Bureau was frequently very appreciably hampered by the fact that even for quite minor expenditure outside the fixed budget, previous sanction had to be obtained from Berlin. Consequently much useful work would have had to remain undone if, particularly in the first months of the war, self-sacrificing German-Americans to whom it was only of the slightest interest that the German point of view should be accurately and emphatically explained, had not placed small sums at the disposal of the leaders of our propaganda. In the two and a half years between the outbreak of war and the rupture between Germany and America the sums paid out from official funds for propaganda work in the Union—including minor contributions for other countries, as, for example, the pictures distributed from New York over South America and Eastern Asia—do not, all told, exceed a million dollars. That is surely only a small fraction of what England and France have expended during the war in order, in spite of very thorough preparation in peace time, to win over American public opinion to their cause. It is actually only a sixth of what, according to the *Chicago Tribune* on the 1st November, 1919, the official American Press Bureau of Mr. George Creel has spent in order to "cement enthusiasm for the war" during the eighteen months between America's entry into the war and the conclusion of the Armistice. The thirty-five to fifty million dollars which, according to the statements of our enemies, were swallowed up by German propaganda in the United States belong, therefore, to the realms of fable.

In this connection I must mention yet another, far more malicious legend, namely, the slander widely spread in America last year, that the funds collected in America for the German Red Cross were used to finance German propaganda. It is a fact that every dollar that went to the German Red Cross Delegation in New York was remitted to the home organization for which it was intended. Of course these funds were in the first place paid into the various New York banking accounts from which Dr. Dernburg drew the funds for the Press Bureau. But, as Captain Hecker has most definitely stated, their equivalent was remitted to Germany through the bank, regardless of the changes in the exchange.

Dr. Dernburg, in organizing the Press Bureau, availed himself of the assistance he found in New York. The suggestion, widely current in America and repeated by a member of the American Secret Service before the Senatorial inquiry, that this Press Bureau had formed, as it were, a part of the German mobilization, and that, therefore, the most skilled propaganda experts from Europe and the Far East had been gathered together in New York in order that, after a preliminary run there, they might be let loose on the American world, is a ridiculous invention. Just as Dr. Dernburg himself became a propagandist without any premeditation, so it was also the case with his colleagues. At first his only assistants were the New York Press Agent of the Hamburg-Amerika line, Herr M. B. Claussen, and after the entry of Japan into the war a Government official from that country who was unable to continue his journey to Germany, because the passport across the Atlantic granted him through the instrumentality of the State Department was rejected by the British authorities. This official, Dr. Alexander Fuehr, the interpreter of the Consulate-General in Yokohama, who had great experience in Press matters and possessed an intimate knowledge of American affairs, assisted by quite a small staff of assistants engaged in New York, issued the daily bulletins of the "German Information Service," which appeared for a year and consisted of translations of the substance of the German newspapers, comments on daily events and occasional interviews with people who had returned from Europe. It was Herr Claussens's duty to circulate the bulletins, the arrival of which was in no way kept secret, among the American Press, and to see to it that they should be reproduced as fully as possible, which was done, especially in the provincial Press.

Later, when the propaganda movement had developed to the extent of publishing and circulating leaflets, brochures and longer pamphlets, Dr. Dernburg decided to employ in the Press Bureau a well-known American publicist in the person of Mr. William Bayard Hale, who had already done good work, by speaking and writing, towards an unbiassed appreciation of the German point of view, and he was assisted by two younger New York journalists. Later, when the bureau took up war-picture and war-film propaganda, these were joined by two more young German Government officials, Dr. Mechlenburg and Herr Plage, who also were held up in America on their way from Japan. More than a dozen persons, including messengers, have never been employed by the Press Bureau at a time. Of the thirty-one trained propagandists imported from Germany who, according to Captain Lester's evidence before the Senatorial Commission, were supposed to have worked in the Press Bureau, in so far as their names were given in the protocols of the inquiry, we are assured by Herr Fuehr that not one was employed there!

In addition to his direction of the Press Bureau Dr. Dernburg, who continued with inexhaustible energy to write articles for the periodicals and instructive letters for the daily Press, was responsible for keeping in touch with the directors of the American Press. He also availed himself of invitations to speak in American and German circles, and sometimes in other places than New York. As far as I know he never founded any societies for propaganda purposes. On the other hand, when such societies which had arisen without his influence turned to him, he of course supported them by word and deed.

For all questions of propaganda Dr. Dernburg had the assistance of a small committee nominated by himself and consisting, in addition to Herren Albert, Meyer Gerhardt and Fuehr, of a few American journalists and business men. It was his custom to confer with this committee once or twice a month, when the general situation, the prevailing fluctuations of public opinion and the probable influence of the propaganda material about to be published, were discussed in detail.

With this entirely improvised and, as will be seen, very modest machinery, Dr. Dernburg began his campaign. The enemy statement that the German propaganda in the United States had been actually organized many years before the war, so that in 1914 we might have ready at our disposal an organization with branches in every part of the country, is unfortunately devoid of any foundation. It is a regrettable fact that, in spite of my repeated warnings to the authorities, nothing was ever done on the German side before the war. It is well known that at that time the power of public opinion in democratic countries was very little understood in Germany. It was thought at home—which is typical of the objective, matter-of-fact German national character—that it was much more important that the right should be done than that it should be recognized as right by the public. Added to this was the under-estimation of the influence of the United States on the development of world politics.

Before the war no one in Germany had thought it possible that the Union would have to be reckoned with as a factor, much less a decisive factor, in a European war. This was a mistake, the effect of which unfortunately was felt until well into 1917—the result was that there was never enough money available to keep in touch and co-operate with the American Press. As a matter of fact I had, in the course of my activities in Washington, personally entered into certain social relations with the proprietors of a few great American newspapers. But from Berlin no advances were made. Even with the German-American papers there was no organized connection, and they themselves did not work together in any way. It is true that for years there had been a business connection between the greatest American news-agency, the Associated Press, and the Wolff Telegraphic Bureau; as, however, the agency was not served direct with Berlin Wolff-telegrams, but by its own representatives there, this did not amount to much. England, on the other hand—quite apart from the close relationship resulting from a common language—had for years maintained and systematically cultivated the closest contact with the American Press. It followed, then, that on the outbreak of war the English influence on the American daily Press was enormous. It did not rest as exclusively as has been assumed in Germany on direct proprietary rights. I do not think that, with the exception of a single newspaper in one of the smaller cities any great American paper was directly bought by England. Here and there considerable blocks of American newspaper shares may have been in English hands and influenced the tendency of certain papers. If, however, it is true—as was credibly stated in Irish-American quarters during the first year of the war—that Lord Northcliffe boasted a year or two before the war of "controlling" seventeen American papers, it is difficult to believe that this influence of the English press-magnates was based on hard cash. Rather is it the case that certain newspapers received their otherwise very costly private news-service from England on very advantageous terms. To others, English writers of leading articles are said to have been attached, without cost to the newspaper—a scheme of which I have often heard in America, but which is difficult to prove, as all American newspapers maintain the strictest secrecy as to the origin of their leading articles. It is, however, common knowledge that with regard to European affairs the American news service was swayed by this entirely English organization. Until the outbreak of the war the American news agencies drew exclusively from English sources. Moreover, those newspapers which in the United States play a very important part, inasmuch as they are the fount of most of the new ideas by which the tone of the Press in influenced, were in a very considerable degree served from England. On the other hand, the wide field of cinematographic production was strongly influenced by the French film. In this way our enemies in the United States had, at the outbreak of war, a boundless and excellently prepared field for the propagation of their news, and the representation of their point of view, but more particularly for their attack on the German cause. In spite of this, however, they immediately inundated the Union with propagandist literature, particularly through the agents of the English shipping lines, who were scattered all over the country, and the well-known author and politician, Sir Gilbert Parker, sent from London tons of this matter to well-known American business men, professors and politicians.

On our side, it is true, and I should like to emphasize this to their credit, that on the outbreak of war the German-American newspapers took up our cause unhesitatingly and as one man. Further, they have, until America's entry into the war, honestly striven to win full justice for the American point of view, and to combat the unneutral leanings of the majority of the Americans and the slanderous attacks of our enemies. As, however, they are not accessible to the general public, who do not know German, and in particular scarcely ever come into the hands of the authoritative American political circles, their support remained more or less academic. Very valuable services were rendered to the German cause by the already-mentioned weekly paper *Fatherland,* which was printed in English; in view, however, of its reputation as a partisan journal, it naturally could not exert so deep an influence as the local daily papers, which carried on the English propaganda without allowing it to become too conspicuous. For telegraphic communication from Germany to America we had to rely solely on the two German wireless stations at Sayville and Tuckerton, erected shortly before the outbreak of war, and we soon succeeded, subject to American censorship, in getting a regular Press-service, which was spread, not only over the whole of the United States, but was also passed on to South America and East Asia. But in the first place, in spite of repeated extension and strengthening, these two stations were quite inadequate; in the second place, the Press-service never succeeded in adapting itself thoroughly to American requirements. The same may be said of most of the German propaganda literature which reached America in fairly large quantities since the third month of the war, partly in German and partly in not always irreproachable English. This, like the Press telegrams, showed a complete lack of understanding of American national psychology. The American character, I should like to repeat here, is by no means so dry and calculating as the German picture of an American business man usually represents. The outstanding characteristic of the average American is rather a great, even though superficial, sentimentality. There is no news for which a way cannot be guaranteed through the whole country, if clothed in a sentimental form. Our enemies have exploited this circumstance with the greatest refinement in the case of the German invasion of "poor little Belgium," the shooting of the "heroic nurse," Edith Cavell, and other incidents. Those who had charge of the Berlin propaganda, on the other hand, made very little of such occurrences on the enemy side, e.g., the violation of Greece, the bombing of the Corpus Christi procession in Karlsruhe, etc. One thing that would have exerted a tremendous influence in America, if its publicity had been handled with only average skill, was the sufferings of our children, women and old people as a result of the British hunger blockade—that they have made no attempt to bring to the notice of the world.

On the other hand they put themselves to the greatest possible trouble to lay "The Truth About the War" before American public opinion. This, however, fell on unfavorable ground, for the American does not care to be instructed. He had no interest in learning the "truth" which the German Press communications and explanatory pamphlets were so anxious to impress upon him. The American likes to form his own opinions and so only requires facts. The possibility of exerting influence therefore lies rather in the choice of the facts and the way in which they are presented, than in logical and convincing argument. It is all the easier to influence him by the well-timed transmission of skilfully disposed facts, since his usually very limited general knowledge and his complete ignorance of European affairs deprive him of the simplest premises for a critical judgment of the facts presented to him from the enemy side. It is quite incredible what the American public will swallow in the way of lies if they are only repeated often enough and properly served up. It all turns on which side gets the news in first; for the first impression sticks. Corrections are generally vain, especially as they appear as a rule in small print and in inconspicuous places. When, for example, the American Press got the first news of the "destruction" of Rheims cathedral from London and in the English version, no German correction, however well-founded, would succeed in removing the first impression.

Particularly ineffective in their influence on American

public opinion—as may be said here in anticipation—
have been the majority of our official Notes. In view
of the subsequent ever-increasing interruption of the
news service from Germany, they were the last and only
means by which the German standpoint could be brought
before the American people. Their effectiveness depended entirely on the impression that they made on
American public opinion and not on the Washington
Government; yet they were nearly always drawn up in
Berlin in the form of juristic précis, propagandist but
quite futile.

All these factors must be taken into consideration in
attempting to estimate the success of our propaganda
in the United States. They show that on the one hand
the prevailing conditions of American public opinion
were extraordinarily unfavorable to our propaganda,
and that the support it received from home, with a few
exceptions, was misguided.

Dr. Dernburg, then, had not a chance during the eight
months of his activity in America of transforming her
into a pro-German country, and it is certain that no one
else could have done it in his place. But he succeeded
to a great extent, and within a comparatively short
time, in more or less crippling the enemy propaganda,
and at least in gradually rendering ineffective the gross-
est misrepresentations of our enemies. By his own
writings and other methods of spreading the truth, and
particularly by the numerous brochures and books, which
at his suggestion were written by American supporters
of the German cause and distributed in thousands
directly or indirectly by the Press Bureau with the help
of a skilfully compiled address-book, he succeeded in
exerting very considerable influence. By keeping in touch
with American journalists and other influential persons
he did much good work, particularly in the first months

of the war. His connection with Irish leaders laid the foundation for a co-operation which in the following year was of great importance to our position in the United States, and which, with a somewhat more intelligent backing by our Government departments at home, might have been more fruitful still.

One branch of our propaganda which was also initiated under Dr. Dernburg, but was chiefly developed after his departure, was the moving-picture propaganda, for which a very efficient company was floated by Privy Councillor Albert. At first it was intended to be an agency for the circulation of films from Germany. As, however, suitable material for the American market could not be obtained there, the "American Correspondent Film Co." decided to send its own agents to Germany and Austria with a view to making suitable films for their purpose. In this way several important film-dramas were produced which have had great success in hundreds of American cinemas. In spite of this the company had finally to be liquidated, chiefly owing to lack of support from the military authorities at home.

With the sinking of the *Lusitania* our propaganda of enlightenment in the United States substantially came to an end. Henceforward the principal aim of its activity, which, after Dr. Dernburg's departure, came under the direction of Privy Councillor Albert, was to keep the United States out of the war. Side by side with this, an attempt was made to influence public feeling against the export of arms and ammunition and against the Anglo-French loan, and to demonstrate the increasingly prejudiced effect wrought by England on American economic interests. In November, 1915, I urged, as I cabled at the time to Chancellor Bethmann-Hollweg, the complete suppression of propaganda. The Press Bureau in New York continued under the direction of Dr. Fuehr, until the breaking off of relations between America and Germany. It concerned itself, however, apart from certain regular literary contributions to certain journals, less with propaganda work than with keeping an eye on the American Press and the development of the news service to and from Germany as well as to South America and Eastern Asia.

CHAPTER III

POLITICAL EVENTS PRECEDING THE "LUSITANIA" INCIDENT

As I mentioned in the first chapter, it was to be expected that public opinion in America would range itself overwhelmingly on the side of the Entente. As a result of the violation of Belgian neutrality, this happened far in excess of expectation. The violence of the statements of the anti-German party called forth strong replies from those who desired a strict neutrality on the part of the United States. The adherents of the latter party were always stigmatized as pro-Germans, although even the German-Americans never called for anything more than an unconditional neutrality. This also was the aim for which the German policy was working through its representatives in America. We never hoped for anything further.

The waves of excitement ran so high that even the private relations of the adherents of both parties contending suffered. President Wilson, therefore, on the 18th August, 1914, issued a proclamation to the American people which is of special interest because it lays down in a definite form the policy to which he logically and unwaveringly adhered until the rupture.

In this proclamation the following sentences occur: "Every man who really loves America will act and speak in the true spirit of neutrality, which is the spirit of impartiality and fairness and friendliness to all concerned." And further: "The people of the United

States . . . may be divided in camps of hostile opinion. . . . Such divisions among us would be fatal to our peace of mind and might seriously stand in the way of the proper performance of our duty as the one great nation at peace, the one people holding itself ready to play a part of impartial mediation and speak the counsels of peace and accommodation, not as a partisan, but as a friend."

The policy outlined in these quotations from Mr. Wilson's proclamation won the approval of an overwhelming majority of the American people, for even among the supporters of the Entente there was only a small minority who desired an active participation in the war by the United States. Apart from the fact that the traditional American policy seemed to preclude any such intervention in European affairs, it was to the interest of the United States to play with unimpaired power the rôle of *Arbiter mundi,* when the States of ancient Europe, tired of tearing one another to pieces, at last longed for peace again. America could not but hope that neither of the two warring parties would come out of the war in a dominating position. There is, therefore, a certain modicum of truth in the view frequently expressed in Germany that the United States would in any case finally have entered the war to prevent the so-called "German Peace." But the question is whether such a peace was possible in face of the superior strength of our enemies. If we had won the first battle of the Marne and had then been prepared to restore Belgium and conclude a moderate peace, it is conceivable that we might have come to terms with England on the basis of a kind of Treaty of Amiens. After the loss of the battle of the Marne a "German Peace" was out of the question. The possibility of such a peace has never recurred. It was therefore necessary for the German policy to strive for a peace by understanding on the basis of the *status quo*. Just as Frederick the Great defended Prussia's newly won position as a great Power against overwhelming odds, so we were fighting under similar conditions for the maintenance of Germany's position in the world.

Our Government had declared *urbi et orbi* that they were waging a defensive war, and were therefore obliged to regulate their policy accordingly. If we had desired a peace like that of Hubertusburg we should have won. It is often contended in Germany to-day that it would still have been possible to attain this end. I have struggled for it in America for two and a half years and am as convinced to-day as I was then, that by acquiescing in the policy of the United States we should have obtained a peace which would have met the needs of the German people, if only those who desired the same thing at home had been in a position to carry their wishes through.

In Germany it is also alleged, contrary to my own opinion, that the German people could not have held out if they had not been driven on by the "Will to conquer." I regard this view as an injustice to the German nation. If our home propaganda, instead of continually awakening vain hopes, had insisted on telling the real truth, the German people would have faced danger to the last. We ought to have repeated constantly that our situation was very serious, but that we must clench our teeth, and our Government must be ready to seize the first opportunity to end the defensive war by a corresponding peace.

The controversy about the "German peace" or "peace by negotiation" must be touched on here because it formed the nucleus of the diplomatic struggle in Washington. At the beginning of the war these catchwords had not yet been invented, but their substance even then controlled the situation. The attitude of the American Government and public opinion towards us depended in the first place on whether they thought that we were striving for world-mastery or were waging a defensive war.

Immediately after my return from Europe I called on President Wilson, who had taken the opportunity of the war and the death of his first wife, to withdraw even more than ever from the outer world. He was generally known as the recluse of the White House. He only received people with whom he had political business to settle. Particularly from diplomats and other foreigners Mr. Wilson kept very aloof, because he was anxious to avoid the appearance of preference or partiality.

After the disillusionment of Versailles it is difficult for a German to form an unbiassed judgment of Mr. Wilson. We must not forget, however, that no serious attempt has ever been made in Germany to get an unprejudiced estimate of Mr. Wilson's personality. In the course of the war he has come to be regarded more and more as unneutral and anti-German, whereas, to the average American public opinion, he appeared in quite a different light. Later, after the defeat of our arms, we hailed Mr. Wilson as the Messiah who was to save Germany and the whole world from dire distress. When, therefore, at Versailles, the President, instead of unfolding and carrying through a far-reaching programme for the general reconstruction of the world, approved all the ultra-chauvinistic and nationalistic mistakes of the European statesmen and proclaimed as the aim of the peace the punishment of Germany, Mr. Wilson was set down in Germany without more ado as a hypocrite.

I think that through all the phases of the war the German opinion of Mr. Wilson has suffered from sheer exaggeration. The chief mistake lay in separating Wilson's personality from public opinion in the United States. In spite of his strong will and his autocratic leanings, Mr. Wilson is still, in the first place, a perfect type of the American politician. In his speeches he always tries to voice public opinion, and in his policy to follow its wishes.

He certainly tries to direct and influence public opinion. But he changes his front at once if he notices that he has strayed from the way that the *aura popularis* would have him follow. In order to form a correct judgment of Mr. Wilson's actions and speeches it is always necessary to ask oneself, in the first place, what end he has in view for his own political position and that of his party in America. He proclaims in a most dazzling way the ideals of the American people. But their realization always depends on his own actual political interests and those of the Democratic party. Mr. Wilson's attitude has always been synonymous with that of his party, because the latter can produce no other personality capable of competing with the President. Therefore, Mr. Wilson always met with little or no opposition within the Democratic party, and he was able to follow for a long time his own inclination to adopt a quite independent policy.

Socially the President is very congenial when once he has made up his mind to emerge from his narrow circle. He has not the reputation of being a loyal friend, and is accused of ingratitude by many of his former colleagues and enthusiastic adherents. In any case, however, Mr. Wilson is an implacable enemy when once he feels himself personally attacked or slighted. As a result of his sensitiveness he has a strong tendency to make the mistake of regarding political differences of opinion as personal antipathy. The President has never forgiven the German Government for having caused the failure of his peace-policy of 1916-17, which was supported by public opinion in America. In Germany his later speeches, in which he drew a distinction between the German people and the Imperial Government, were regarded as hypocrisy. Such a differentiation was at that time based on American public feeling, which held autocracy and militarism responsible for the disasters which had been brought upon the world. The question has, however, never been answered why this distinction was abandoned by Mr. Wilson at Versailles. Without wishing in any way either to accuse or defend him I consider the answer to this riddle to be that the President allowed himself to be convinced of the complicity of the German people by the statesmen of the Entente. He was at the time in a mood with regard to us which predisposed him to such influences. Mr. Wilson was by origin, up-bringing and training a pacifist. When it is remembered that with us and in neutral countries it was the pacifists themselves who were the most indignant at the Peace of Versailles, that they were the very people who for the most part advised against the signature of this peace, one can imagine the feelings aroused in a disillusioned pacifist like Wilson by those whom he regards as responsible for having thwarted the possibility of an ideal pacifist peace.

Apart from this, Mr. Wilson at Versailles no longer dominated American public opinion, and his political power consequently collapsed. In the United States the old indifference to European affairs regained the upper hand. Men were satisfied with having brought about a victory over autocracy and militarism. They wanted nothing further. The American troops were crowding home, and, finally, feeling in the United States was still so strongly against us that no one would have understood the President if he had caused a rupture with his Allies on our behalf.

At Versailles, too, an outstanding peculiarity of Mr. Wilson's may have played a part which even during the earlier negotiations had been of great importance. He is a man who is slow to make up his mind, and likes to postpone decisions until they are inevitable. He is always ready to wait and see whether the situation may not improve or some unexpected event occur. How often during the Washington negotiations did, first I and then our enemies, believe that we had set President Wilson on a definite course. But again and again the requisite decision would be postponed. In Washington it was generally taken under the strong pressure of public opinion. In Versailles the Entente statesmen may well have forced a decision by displaying a stronger will and a wider knowledge of European affairs. Mr. Wilson was at Versailles in the position of the giant Antæus, who drew his strength from his native soil. Once away from American ground Hercules (Clemenceau) was able to crush him.

At the time I am now describing the circumstances were quite different, because at that time Mr. Wilson had a reliable support for his policy in American public opinion. In Germany, at the very beginning of the war, great resentment was felt against Mr. Wilson for the cold negative in his reply to the Emperor's telegram in which Mr. Wilson was asked to condemn the atrocities perpetrated by the Belgian population and *francs-tireurs*. It was not, however, noticed in Germany that the President at the same time likewise refused to receive a Belgian deputation which came to America to beg for his help.

During my conversation with the President already

mentioned, he made a statement on the lines of his proclamation of neutrality of which I have already given the substance. My reply that the American neutrality seemed to us to be tinged with sympathy for our enemies Mr. Wilson contradicted emphatically. He thought that this appearance was the result of England's naval power, which he could do nothing to alter. In this connection the President made the following remark, which struck me very forcibly at the time:

"The United States must remain neutral, because otherwise the fact that her population is drawn from so many European countries would give rise to serious domestic difficulties."

My remark about the benevolence of the United States' neutrality towards our enemies was at the time chiefly prompted by the differences that had arisen with regard to the wireless stations.

The fact that this question arose gives yet another proof of how little we were prepared for war. By German enterprise two wireless stations had been erected on the east coast of the United States as a means of direct communication with Europe, one at Sayville (Long Island, the other at Tuckerton (New Jersey). Both were partly financed by American and French capital. As at the beginning of the war the cable fell entirely into English hands and was destroyed by them, we had no telegraphic communication with home at our disposal. We had to fall back exclusively on the wireless stations, when, as frequently happened, we were unable to make use of the circuitous routes via neutral countries. Unfortunately it appeared that the legal position with regard to the proprietorship of the two stations was not clear. Actions were immediately brought on the French side, and the closing of the stations by decree of the courts demanded. Under these circumstances it was fortunate for us that the American Government, after tedious negotiations with me, took over possession of both stations. Otherwise they would have been closed and we should have been unable to use them.

Our satisfaction at this decision was modified by the establishment of a censorship of radio-telegrams on the part of the American Government on the strength of the Hague Convention, which prohibits the communication by wireless from a neutral country with the military or naval forces of a combatant. If the stations had been publicly used before the war we should have stood on firm legal ground, for such cases are excepted by the Hague Convention. Unfortunately the stations were in 1914 only partially completed, and the application of the clauses in question was therefore doubtful. It is true that the stations were ready for immediate use, but as a result of the French protest the American Government held strictly to the legal standpoint. In these negotiations we had to content ourselves with pointing out that whereas our enemies could pass on military information to their Governments by means of coded cablegrams, we should be confined to the use of the wireless stations. Finally we came to an agreement with the American Government that they should have a copy of the code which we used for the wireless telegrams. In this way their contents were kept secret from the enemy, but not from the Washington Government. This course we only agreed to as a last resource as it was not suitable for handling negotiations in which the American Government was concerned.

The course of this controversy was typical of the fate of German interests in America throughout the whole period of American neutrality. Unfortunately we had absolutely no means at hand for putting any pressure on

America in our own favor. In comparison with the public opinion in the Eastern States, which followed in the wake of the Entente, and with the authoritative circles of New York, Wilson's Administration without question strove for an honorable neutrality. In spite of this most of their decisions were materially unfavorable to us, so that a German observer from a distance might, not without reason, obtain the impression that the neutrality of the American Government was mere hypocrisy and that all kinds of pretexts were found for helping England.

This was not the chief impression made on a near observer. In politics the Americans are first and foremost jurists, and indeed in a narrower and more literal sense than the English Imperialists, with whom, according to their old traditions, justice only serves as a cloak for their political ambitions. I cannot judge how far the Americans have become full-blooded Imperialists since their entry into the war, i.e., since about 1917. At the time of which I speak this was far from being the case. If, moreover, it is a fact that the majority of the decisions of the United States turned out unfavorably to us, the question of the American motives should have been carefully differentiated from the other question as to what inferences may be drawn from the state of affairs. Even if we had had just reason to complain of unfair treatment it was for us to be as indulgent towards America as was compatible with our final aim not to lose the war. The question is not whether we had cause for resentment and retaliation, but simply what benefit could be extracted for Germany out of the existing situation.

At this visit to the White House, the only question that was acute was that of the wireless stations. This and the negotiations which I shall mention later, dealing with the coaling of our ships of war and the American export of arms and ammunition, I discussed with Secretary of

State Bryan. The first time I visited this gentleman he exclaimed with great warmth: "Now you see I was right when I kept repeating that preparation for war was the best way of bringing war about. All the European Powers were armed to the teeth and always maintained that this heavy armament was necessary to protect them from war. Now the fallacy is obvious. We alone live in peace because we are unarmed."

Mr. Bryan has always been a genuine pacifist, and later sacrificed his Ministerial appointment to his convictions. So long as he remained in office he continued to influence the American Government to maintain neutrality and constantly strove to bring about peace.

A first attempt in this direction was made from Washington immediately after the outbreak of the war, but met with no response from the combatant Powers. At the beginning of September, Mr. Bryan repeated the offer of American mediation.

At that time a vigorous agitation had begun in New York for the restoration of peace. Mr. William Randolph Hearst, the well-known editor of widely circulated newspapers, and other well-known personalities, called together great meetings at which America's historical mission was said to be the stopping of the wholesale murder that was going on in Europe. At this time I was, together with several other gentlemen, staying with James Speyer, the banker, at his country house. The host and the majority of the guests, among whom was the late ambassador in Constantinople, Oscar Straus, were supporters of the prevailing pacific movement. The question of American mediation was eagerly discussed at the dinner table. Mr. Straus was an extremely warm adherent of this idea. He turned particularly to me because the German Government were regarded as opponents of the pacifist ideas. I said that we had not desired the war and would certainly be ready at the first suitable opportunity for a peace by understanding. Thereupon Mr. Straus declared that he would at once travel to Washington and repeat my words to Mr. Bryan. Immediately after dinner he went to the station and on the following day I received a wire from the Secretary of State, asking me to return to Washington as soon as I could to discuss the matter with him. There we had a long interview in his private residence, with the result that an American offer of mediation was sent to the Imperial Chancellor. Meanwhile Mr. Straus had gone to the ambassadors of the other combatant Powers, who all more or less rejected the proposal. The friendly reply of the German Government coincided in principle with what I had said, but added that Mr. Bryan should first address himself to the enemy, as the further course of the negotiations depended on their attitude, which was not yet known. The American Government never returned to the question and I had no reason to urge them to do so. Any importunity on our side would have given an impression of weakness. Nevertheless this interlude was so far favorable to us that it contrasted our readiness for negotiation with the enemy's refusal.

In consequence of the failure of their first attempt to intervene the American Government thought it necessary to exercise more restraint. In spite of this, however, President Wilson, before the end of the winter of 1914-15, sent his intimate friend, Colonel Edward M. House, to London, Paris and Berlin, in order to ascertain semi-officially whether there were any possibilities of peace.

Mr. House, who lived in an unpretentious abode in New York, occupied a peculiar and very influential position at the White House. Bound to the President by intimate friendship, he has always refused to accept any

Ministerial appointment, either at home or abroad, although he was only possessed of modest means and could certainly have had any post in the Cabinet or as an ambassador that he had liked to choose. In this way he remained entirely independent, and since President Wilson's entry into office, was his confidential adviser in domestic, and particularly in foreign politics. As such Colonel House had a position that is without precedent in American history. During his stay in London, at this time, he is said to have described himself to the wife of an English Cabinet Minister, herself not favorably disposed towards America, as the "eyes and ears of the President." I know from my own experience how thoroughly and effectively he was able to inform his friend on the European situation, and how perfectly correctly, on the other hand, he interpreted Mr. Wilson's views.

It was not easy to become more closely acquainted with Colonel House, whose almost proverbial economy of speech might be compared with the taciturnity of old Moltke.

Unlike the majority of his fellow-nationals, and particularly his immediate fellow-countrymen of the Southern States, Colonel House, while possessing great personal charm and the courtesy that is characteristic of the Southern States, is reserved and retiring. It took a considerable time before I got to know this able and interesting man at all intimately. I did not become intimate with him until the time of the journey to Berlin already mentioned. Even then it was the earnest wish of Colonel House to obtain for his great friend the chief credit of being the founder of peace. Colonel House was particularly well fitted to be the champion of the President's ideas. I have never known a more upright and honorable pacifist than he. He had a horror of war because he regarded it as the contradiction of his ideals of the nobility of the human race. He often spoke with indignation of the people who were enriching themselves out of the war, and added that he would never touch the profits of war industry. He afterwards repeatedly told me that he had spoken as energetically in London against the blockade, which was a breach of international law, as against the submarine war in Berlin. Both these types of warfare were repugnant to the warm, sympathetic heart of Colonel House. He could not understand why women and children should die of hunger or drowning in order that the aims of an imperialist policy, which he condemned, might be attained. At the same time he was convinced that neither of these types could decide the war, but would only serve to rouse in both the combatant countries a boundless hatred which would certainly stand in the way of future co-operation in the work of restoring peace. In many of his remarks at that time, Colonel House proved to be right, since the war was decided mainly by the entry of America and the consequent overwhelming superiority in men, money and material.

Meanwhile, as a result of the traffic in munitions, feeling in Germany had turned sharply against the United States. Our position with regard to this question was very unfavorable as we had no legal basis for complaint. The clause of the Hague Convention which permitted such traffic had been included in the second Hague Convention at our own suggestion. Nevertheless it was natural that the one-sided support of our enemies by the rapidly growing American war industry roused strong feeling in Germany. As a result there began a controversy with the American Government similar to that with England during the war of 1870-71. Even in the United States there was a considerable minority which disapproved of the munitions traffic, though on moral rather than political or international grounds. It goes without saying that the agitation of this minority was supported in every way by the German representatives. There was no law in America to prohibit such support, which could not, moreover, be regarded as a breach of American neutrality. It is true that in this way a few Germans got themselves into an awkward position because they were suspected of stirring up the German-Americans, who together with the Irish played a leading part in the agitation against the Government. In particular, Dr. Dernburg became unpopular in America, since he began to address meetings in addition to his journalistic work. The Washington Government regarded him as the leader of the "hyphenated Americans" who were opposing the policy of the President's Administration, because the latter took up the strict legal standpoint that the traffic in munitions was permissible, and that it would therefore be a breach of neutrality in our favor if such traffic were forbidden after the outbreak of hostilities. President Wilson himself even had an idea of nationalizing the munition factories, which would have rendered traffic with the combatant Powers a breach of international law. When, however, he sounded Congress on this matter, it became evident that a majority could not be obtained for such a step. The United States had already brought forward a similar proposal at the Hague Conference with the intention of conceding one of the chief demands of the pacifists. It was in wide circles in America an axiom that the munitions factories were the chief incentives to war. As during the first winter of the war there were very few such factories in America the President's plan was not merely Utopian but meant in all seriousness, in which connection it should be noted that American industrial circles were among Mr. Wilson's bitterest opponents. If Mr. Wil-

son's proposal had been known to German public opinion
he would have been more favorably judged.

The negotiations which I had to carry out on this question of the munitions traffic concerned themselves also
with the question of the coaling of our ships of war.
This was based on an agreement between the American
Government and the Hamburg-Amerika line. The port
authorities had at first shown themselves agreeable. As
a result of the English protest the attitude of the American Government became increasingly strict. With the
actual coaling I had nothing to do. That came within
the sphere of the Naval Attaché, who, for obvious reasons connected with the conduct of the war at sea, kept
his actions strictly secret. My first connection with this
question was when I was instructed to hand over to the
American Government the following memorandum, dated
15th December, 1914:

"According to the provisions of general international
law, there is nothing to prevent neutral States from
allowing contraband of war to reach the enemies of Germany through or out of their territory. This is also
permitted by Article VII. of the Hague Convention of
the 19th October, 1907, dealing with the rights and duties
of neutrals in the case of land or sea war. If a State
uses this freedom to the advantage of our enemies, that
State, according to a generally recognized provision of
international law, which is confirmed in Article IX. of
the two aforesaid Conventions, may not hamper Germany's military power with regard to contraband
through or out of its territory.

"The declaration of neutrality of the United States
takes this view fully into account since the furnishing
of contraband of war to all combatants is likewise permitted: 'All persons may lawfully and without restric-

tion by reason of the aforesaid state of war, manufacture and sell within the United States, arms and ammunitions of war and other articles ordinarily known as contraband of war.'

"This principle has been accepted in the widest sense by the public declaration of the American State Department of the 15th October, 1914, with regard to neutrality and contraband.

"Nevertheless different port authorities in the United States have refused to supply the necessary fuel to merchant vessels in which it might be carried to German ships of war on the high seas or in other neutral ports. According to the principles of international law already mentioned, there is no need for a neutral State to prevent the transport of fuel in this way; such a State then ought not to hold up merchant ships loaded in this way nor interfere with their freedom of movement, once it has countenanced the supply of contraband to the enemy. The only case in which it would be the duty of such a nation to hamper the movements of these ships in this one-sided fashion would be one in which such traffic might be turning the ports into German naval bases. This might perhaps have been the case if German coal depots had been situated at these ports, or if the ships used them for a regular calling port on their way to the German naval forces. It is, however, unnecessary to urge that the occasional sailing of a merchant ship with coal for German ships of war does not make a port into a base for German naval enterprises out of keeping with neutrality.

"Our enemies are obtaining contraband of war from the United States, in particular rifles, to the value of many milliards of marks; this is within their rights. But toleration becomes serious injustice if the United States refuses to allow the occasional provisioning of our ships of war from her ports. This would mean unequal treatment of the combatants and a recognized rule of neutrality would be infringed to our disadvantages."

This memorandum played an important part in the subsequent negotiations, because Mr. Flood, the president of the Committee for Foreign Affairs of the American House of Representatives, interpreted it as amounting to a German agreement to the supply of arms and ammunition to her enemies.

In view of the situation in the United States, it was to our interest to leave the struggle for a prohibition of the munitions traffic to our American friends. The efforts of Senator Stone in this direction are well known, and have been recently quoted before the Commission of the German National Assembly. If a considerable number of influential Americans took up the case for the prohibition there was far more hope of bringing it about than if it was apparent that the American Government were surrendering to German pressure. The pacifist Mr. Bryan was very sensitive on this point and visited me frequently to assert his neutrality.

I therefore advised the Imperial Government in this matter not to send an official Note for the moment, so that the American agitation in favor of the prohibition of munition traffic might have full freedom for development. As, however, our enemies continually harked back to the idea that the Imperial Government did not take exception to the supply of munitions, I was forced, as the result of continual pressure from our American friends, to alter my attitude, and, after receiving permission from Berlin, to hand to the Washington Government on 4th April, 1915, a memorandum, of which I give the most important part here.

"Further I should like to refer to the attitude of the

United States towards the question of the export of arms. The Imperial Government is convinced that the Government of the United States agree with them on this point, that questions of neutrality should be dealt with not merely with regard to the strict letter, but the spirit also must be taken into consideration, in which neutrality is carried through.

"The situation arising out of the present war cannot be compared with that in any previous war. For this reason no reference to supplies of arms from Germany in such wars is justified; for then the question was not whether the combatants should be supplied with material but which of the competing States should secure the contract.

"In the present war all the nations which possess a war-industry of any importance are either themselves involved in the war, or occupied with completing their own armament, and therefore have prohibited the export of war material. The United States are accordingly the only neutral State in a position to supply war-material. The idea of neutrality has, therefore, assumed a new significance, which is quite independent of the strict letter of the laws that have hitherto prevailed. On the other hand the United States are founding a gigantic war industry in the broadest sense, and they are not only working the existing plant but are straining every nerve to develop it and to erect new factories. The international agreement for the protection of the rights of neutrals certainly arose from the necessity of protecting the existing branches of industry in neutral countries as far as possible against an encroachment upon their prerogatives. But it can in no way accord with the spirit of honorable neutrality, if advantage is taken of such international agreements to found a new industry in a neutral State, such as appears in the development in the

United States of an arms-industry, the output of which can, in view of the existing situation, be solely to the advantage of the combatant powers.

"This industry is at present only delivering its wares to the enemies of Germany. The readiness, in theory, to do the same for Germany, even if the transport were possible, does not alter the case. If it is the desire of the American people to maintain an honorable neutrality, the United States will find the means to stop this one-sided traffic in arms, or at least to use it for the purpose of protecting legitimate commerce with Germany, particularly in respect of foodstuffs. This conception of neutrality should appeal all the more to the United States in view of the fact that they have allowed themselves to be influenced by the same standpoint in their policy in regard to Mexico. On the 4th February, 1914, President Wilson, according to a statement of a member of Congress on 30th December, 1914, before the commission for foreign affairs with regard to the withdrawal of the prohibition of the export of arms to Mexico, said: 'We shall be observing true neutrality by taking into consideration the accompanying circumstances of the case. . . . He then took up the following point of view: 'Carranza, in contrast to Huerta, has no ports at his disposal for the importation of war-material, so in his case we are bound, as a State, to treat Carranza and Huerta alike, if we are to be true to the real spirit of neutrality and not mere paper neutrality.'

"This point of view, applied to the present case, indicates prohibition of the export of arms."

Although during the war all Notes were at once made public, the American Government were very annoyed at my publishing this memorandum, which in any case would have met with no success. The agitation for the prohibition of the export of arms and munitions was vigorously pressed, and in spite of the "*Lusitania* incident" never completely subsided. But the American Government held to their point of view, which they explained to me on the 21st April, as follows:

"In the third place, I note with sincere regret that, in discussing the sale and exportation of arms by citizens of the United States to the enemies of Germany, Your Excellency seems to be under the impression that it was within the choice of the Government of the United States, notwithstanding its professed neutrality and its diligent efforts to maintain it in other particulars, to inhibit this trade, and that its failure to do so manifested an unfair attitude toward Germany. This Government holds, as I believe Your Excellency is aware, and as it is constrained to hold in view of the present indisputable doctrines of accepted international law, that any change in its own laws of neutrality during the progress of a war which would affect unequally the relations of the United States with the nations at war would be an unjustifiable departure from the principle of strict neutrality by which it has consistently sought to direct its actions, and I respectfully submit that none of the circumstances urged in Your Excellency's memorandum alters the principle involved. The placing of an embargo on the trade in arms at the present time would constitute such a change and be a direct violation of the neutrality of the United States. It will, I feel assured, be clear to Your Excellency that, holding this view and considering itself in honor bound by it, it is out of the question for this Government to consider such a course."

In the meantime, Colonel House returned from Europe without having met with any success, but he had opened useful personal relations. The Governments of all the combatant Powers then held the opinion that the time had not yet come when they could welcome the mediation of President Wilson. Colonel House, however, did not allow the lack of success of his first mission to deter him from further efforts, and remained to the last the keenest supporter of American mediation. Since this journey Colonel House and I became on very friendly and intimate terms, which should have helped to bring about such a peace.

CHAPTER IV.

ECONOMIC QUESTIONS

In the preceding chapter I mentioned that Dr. Dernburg's plan for raising a loan in the United States had failed. Later the direction of all our economic and financial affairs passed into the hands of Geheimrat Albert. His original task was to organize in New York extensive shipments of foodstuffs, particular wheat and fats, which were to be exported through the New York office of the Hamburg-Amerika line. This depended, in the first place, on the possibility of raising the necessary funds, and in the second, on the possibility that England, out of regard for the neutrals, and particularly the United States, would be compelled to abide by the codified principles of international law. Neither of these premises materialized.

As the necessary means for carrying through the scheme could not be raised it might have been possible to finance it if the Government had taken over the not inconsiderable funds of the German banks and the great industrial enterprises, e.g., the chemical factories in the United States, and used them for the shipments. The suggestions we made to this effect were not answered until the end of August, when we arrived in New York and had already lost many weeks in trying to negotiate the loan. One organ, which immediately after the war had taken up these questions on its own initiative, failed, and so nothing was done in the whole wide sphere of credit, supply of raw materials and foodstuffs and shipping until my arrival with the other gentlemen, so that the most favorable opportunity was lost. Remittances from Germany did not arrive until long afterwards, and then only to a very modest extent. Consequently the whole economic scheme was considerably narrowed and hampered from the beginning.

The second assumption, that the United States, in consideration of her great commercial connections with Germany, would maintain her rights as a neutral State to unrestricted sea trade within the provisions of international law, proved to be unfounded. The United States, at any rate according to the view of some very distinguished Americans, as, for example, in the journal *New Republic,* violated the spirit of neutrality when she allowed commerce of the neutrals one with another to be strangled by England. To the interest in traffic with the neutral States, and indirectly with Germany, was opposed the interest in the still greater trade with our enemies, to which was added, and indeed to a rapidly increasing extent, the supply of war material. The United States did not realize the extent of their economic power in respect of England, as the inexperienced, newly-appointed Democratic Government had no statistics to which to refer, and from a military point of view were defenceless for want of an army or fleet. So England was able, slowly and cautiously, but surely, to cut off the Central Powers from the American market. In view of this state of things the important thing was to pass all shipments off as neutral. The exporter had to be an American or a subject of neutral Europe. The financing had also to be European, at any rate outwardly. The destination could only be a port in Holland, Scandinavia, Spain or—at that time—Italy. Consequently it was not long before the consignments could no longer be made through the New York representative of the Hamburg-Amerika line, but were taken in hand by Herr Albert himself, who merely availed himself of the professional advice of the Hamburg-Amerika line.

All decisions therefore could emanate from the same source, which prevented loss of time, especially as the financial responsibility also rested with Herr Albert. The most important thing, however, was that attention was distracted from the shipping, as for a long time Herr Albert remained unknown, whereas the Hamburg-Amerika line from the first was kept under the closest observation by England. On the other hand, this arrangement exposed the cargoes to condemnation by the English prize courts as they were now State-owned. But Herr Albert could assume—and, as it turned out, rightly—that so long as the English respected neutral property, it would be difficult as a rule to trace the shipments back to him. Otherwise there would have been no security for a German private undertaking.

In carrying out his task, Herr Albert at first shipped the purchased goods by the usual lines (Scandinavia-American line). Soon, however, difficulties arose, because these lines, in order to avoid being held up in English ports, would no longer accept cargoes which were intended, if possible, for Germany, so a special line was formed sailing under the American flag. The direction of this line was in the hands of an American firm who represented themselves as the owners, whereas, in reality, the ships were chartered by Herr Albert. As, at the beginning of the war, the American flag was more respected by the English than those of the other neutrals, a number of these ships got through without much delay. Later this method of shipping also became impossible. Then single ships were chartered—mostly under the American flag—and when the owners, from fear of loss, refused the charter, or when outrageous conditions made chartering impossible, they were bought out-right. The ships were consigned as blockade runners to a neutral port, and later either made direct for Germany or were taken in by a German ship of war. As the most important examples I may mention the *Eir, Maumee, Winneconne, Duneyre, Andrew, Welch* and *Prince Waldemar.*

With the tightening up of the English measures and blockade these undertakings became increasingly difficult, and finally had to be abandoned. Moreover the cost and the trouble of preparation grew out of all proportion to the results. Every individual shipment had to be prepared long beforehand. Out of ten attempts often only one would succeed. Very often an attempt which had cost weeks of work would fall through at the last moment owing to the refusal of credit by the banks, particularly when the political position was strained, or to an indiscretion, or English watchfulness, or difficulties with the American port authorities.

The English surveillance had assumed dimensions that would not have been possible without the tacit connivance, which at times became active support, of the American authorities. Not only did the English consuls demand that in each individual case the bills of lading should be submitted to them, but in addition to this an efficient surveillance and spy service was organized, partly by American detective bureaus and partly by a separate and wide-reaching service. The English had confidential agents in all the shipping offices, whose services had for the most part been acquired by bribery. At various times attempts were made to break into Herr Albert's office, to learn the combination for opening his safe, to get hold of papers through the charwomen and other employees, and even to rob him personally of papers. The control of the American port authorities was within the letter of the law, but in practice it worked very unfavorably to us. The regulation was that ship and cargo must be consigned to a definite port. This regulation was drawn up purely for purposes of statistics, and consequently no importance was attached to it before the war. As a rule the bills of lading were filled in by subordinate employees of the exporter. Soon after the outbreak of the war a special "neutrality squad" was attached to the "Collector of the Port of New York" whose duty it was to maintain strict neutrality by seeing that the said laws were properly observed. This led, in cases where there was a suspicion that the cargo was not intended for the given port of destination, but for Germany, to an exhaustive inquiry. This measure could not fail to act as a deterrent, and even Herr Albert was seriously hampered in his enterprises. The whole system amounted to a complement of the English blockade. When Herr Albert finally succeeded in coming to an agreement with the Customs authorities in this matter a great number of opportunities had been missed and the shipments had been made practically impossible by the tightening of the English blockade.

There was no question of entrusting the shipping to American exporters who had had long experience of German trade. Herr Albert from the first considered it advisable to interfere as little as possible with the existing business relations between the two countries, and he left it to the firms trading with Germany to carry through their commissions as best they could. This method of supplying Germany with food, however, completely failed. The fault also lies partly with the importers in Germany. In these circles it was for a long time hoped, but in vain, to obtain consignments from American firms. Further, they clung too long to the business methods of peace, demanded estimates, bargained about prices, and, most important of all, did not realize that the risk to the exporter as a result of the English blockade made special compensation or payment necessary. In consequence the valuable time at the beginning of the war was lost. Very soon, however, the American exporters withdrew completely, because those who had had previous business relations with Germany were known to the English, and so were suspected and finally placed on the black list. A shipment by one of these firms would then at once have been marked down as destined for Germany, and would have run risk of capture. Herr Albert, therefore, made use of special agencies. At first, in addition to employing Danish firms, he founded several new American export companies. These new organizations were of course only available for a short time, and, as soon as they came under English suspicion and were consequently rendered useless, had to be replaced by others.

The reproach that has been made from time to time that these enterprises were confined to a small clique of confidential persons and firms seems to be unjustified by the facts. The circumstances demanded the closest possible secrecy, for otherwise the origin and destination of the cargoes would have been discovered by the English secret service before they left New York. This would have involved the complete loss of the cargo as a result of the English embargo. That firms already engaged, even though for a short time, in German-American commerce could not be considered is obvious. Not only were they known to the English, but in some cases their German names already laid them open to suspicion. Accordingly, their occasional requests that they should carry through enterprises of this nature were consistently refused. This criticism is only made by a small circle of German-American firms grouped round the German Union and the so-called German-American Chamber of

Commerce, and originated in an anxiety, understandable but based on an inadequate knowledge of the facts, to participate in the undertakings.

Although the export of raw material did not actually come within the scope of Herr Albert's original commission, it often became necessary, at special request or from the nature of the case, to lend a helping hand in the export of raw material, particularly wool and cotton. In this way, in the autumn of 1914, the American steamer *Luckenbach* was successfully run through direct to Germany with several million pounds of wool on board. With regard to cotton, Herr Albert, also in the autumn of 1914, by negotiations which he carried on through me with the State Department and the Foreign Trade Adviser, succeeded in obtaining English recognition that cotton should not be regarded as contraband of war. Even after this recognition, England made the export of cotton practically impossible by intimidating the cotton exporters in every possible way, among others by spreading the rumor that the ships would be captured nevertheless, and by prohibiting English insurance companies from underwriting such cargoes. Here Herr Albert intervened by effecting the insurance through German insurance companies, and proved by the loading and arming of cotton ships, e.g., the American ship *Carolyn,* that the threat of capture was not to be taken seriously but was simply an attempt at intimidation on the part of the English. In this way, confidence was so far restored that in the autumn of 1914 and the beginning of 1915 a large number of other firms joined in the business. When, later, cotton was made unconditional contraband of war, Herr Albert made attempts to fit out blockade runners —which ended with the arrival at a German port of the *Eir* with 10,000 bales of cotton.

The various attempts to export copper, rubber and

other raw materials which were unconditional contraband, apart from the cases already mentioned of wool and cotton, proved impossible, in spite of repeated, extensive and very cautious preparation. A very ambitious scheme of this kind with the S.S. *Atlantic* had to be abandoned at the last moment owing to difficulties with the port authorities.

All these enterprises, the purchase, sale and shipment of foodstuffs and raw material, the chartering, buying and selling of ships, the founding of shipping lines, new companies, etc., as well as the financial business had their political as well as their purely business side. They were either intended to serve as precedents in the definite phases of development of international maritime law or to exert influence on American public opinion from an economic point of view.

When the result of these shipping enterprises is weighed after the event, it will be seen that they did not play a decisive part in the supply of Germany with foodstuffs and raw material. Germany would during the first year of war have managed to get along even without the few hundred thousand tons which in this way were brought in via neutral countries. Nevertheless, in conjunction with the imports from neutral countries, they several times served to relieve the situation. Very important in this respect was the successful struggle for the free import of cotton at the end of 1914 and the beginning of 1915, quite apart from our own shipments. Without this we should have come to an end of our supplies considerably earlier.

The question of war and marine insurance very soon called for particular attention to the interests of our own shipping. The American insurance market was dominated by the English companies. The latter not only conducted about two-thirds of the whole insurance business of the country, but also exerted a decisive influence on the American companies. In addition to this, they held an authoritative position as holding a share of the capital. England very soon gave instructions that English insurance companies should not participate in any business in which German interests were in any way involved. Consequently in making shipments to neutral countries, we were faced with great difficulties, for the power of the German insurance companies and the few American companies that were independent of England did not suffice.

The two most important German companies with branches in New York, the *Norddeutsche Versicherungsgesellschaft* and the *Mannheimer Versicherungsgesellschaft*, which was excellently, actively, and very loyally represented in New York by the firm F. Hermann & Co., at first offered an insurance limit of about 75,000 dollars, that is 150,000 dollars together, which in any case was insufficient. At first they had no authority to undertake war insurance.

The economic importance of the insurance question is obvious on the face of it. No marine insurance was possible without war insurance. In particular the American Government bureau for war insurance made the covering of the marine insurance an essential condition. This example was followed by all the American insurance companies. A satisfactory settlement of the insurance—both war and marine—on the other hand was a necessary condition for the financing of the shipments. The shippers only obtained credit from the bank on handing over the insurance policies. In addition to this it came about later that the few American shipping lines which remained independent of England, and so were on the black list, were no longer in a position to cover the "Hull Insurance," i.e., the insurance of the ship herself, and therefore the solution of the insurance question became a necessary condition for obtaining freight space. Here too, then, it was to our interest to come to the rescue, because otherwise the lines in question would have been forced to come to an understanding with the English firms, which would have placed their tonnage at the service of our enemies.

To begin with, Herr Albert himself undertook the insurance in cases of exceptional importance. It was at most a question of a small balance, by the furnishing of which an immediate risk or a dangerous delay in shipment was avoided. Our chief efforts were directed towards raising the insurance limit of the German companies. As a result a pool of German insurance companies was formed whose limit for marine and war insurance was gradually raised more and more. In this way it was possible to carry through a number of shipments to European countries, to keep a not inconsiderable tonnage—about 30,000 tons—out of the hands of the Allies, as well as to enable a number of important German firms in South America to carry on extensive trade between North and South America, and so to maintain their business activity in spite of the measures adopted by the English.

About our propaganda I have already spoken in detail in the second chapter. It may be mentioned again here that the centre of gravity of our active propaganda lay in the economic question, which was to a certain extent the key to the understanding of our American policy during the war.

Though the vast and rapid development of American export trade through the trade in war material, and the change in position from debtor to creditor, was only effected gradually, and the loss of the German market at first made itself adversely felt both actively and passively, the size of the contracts from the Allies and the consequent profits at once acted like a narcotic on public opinion. This was all the more the case as a result of the extraordinarily skilful way in which the English handled the question. They always proceeded cautiously and gradually. For instance, they at first accepted the Declaration of London in principle, but made several alterations which to the public, who did not realize the extent of their effect, seemed unimportant and which yet formed the basis for the gradual throwing overboard of the Declaration of London. After public opinion had grown accustomed to the English encroachments and the interests affected had been pacified by the Allied contracts, the blockade was introduced after careful preparation in the Press; it was not at first described as a blockade, but was gradually and systematically tightened. Among other things, the export of cotton to Germany was expressly agreed to at the end of 1914, but was afterwards hampered in practice by various measures, as, for example, the holding up of individual ships, and the refusal of marine insurance, and finally brought to an end by the declaration of cotton as unconditional contraband. It is characteristic that the declaration of cotton as unconditional contraband was made public on the very day on which the whole American Press was in a state of great excitement over the *Arabic* case, so that this comparatively unimportant incident filled the front pages and leading articles of the newspapers, while the extremely important economic measure was published in a place where it would hardly be noticed.

We made vigorous efforts to oppose this English step. We got into touch with the importers of German goods, who formed an association and forwarded a protest to Washington. Without attracting attention, we gave the association the assistance of a firm of solicitors, whose services were at our disposal, as legal advisers. Relations were entered into with the cotton interest, which, through the political pressure of the Southern States, exerted great influence on public opinion and in Congress. Various projects for buying cotton on a large scale for Germany were considered, discussed with the cotton interest and tested by small purchases. In the same way negotiations were entered upon with the great meat companies, the copper interest and others by systematic explanation and emphasis of the interests with regard to the German market. The result, partly for the reasons given, partly owing to the political development of the general relations between Germany and the United States, was small. This, however, can hardly be taken as an argument against the expediency of the steps taken as at that time. No one could foresee the later development of the war and particularly the length of time it was going to last; whereas had the war been shorter there is no doubt that these measures would have attained their object.

An important part of the economic propaganda was the institution of the so-called "Issues," i.e., the attempt by carefully construing individual incidents to make clear to public opinion the fundamental injustice of the English encroachments and their far-reaching consequences in practice. The most important case in this direction is that of the *Wilhelmina*. According to the prevailing principles of international law, foodstuffs were only conditional contraband. They might be imported into Germany if they were intended for the exclusive use of the civil population. As, however, England succeeded in restraining the exporters from any attempt to consign foodstuffs to Germany, especially as in view of the enormous supplies that were being forwarded to our enemies they had little interest in such shipment, the question never reached a clear issue. Herr Albert therefore induced an American firm to ship foodstuffs for the civil population of Germany on the American steamer *Wilhelmina,* bound for Hamburg, by himself undertaking the whole risk from behind the scenes. This was arranged in such a way as to preserve in appearance the good faith of the American firm, and to make the shipment seem purely American in the eyes of the American Government and the English.

The *Wilhelmina* was taken by the English into Falmouth and detained on the grounds that Hamburg was a fortified town, and that, according to the measures adopted by Germany for supplying the civil population with food—requisitioning, centralization of distribution, etc.—there was no longer any distinction between the supply of the military and the civil population. While the negotiations on this question were still in the air, and seemed to be progressing favorably for us, England resorted to a general blockade. Consequently the case lost its interest, both practical and as a question of principle, especially as England declared her readiness to pay for the goods at Hamburg prices. As, on the other hand, insistence on the purely theoretical claims would give rise to the danger that the English or American secret service might in the end succeed in proving the German origin of the undertaking, Herr Albert accepted the proffered payment of the English Government, and received as compensation a sum which covered all the expenses.

Such incidents could have been construed in several ways. One of the most important, and also the most popular, was the shipment of cotton to Germany for the civilian population between the autumn of 1915 and the middle of 1916. The declaration of cotton as absolute contraband was at first only on paper, as no American exporters had hitherto ventured to ship cotton. Consequently, detailed discussions took place as to whether such an undertaking should be entered upon in the full light of publicity. Great excitement among the cotton growers proved the extremely keen and widespread interest. England would have been forced to act on her declaration at a time when the American Government could not afford to ignore the interests of the cotton industry, with its influence on domestic politics. The full effect of the meagreness of the crops, and on the other hand the increase of consumption in the United States, and consequent rise in price, was not yet realized by the public, nor even in cotton circles. The cotton industry viewed with anxiety the increased difficulty of finding a market, and were anxious for a reopening of that of the Central Powers.

Certainly a shipment of cotton to Germany would only have been justified in conjunction with comprehensive other measures, particularly purchases on the American cotton market on German account. As a result of detailed discussion with American interested parties, who repeatedly urged us to such a step, we forwarded proposals to Berlin on these lines. Their general purport was that about a million bales of cotton should be bought outright on behalf of Germany, and that in addition options should be secured on a further million or two million bales on the understanding that the taking up of the options should be dependent on the possibility of shipment to Germany. On the strength of these measures the shipment of one big consignment should have been undertaken. The plan had sound prospects of success. In any case there would have been no risk worth mentioning, as, to the initiated, there was no doubt as to the rise of prices. In view of the new bank legislation (Federal Reserve Act), no insuperable difficulties would have stood in the way of financing the shipment. The indirect political pressure on the American Government and public opinion, with its reaction on England, would have been considerable.

Unfortunately the plan was frustrated by the taking up of the matter in America direct from Germany, without regard to the shipment difficulty, without going into the question of the options and without knowledge of the political or economic situation. Bremen actually placed a contract in New York for one million bales to be delivered in Bremen at a fixed price. It was, however, clear from the first to anyone acquainted with the circumstances that such a step was bound to be futile. The whole thing turned on the question of shipping. The American Press, again under English influence, at once pointed the finger of scorn, saying that the contract was not meant seriously, but was merely a piece of bluff for purposes of German propaganda.

After this had brought about the collapse of the more ambitious plan, the shipment of a single cargo still continued to be discussed and detailed preparations were made. The idea had, however, to be abandoned, because the difficulties of passing off the shipment as a purely American enterprise were practically insuperable without the background of great economic measures, which placed the cost out of all proportion to the chances of success. The whole cost, as in the "*Wilhelmina* case" would have to be guaranteed from Germany, and would of course have been lost if the English secret service succeeded in establishing the German connection.

The propaganda for preventing and hampering the supply of war material to our enemies turned at first on the question of principle whether such supplies were reconcilable with neutrality. The attempt was made—as has been briefly mentioned already—with the special support of the German-American circles, to impress upon the

American people the immorality and essentially unneutral nature of the supplies, especially in view of the vast scale they were assuming. It is well known that these attempts, which extended to a strictly legal exertion of influence on Congress, failed. The lack of unity and limited political experience of the German-Americans contributed to this result, but the economic interest of the nation in the supplies, in which the whole American Administration and industry were finally concerned, formed the decisive factor.

Attempts too were very soon made to hamper the supplies in a practical way. In August, 1914, it might perhaps have been possible to buy up the Bethlehem Steel Works, if the outlay of the necessary capital had been promptly decided upon. At that time the Americans themselves did not foresee what a gigantic proportion these supplies were to assume. The purchase of these works would have deprived the whole munition industry of its main support. Similar proposals have repeatedly been worked out by us, as, for example, the proposal to amalgamate the whole shrapnel industry of the United States. The fear, well grounded in itself, that such an arrangement was scarcely within the bounds of practical politics and could have been got round, could be ignored. In case of disputes as to the validity of such a step we should have gained more by the publicity than we stood to lose. At that time, however, the Berlin Government took up a negative attitude, and did not interest itself in the question until the beginning of 1915, when the vast supplies of material from America began to make themselves felt and the concentration of German industry on the production of munitions was not yet complete. The Military Attaché received instructions to do everything possible to hamper the fulfilment of the great outstanding French and Russian contracts for shrapnel, which was at that time still the chief shell used by the Allies. This was done successfully, if on a small scale, by founding an undertaking of our own, called the Bridgeport Projectile Company, and entering into contracts to establish the most important machinery for the manufacture of powder and shrapnel. Through this company, which originally passed as entirely American, the special machinery required for the manufacture of shrapnel was bought on a scale which seriously affected the American output, and in particular hindered the acceptance and carrying through of further contracts from the Allies for a considerable time. Herr Albert assisted and advised the Military Attaché in making these contracts, arranged the financing of the enterprise later on, and worked at its development after Herr von Papen's departure.

Still more successful were the efforts to remove from the market the surplus benzol, which is the raw product for the production of picric acid. The benzol was bought up by a company specially formed for the purpose, who sent it to a chemical works under German management to be manufactured into salicylic preparations. These products were sold for the most part for the American market, and also, with the approval of the Ministry for War, exported to neutral countries. The undertaking was eventually closed down after making considerable profits for the Imperial Treasury. In the same way, for some time, all the bromine coming on to the market, the products of which were used to manufacture and increase the density of gas, were bought up.

To these efforts to hamper and delay the supply of war material belonged also the much-discussed agreement with the Bosch Magneto Company, the American branch of the Stuttgart firm. The substance of the arrangement was that this company, which was under German direction, should not immediately refuse Allied contracts for fuses, but should appear to accept them and delay their fulfilment, and, to complete the deception, even occasionally deliver small quantities, and finally, at the last moment, refuse to complete the contract. This procedure was attacked at the time by a German-American journalist, von Skal. On the strength of short notices which Herr von Skal published in the German Press, in ignorance of the real state of the case, public opinion in Germany turned against the parent firm, the Bosch works in Stuttgart. The question then became the subject of my reports, and was submitted to an inquiry by the home authorities and the courts. I still hold to my opinion that the whole affair was unnecessarily exaggerated by German public opinion, and that the detailed investigation into its legality by the home authorities and courts was unnecessary, as the managing director of the American branch and the directors of the German company had acted in perfect good faith in an attempt to advance the interests of the German cause. It was merely a question of the result. If their policy of procrastination had succeeded in delaying the contracts and had kept our enemies for a considerable time from building their own factory for fuses and aeroplane magnetoes, their action would have been justified; in the contrary event it would have been vain, but blameless from a moral and legal point of view. The fact that at the beginning the English relied on the possibility of the production and supply of such fuses from America, and only later gradually came to a decision to build and fit out their own factories, consequently under much more difficult circumstances, offered an opening for this procedure. That difficulties were caused to the enemy in this respect until quite recently is unmistakably shown by the messages that reached America from England.

As a result of the extensive purchases of the Allies, there came about a gradual change in the attitude of the American Government to the question of issuing loans. At the end of March, 1915, we succeeded, acting on instructions from Berlin, in raising a small loan. It involved an unusual amount of trouble. The American financial world was already completely dominated by the Morgan trust. This domination resulted from the fact that the Allied commissions were concentrated in English hands and were placed by England in the hands of J. P. Morgan & Co., who acted as the agents of the English Government. As these commissions finally included every sphere of economic life, all the great American banks and bankers were called upon, and so drawn into the Morgan circle. The result was that no big firm could be induced to undertake a German loan. However, several trust companies of repute, who already had or wished to have business relations with Germany, declared their readiness to become partners in a syndicate if we succeeded in finding a "Syndicate Manager." A certain New York firm which afterwards made a name for itself, but at that time was comparatively unknown, seemed suited for this position. When all the preparations and preliminary agreements had been carried through, the trust companies, under the pressure of the Morgan influence, declared that their names must not be associated with the syndicate. Meanwhile the matter had gone so far that withdrawal would have meant a moral surrender which would have been dangerous for our credit. Consequently, we had to make up our minds to negotiate the loan under the signature of this one firm, which was naturally undesirable for the general interest.

Looking back, I am of the opinion that we should have done better not to consider a loan in the United States, but to remit the necessary funds from Berlin. This had to be done later to redeem the loan, and at a time when the rate of exchange was much more unfavorable. When the loan was raised we had certainly no idea that it would have to be redeemed during the war, as we had reckoned on a shorter duration of hostilities. On the other hand there is no truth in the statement that this loan in some way cleared the way for further Allied loans. These loans, which were the natural result of the great supplies of material to the Allies, would have come in any case. We did, however, deprive ourselves by this loan of an argument to prove the defective neutrality of the United States.

In 1916 we succeeded in getting hold of some five millions in Treasury notes without formal loan negotiations.

Another economic question which occupied my attention was connected with the export of German dye-stuffs to the United States. In Berlin it was held that German dye-stuffs should be withheld from the United States as a lever for inducing them to protest against the English blockade, and possibly have it raised. The same point of view was adopted with regard to other goods which were necessities for the United States, as, for example, potassic salt, sugar beetroot seed and other commodities. A change of view did not occur until the spring of 1916 at my suggestion. It is my belief that the withholding of these goods proved a serious mistake. The political aim of bringing pressure to bear on England with a view to the raising of the blockade was not realized. The American industry partly got over the difficulty by obtaining dye-stuffs in other ways—importation of German dyes from China, where they had been systematically bought, smuggling of German dyes via neutral countries, importation of Swiss dyes, introduction of natural dyes and dye-substitutes—but more especially by the foundation of a dye industry of their own. In the case of potash, they had simply to do with what little they could get; which was all the easier as the American manure manufacturers and dealers had already in their own interests begun a systematic propaganda to prove that potash was not indispensable, but could be replaced by their own products. It might be observed as a generalization that ultimately no individual product has proved to be really indispensable. The result of holding back our exports was therefore simply—apart from a quite unnecessary straining of political relations, since England succeeded in diverting all the odium on to us— a scarcity of important German commodities in the United States and the substitution of their own production.

In negotiating the German loan, the chief difficulty was that grasping speculators got hold of the market, discredited the war loan by underbidding one another and in part by direct dishonorable dealing, and also that owing to the impossibility of producing ready money, interest in the war loan flagged. Early on I suggested the issue of bills *ad interim*. The scheme, however, failed, because the representative of the Deutsche Bank opposed it, and because the natural opposition of two great institutions, who were making a profitable business out of the sale of war loans and the speculations on the value of the mark, which were closely connected with it, could not be overcome. I am still of the opinion that with well-timed organization the sum raised by the war loan could have been increased by several millions.

CHAPTER V

THE SO-CALLED GERMAN CONSPIRACIES

IMMEDIATELY after the outbreak of war, our cruisers in foreign waters were cut off from their base of operations, and the German Reservists in North and South America were prevented from returning home owing to the British Command of the Sea. Measures to assist them were therefore taken by the German Nationals and German Americans in the United States, which although not in themselves aimed at the Union, certainly transgressed its laws. Moreover during the year 1915 and succeeding years, several deeds of violence against the enemies of Germany, or preparations for such deeds, were discovered, involving more or less serious offences against the laws of America. Both kinds of activity, comprised under the suggestive term "German Conspiracies" or "German Plots against American Neutrality," were skilfully used by our enemies to discredit us, and these agitations did considerable harm to the German cause, besides being a serious obstacle in the way of my policy.

Among the measures for assisting the German fleet may be mentioned, in the first place, the case of the Hamburg-Amerika Line, which has already been noticed. The New York branch, acting in accordance with the instructions of their head offices in Hamburg, dispatched about a dozen chartered vessels, laden with coal and provisions, to the squadron of German cruisers and auxiliary cruisers then on the high seas. This cargo was declared in

the ships' clearing papers to be consigned to ports beyond the area of open sea where the German cruisers
were known to be. When it came out later that the New
York branch of the Hamburg-Amerika Line had made
use of this device for coaling German men-of-war, the
chief officials were brought up on the charge of deliberately making false declarations in their clearing papers,
and their chief, Dr. Bünz, a man of the highest character,
with three of his subordinates, was condemned, in December, 1915, to eighteen months' imprisonment in the
first instance.

The severity of the penalty thus inflicted on a man so
universally respected, who had, during his long tenure of
the office of Consul-General in Chicago and New York,
gained the warm affection of many Americans, was regarded merely as a manifestatoin for the benefit of the
outside world of the American Government's intention
to preserve a strict neutrality. No one supposed that the
aged Dr. Bünz would really have to undergo his sentence,
and as a matter of fact he remained at liberty for some
time even after America's declaration of war. In the
summer of 1917 a violent press-campaign broke out
against him, whereupon, despite his ill health, he offered
of his own accord to serve his sentence and was removed
to the State prison at Atlanta, where he died in 1918.
All honor to his memory!

Considering that his offence was nothing more than a
technical violation of the letter of the American Customs regulations and was actuated by no base motive,
nor by hostility to the United States, the punishment inflicted was excessively harsh. It was pleaded on his behalf in the speech for the defence that America during
the war against Spain had acted in exactly the same way,
when ships were dispatched from the neutral harbor of
Hong Kong to coal Admiral Dewey's fleet before Manila

and their cargo was declared as being scrap-iron consigned to Macao. An indication of the state of public opinion in the Eastern States of America at the end of 1915 may be found in the fact that the heavy sentence on this "German Conspirator" met with general approval apart from a few emphatic protests on the part of the German-American papers.

A number of German Reserve officers domiciled in America succeeded, despite the close watch maintained by England on the seas, in effecting their return to the Fatherland, thanks to a secret bureau in New York, organized by German-Americans, which provided them with false or forged American passports. This bureau was closed by the American police consequent on the discovery in January, 1915, of four German Reservists, with such papers in their possession, on board a Norwegian ship in New York harbor. The organizer had apparently fled from New York some time before, but finally fell into the hands of the British, and was drowned in a torpedoed transport. The Reservists were discharged on payment of heavy fines. One, however, was sentenced to three years' penal servitude. In estimating this affair, it must be remembered that according to the recognized conventions of international law, British men-of-war were not justified in making prisoners of individual unarmed Germans returning to their homes in neutral vessels. The American Government itself explicitly affirmed as much when a ship flying the Stars and Stripes was held up in mid-ocean for examination. As a rule, however, neutral Powers were too weak to stand up for their rights against British violations of international law, and so all Germans who were discovered by the British on their homeward voyage were made prisoners of war. Our countrymen, therefore, if they wished to do their duty by going to the defence of their Fatherland, were compelled, in face of this flagrant violation of the Law of Nations, to provide themselves with false passports. They had thus to choose between two conflicting duties, a dilemma all too common in life, and one which the individual must solve according to his lights. The bearers of such false passports certainly risked heavy penalties, but shrank still more from incurring any suspicion of skulking or cowardice.

It would seem, moreover, that there is little to choose, from the moral point of view, between their "sailing under false flags," for the purpose of evading the British guardians of the sea, and the hoisting of neutral ensigns by British ships to escape from German submarines.

There can, at all events, be no question of a "German conspiracy" in these cases of forged passports, as I had officially announced on behalf of the German Government, that under the circumstances no one who remained in America would, on his arrival in Germany, be punished for not answering the call to the Colors. I can repudiate in the most express terms any personal responsibility for the activities of the above-mentioned secret bureau in New York, although attempts have been made to connect my name with it on the sole ground of a letter, said to have been written to me by von Wedell before his departure, which was, as a matter of fact, first made known to me by its publication in the Press. It is true that this gentleman, a New York barrister before the war, was a personal acquaintance of mine; he had, however, immediately after the outbreak of hostilities, hastened back to Germany to join his own regiment, and later returned secretly to America, presumably under orders from his superiors, only to disappear again with equal secrecy after a short stay. I had never even heard the name of Rueroede before his arrest, but in view of his denial that any personal profit accrued to him from his services in providing his fellow-countrymen with documents for the purpose of facilitating their escape from British vigilance, I much regret the severity of the penalty inflicted on him.

If the cases of the Hamburg-Amerika Line and the falsification of the passports damaged the German cause in America, this was still more true of the acts of violence planned or carried out by Germans or German-Americans against individuals known to be hostile to our cause. The few authentic cases of this sort of thing were, as every impartial person must recognize, engineered by a few patriotic but foolish hotheads; the more sober and responsible German elements in the United States were certainly no party to them.

To the list of these outrages, the enemies of Germany deliberately added others which probably had no foundation in fact. Thus, for every accident which occurred in any American munition factory—and many accidents were bound to happen in the new works which had sprung up like mushrooms all over the land, and were staffed with absolutely untrained personnel—"German agents" were regularly held responsible, and the anti-German Press, particularly the *Providence Journal,* announced these accidents as "a clear manifestation of the notorious German system of frightfulness." Worse still, these papers instilled into their readers the firm conviction that these crimes were an essential part of German propaganda, and in their cartoons represented the German, more particularly the German-American, as a bearded anarchist with a bomb ready in his hand.

I myself was frequently libelled in this manner by the "Yellow Press," and represented both by pen and pencil as the ringleader and instigator of the so-called "conspiracies"; this accusation, at first tentative, later grew increasingly clear and unmistakable. The campaign of calumny in which even the more respectable Press took its share, was, however, directed more particularly against the Military Attaché, Captain von Papen, and the Naval Attaché, Captain Boy-Ed, whose names were openly coupled with some of the crimes which came before the American Courts of Justice. Both these officers finally fell victims to this agitation, and had to be recalled from America in December, 1915, in accordance with a request from the United States Government. At the same time, in the annual Presidential message to Congress, statutory measures were laid down against Americans implicated in these conspiracies, or, as the phrase ran, against all those "contriving schemes for the destruction of the independence, and implicated in plots against the neutrality, of the Government." Not until the declaration of war against Germany, on April 2nd, 1917, did President Wilson venture openly to accuse the official German representatives in America of complicity in these designs, in the following words: "It is unhappily not a matter of conjecture but a fact proved in our courts of justice, that the intrigues which have more than once come perilously near to disturbing the peace and dislocating the industries of the country have been carried on at the instigation, with the support, and even under the personal direction of official agents of the Imperial Government accredited to the Government of the United States." Since then my own name has been mentioned as the supreme head of the German "Conspiracy" in America, in the innumerable propaganda pamphlets with which the official "Committee of Public Information" has flooded America and Europe. And I have been openly accused of having instigated and furthered, or at the very least been privy to, all manner of criminal activities. In interviews with American journalists I have more than once refuted these calumnies, which can be supported by no evidence, and were solely intended to arouse popular feeling against Germany; but I must now refer again to the more definite of these accusations.

It must be left to the impartial historian of the future to establish the full truth concerning the German conspiracies in the United States; any evidence given under the influence of the passions arising out of the war can, of course, possess only a limited value. It is obvious from the proceedings concerning the constitution of the Senate Committee that much of the evidence was prejudiced and unreliable, probably because it was based solely on information given by Germans or former Germans, whose identities were kept strictly secret, and who told deliberate lies, either because, like Judas, they had received a reward for their treachery, or because, having severed all ties with their old country, they wished to secure their footing in the new.

In any case I myself was never a partner to any proceedings which contravened the laws of the United States. I never instigated such proceedings, nor did I consciously afford their authors assistance, whether financially or otherwise. I was in no single instance privy to any illegal acts, or to any preparations for such acts. Indeed, as a rule I heard of them first through the papers, and even then scarcely believed in the very existence of most of the conspiracies for which I was afterwards held accountable. I shall hardly be blamed for this by anyone who remembered the number of projects which we were all duly accused of entertaining, such as the various alleged plans for the invasion of Canada with a force recruited from the German-American rifle clubs, and many another wild-cat scheme attributed to us in the first months of the war.

Such offences against the laws of America as were

actually committed were certainly reprobated by none more sincerely than by myself, if only because nothing could be imagined more certain to militate against my policy, as I have here described it, than these outrages and the popular indignation aroused by them. I fully realized that these individual acts, in defiance of the law of the land and the resulting spread of Germanophobia, were bound to damage me in the eyes of the United States Government and public opinion. It is thus obviously absurd to accuse me of being responsible in any way for the acts in question, seeing that any such instigation, or even approval on my part, would have involved the utter ruin of my own policy!

Another accusation against my conduct while in America is that I at all events connived at the commission of crimes under the direction of officers attached to the Embassy of which I was in charge, or of other German Secret Service agents. The evidence for this consists of certain cipher telegrams from the military authorities in Germany, addressed to the Embassy in Washington; these were decoded in England and said to contain instructions for outrages to be committed in Canadian territory. I cannot say if these messages were genuine or no. Military cipher telegrams, formally addressed to the military attaché, were frequently received at the Embassy, but were always sent forward at once by the registry to Captain von Papen's office in New York, as a matter of routine, and without being referred to me in any way. Von Papen certainly never told me a word about any instructions from his superiors that he should endeavor to foment disorders as alleged. For the present, then, I consider that there is insufficient evidence for his having received any such orders; but in all these matters I can, of course, speak only for myself, military matters being entirely out of my province.

Soon after von Papen's recall I entered a protest against the sending of a successor, as there was no longer any useful purpose to be served by the employment of a Military Attaché, whose presence would only serve as a pretext for a renewed hostile agitation against us.

Whether the illegal acts of the Secret Agents sent to the United States by the military authorities were committed in accordance with their orders or on their own initiative I had no means of knowing at the time, nor have I been able to discover since my return home. I may observe, however, that I more than once urgently requested the Foreign Office to use all their influence against the dispatch of Secret Service men to America. Moreover, I had published in the Press a notice, couched in strong terms and signed by myself, warning all Germans domiciled in the United States not to involve themselves in any illegal activities under any circumstances whatever. And I think I am justified in saying that twelve months before the severance of diplomatic relations, I had made a clean sweep of all "conspiracies" and extorted a promise that no more "agents" should be sent over from Germany. On my arrival home, I was held by some to have been at fault for not having put down the movement earlier; to which my reply must be that as a matter of fact it was the cases of Rintelen and Fay that first earned us the reputation of "conspirators"; all the rest came to light later, and were in great measure connected with their machinations. I took steps, as soon as I heard of these two affairs, to avoid any repetition of them, in which effort I was successful.

The following throws some light on the attitude of the United States Government towards me in the matter of the "conspiracies." When in November, 1915, the Press campaign had reached the height of its violence,

I forwarded a Note to Mr. Lansing, the Secretary of State, protesting strongly against the unjustifiable attacks aimed at myself and my colleagues of the Embassy and requesting that some effort should be made to suppress them, as follows:

"Washington, Nov. 16, 1915.

"The continuance of the baseless attacks on myself and the colleagues of my Embassy in the columns of the *Providence Journal* impels me to ask whether your Excellency cannot see your way to make it clear that these attacks are not countenanced by the American Government. Such slanders against the representatives of a friendly Power who have a right to claim the protection and hospitality of the United States authorities would be incomprehensible, were it not a matter of common knowledge that the *Providence Journal* is a 'hyphenated' Anglo-American paper. To borrow the phrase of the United States President, this journal is obviously a greater friend of other countries than its own.

"For the last fifteen months I and all my colleagues have had, if I may say so, a whole army of American private detectives on our track. Day and night they have pursued us in the service of our enemies. Yet, although official German documents have been stolen, no one has yet succeeded in producing a single proof of illegal activities on the part of any one of us.

"I should esteem it a great favor if your Excellency could see your way to secure this Embassy against a repetition of these baseless attacks, which have as their sole foundation the pre-supposition of conspiracies which have no existence in fact."

I never received any reply to this letter, but a short time after Mr. Lansing while informing me that the

American Government felt itself compelled to ask for the recall of Captains Boy-Ed and von Papen, as being no longer acceptable to them (this affair I propose to refer to again in another place), stated in the most explicit terms that I was in no way implicated in the matter. The fact that the American Government, even after the departure of the two attachés, maintained the same intimate relations with me throughout the fourteen months which elapsed before its diplomatic representatives were recalled from Germany, proves that this was no empty compliment, but was meant in all sincerity.

I feel myself compelled to insist on these facts, in view of the efforts subsequently made to represent me as the originator or leader of the famous "conspiracies," which were later immeasurably exaggerated by American propaganda. This propaganda has poisoned the mind of the average American citizen to such an extent that he firmly believes the German Embassy to have been a nest of anarchists, who even during the period of his country's neutrality "waged war" in the most dastardly manner against her.

And yet these stories of so-called "conspiracies," with their legions of conspirators, and resulting lengthy lists of German outrages in America, will not bear serious examination.

Irrefutable evidence on the subject can be found in the official report of the Senate Committee of Inquiry into the activities of German propaganda, which has already been mentioned more than once. After the depositions of Mr. Bruce Bielaski on this subject had gone on for two days, Senator Nelson, being tired of this dry recital—he had already expressed the opinion that most of the evidence given so far was too academic—asked this officer of the Department of Justice for a report on the German attempts "to foment strikes and cause explosions in munition factories" which he apparently considered to be an integral part of German propaganda. Mr. Bielaski then referred to the "more important cases of offences against the law, which had been fathered by the German Government." He prefaced his statement with the remark that the list he was about to give was complete in every way; twenty-four cases were dealt with, and the names of the incriminated individuals given, as reproduced below:

1. Falsification of passports (von Wedell, Rueroede).
2. Destruction of a bridge in Canada (Horn).
3. Falsification of passports (Stegler, Madden, Cook).
4. Falsification of passports (Lüderitz).
5. Attempted destruction of a canal in Canada (von der Goltz, Tauscher, Fritzen).
6. Falsification of passports (Sanders, Wunmerburg, and two accomplices).
7. Supplying of coal, etc., to German men-of-war at sea (Bunz, Koeter, Hofmeister, Poppinghaus).
8. Attempt to bring about a revolution in India (Bopp, von Schack, von Brinken, Ram Chandra, and twenty-five accomplices).
9. Attempt to blow up a railway tunnel in Canada (Bopp and three accomplices).
10. Attempted destruction of munition factories and railway bridges in Canada (Kaltschmidt, and five accomplices).
11. Plot to destroy Allied munition ships by infernal machines (Fay, Scholtz, Dächer and three accomplices).
12. Plot to destroy Allied munition ships by incendiary bombs (Scheele, von Kleist, Wolpart, Bode).
13. Attempt to foment strikes in factories engaged in the making of war materials (Rintelen, Lamar, Martin).

14. Attempt to foment strikes among the dockers (no convictions).
15. Sending of spies to Canada (König).
16. Perjury in the matter of the arming of the *Lusitania* (Stahl).
17. Attempt to smuggle rubber to Germany (Jaeger and five accomplices).
18. Attempt to smuggle ashore chronometer of an interned German ship (Thierichens).
19. Attempt to smuggle nickel to Germany (Olsen and two accomplices).
20. Attempt to smuggle rubber to Germany (Newmann and accomplices).
21. Sinking of a German ship at the entrance of an American harbor (Captain and crew of the *Liebenfels*).
22. Attempt to smuggle rubber to Germany (Soloman and accomplices).
23. Falsification of passports (Rintelen and Meloy).
24. Plan to destroy Allied army horses by means of bacteria (Sternberg).

The above is the substance of the evidence given by Bielaski. I have no wish to extenuate, in the slightest degree, the few serious offences against common law included in this list, but I imagine that the unprejudiced reader will not fail to observe that Mr. Bielaski found it necessary to rake up everything possible in order to be able to present the Committee with a respectable catalogue of crimes instigated by the German Government in the United States. Apparently his only object was to produce a list of imposing length, and for this purpose he included in it cases in which it would be difficult for even the most suspicious mind to discover the hand of the German Government. Moreover even he himself did not venture directly to assert the complicity of the representatives of the German Empire in any single one of these offences. In reply to Senator Overman, who asked if Captains von Papen and Boy-Ed were held to be implicated in all these illegal acts, Mr. Bielaski gave the following evasive answer: "The most important, and most serious of these illegal acts, were, generally speaking, inspired, financed and conducted by one or other of the accredited representatives of Germany." Officials or agents in the service of Germany were, however, mentioned by name as leaders or accomplices only in the first fourteen and the two last cases, and I may be allowed to emphasize the fact that by the admission of Mr. Bielaski himself, my own name was coupled only with the agitation for a revolution in India, which was supposed to be a part of Germany's designs. Even if we take Mr. Bielaski's unconfirmed evidence as being reliable, the total number of individuals convicted on these charges in the American Courts of Justice amounts only to sixty-seven, of whom apparently only sixteen were German nationals; and their offences fall under the following heads: the case of the Hamburg-Amerika Line and the five cases of falsification of passports already mentioned: the so-called Indian plot: one case of successful and three of attempted sabotage in Canada: and finally the cases numbered ten to fourteen and twenty-four in Bielaski's list of the illegal acts planned by the agents Rintelen, Fay and Sternberg.

I propose to go into the details of these cases later. What I am now concerned to establish is that the list in question is from one point of view more interesting for what it omits than for what it includes.

In the first place one may notice the absence of the accusation previously made against us more than once, that we had plotted to embroil the United States in war with Mexico and Japan; from the fact that Mr. Bielaski made no mention of this in his evidence before the Senate Committee it must be supposed that these ridiculous stories with which American public opinion had been at one time so assiduously spoon-fed were finally exploded.

As a matter of fact, during my service in Washington, nothing was further from my thoughts than to conspire with Mexican Generals, as any such action would have seriously interfered with my chosen policy. As concerning Japan I may, incidentally, remark that Mr. Hale, when he was acting in collaboration with us in propaganda work, particularly stipulated that we should not undertake anything which might inflame the existing antagonism between America and Japan—a condition which Dr. Dernburg accepted without hesitation, since both he and his assistant Dr. Fuehr, who knew Japan well, were decidedly opposed to any such agitation.

In order to avoid misunderstanding, I wish expressly to state that I do not deny that instructions were sent by Zimmermann, the Secretary of State, to our Embassy in Mexico, which envisaged co-operation with that country against the United States as well as an understanding with Japan, but must point out that this was recommended in the event—*and only in the event*—of the United States declaring war on us.

I shall return to these instructions later, only remarking here that it was my duty to pass them on to von Eckhardt.

It should further be noted that the design, frequently imputed to us in earlier days, of endeavoring to stir up a negro rising in the United States was also omitted from Mr. Bielaski's list. To the request of a Senator of a Southern State for his opinion on this point, he replied without hesitation that no efforts in this direction had been made by any of the official representatives of Germany.

It is noteworthy, moreover, that this agent of the Department of Justice, who had heretofore consistently held us guilty of promoting strikes in munition factories and sabotage of all kinds, failed to follow up his charges. I must admit that, in view of what had already appeared in the Press on the subject of German "conspiracies," I had expected that definite proceedings would be taken on this charge, if they were taken at all; and apparently the members of the Senate Committee were also of this opinion, for one of them expressly asked Mr. Bielaski if he had any evidence to produce on the subject. His reply was: "I know very little, if anything, of that; I don't think that during our neutrality there were any instances of criminal activities of that kind."

Again, the Bureau for the Employment of German Workers, which was likewise at one time proclaimed as a device or cloak for a dangerous "German Conspiracy," was not mentioned in Bielaski's catalogue, which conclusively proves that this calumny had been allowed to drop. The office in question, which was known as the Lübau Bureau from the name of its chief, was started by Captain von Papen with the assistance of the Austro-Hungarian Ambassador, after Dr. Dumba and I had pointed out clearly to our fellow-countrymen working in the American munition factories that any of them who took part in the manufacture of arms or supplies for our enemies would render themselves liable to be tried for high treason in their native land. After this it was the bounden duty of both Embassies to find employment for all those who voluntarily resigned from the factories working for the Entente; and from first to last this office, which had branches in Philadelphia, Chicago, Pittsburgh and Cleveland, and provided about

4,500 men with fresh employment of an unobjectionable nature, was never guilty of any illegal act.

My open reference to the German law of high treason, however, was much criticized by the greater part of the American Press, which stigmatized it as an attempt "to introduce the German criminal code into America," and as an infringement of the sovereignty of the United States. Such criticism appears somewhat unwarranted in view of the wide application given to the law of treason by the Americans themselves shortly afterwards.

After this digression on the subject of the conspiracies which had been previously imputed to us, but were now dropped out of Bielaski's list, I propose to return to the instances of illegal action which were definitely laid to our charge.

The first of these is the action of Werner Horn, a retired German officer, which gained us for the first time the opprobrious epithet of "dynamiters." Horn, of whose presence in America I was not aware until the story of his crime appeared in the papers, contrived in February, 1915, to blow up a railway bridge near Vaneboro, in the territory of Canada, on the line running through the State of Maine to Halifax. Apparently he believed, as did many other people, that this railway was being utilized for the transport of Canadian troops. As the act was quite senseless, and could at worst only have held up traffic for a few hours, Captain von Papen saw no objection to advancing to Horn, who was without means, a sum sufficient to pay the fees of his defending counsel. To the best of my knowledge Horn was simply kept under observation for some time, and it was only after America's entry into the war that he was sentenced to a term of imprisonment for a breach of the regulations with regard to the transport of explosives (he had apparently carried his dynamite with him in a hand-bag).

Of the three attempts at sabotage in Canada, the Welland Canal affair caused at the time the greatest sensation in New York. The Welland Canal connects Lake Ontario with Lake Erie, west of Niagara Falls, i.e., through Canadian territory, and it is a highway for all seaborne traffic on the great lakes, and particularly for the transport of corn to the coast. It was, therefore, considered advantageous from a military point of view to attempt the destruction of the canal. This had apparently already been projected in September by a German adventurer, calling himself Horst von der Goltz, but for some unexplained reason the idea had been abandoned at the last moment.

Captain Hans Tauscher, Krupps' representative in New York, was charged in 1916 with having supplied dynamite for this scheme, but was acquitted, on his calling evidence to prove that he had no knowledge of the use which was to be made of the explosive.

The first information that I had about the attempt on the Welland Canal was the report of the proceedings against Captain Tauscher. Even to-day the full truth of the matter has not yet come to light. The leading figure of the drama, von der Goltz, while on his way to Germany in October, 1914, fell into the hands of the British. When Captain von Papen returned to Germany in December, 1915, under safe conduct of Great Britain, his papers were taken from him at a Scottish port; among them was his American check book, and an examination of this led to the identification of von der Goltz as the individual who had planned the destruction of the Welland Canal. The latter, it would seem, was thereupon offered, by the English authorities, the alternatives of being shot or of returning to America under a guarantee of personal safety, and giving evidence against Germany in open court. He chose the latter course, and turned "State's evidence" in New York, where he was kept under constant supervision. His statements, however, in view of the pressure brought to bear upon him, and of his doubtful past, can only be regarded as of somewhat doubtful value.

During the whole course of my period of office in the United States I heard nothing about the case of Albert Kaltschmidt, the German resident in Detroit, who, after America's declaration of war, was arrested on a charge of conspiring—apparently some time in 1915—to blow up a munition factory, an arsenal and a railway bridge in Canada, and sentenced in December, 1917, to penal servitude, together with four of his confederates, and the statements made in the American Press which fastened upon me the responsibility for the deeds of violence then simmering in the brain of this individual, on the ground that, in October, 1915, he had received a considerable advance from a banking account opened in my name and that of Privy Councillor Albert, I most emphatically deny. Kaltschmidt, who was a well-known business man, had acted on behalf of Albert and von Papen in several negotiations, with the object of forestalling the Entente's agents in the purchase of important war material, and had consequently been in receipt of considerable sums of money for this purpose, both from von Papen and from the general funds of the Embassy. This had, of course, earned him the undying hatred of the outwitted agents of our enemies, and he had also, in company with his sister and brother-in-law (both of whom were later convicted of complicity in his designs), got himself disliked for the prominent part he played in the agitation for an embargo on the export of arms and munitions of war. It seems quite possible that the charges against him were the work of private enemies, and that the American Criminal Court, which condemned him, was hoodwinked by the schemings of certain Canadians; the fact that these criminal designs on Kaltschmidt's part only came to light after the United States had become a belligerent adds probability to the supposition. One thing, however, is certain, that even if the alleged plot on the part of Kaltschmidt and his relations had any real existence, the initiative was theirs alone, and cannot be laid at the door of the Embassy.

The affair of Bopp, the German Consul-General at San Francisco, was also one which aroused much feeling against Germany. This gentleman had already, as early as 1915, been accused of having delayed or destroyed certain cargoes of military material for Russia, with the aid of certain abettors; his subordinates, von Schack, the Vice-Consul, and von Brinken, the Attaché, were also believed to be implicated. In the following year he was further charged with having incited one Louis J. Smith to blow up a tunnel on the Canadian Pacific Railway, with the idea of destroying supplies on their way to Russia. All three officials were therefore brought to trial, but dismissed with a caution. However, at the end of 1916, he and his two subordinates were again brought up on a serious charge and sentenced on the testimony of their chief lieutenant, Smith, who turned State's evidence* against them, to a term of imprisonment.

All three resigned from their posts and lodged an appeal, but were again found guilty in the second instance, after America had entered the war. Consul-General Bopp and his colleagues if they had in reality committed the offences of which they were accused, were

---

*For the benefit of the reader not familiar with American legal procedure, it should be explained that in cases where several individuals are charged in common with an offence, any one of them may be assured of a pardon if he turns State's evidence and informs against his associates. This course of action, reprehensible as it undoubtedly is, from a moral point of view, has the advantage of facilitating the task of police spies!

certainly actuated in no way by the Embassy or any high authorities, but must be held solely and entirely responsible for the course they adopted. In his reports to me, Bopp invariably asserted his innocence, and I am rather inclined to believe that he really fell into one of the traps which the Allied Secret Service were always setting for our officials in America.

According to common report, Consul-General Bopp, Schack and von Brinken later underwent yet a further term of imprisonment for their complicity in the so-called Indian conspiracy. I am quite certain that nothing was ever heard of this affair until after the American declaration of war; then, however, newspaper reports were shown me, the effect that in the year of 1916 an attempt had been made by the Indian Nationalists in San Francisco, with German co-operation, to bring about an armed rising in British India—an absolute "wild-goose chase," which, of course, came to nothing. It was asserted in this connection that a cargo of arms and ammunition on board the small schooner *Annie Larsen*, and destined for our forces in German East Africa, was, in reality, dispatched to India via Java and Siam; but no proofs were brought forward in support of this statement. In connection with this design, four persons were sentenced at Chicago, in October, 1917, and ten (according to Bielaski twenty-nine in all) at San Francisco, in August, 1918, to long terms of imprisonment, for having "illegally conspired in the United States to make war against the territories and possessions of His Majesty the King of Great Britain and Ireland and Emperor of India." It seems that this affair was exploited with great success by the American propaganda service to inflame the minds of its people against Germany. As a matter of fact, I cannot too strongly condemn on principle all military enterprises undertaken from neutral territory; but, from the purely moral point of view, I cannot but remark that it ill befits America to give vent to righteous indignation over such activities, considering the facilities she afforded to Czechs and Poles, during her period of neutrality, for supporting to the utmost of their power their blood brothers in their designs against the Central Powers. Besides, even if it be admitted that the schooner in question was actually sent by the Indian Nationalists with her cargo of arms, it is absurd to regard the dispatch of this small supply of war material as a crime, and gloss over the fact that whole arsenals and ammunition columns were being shipped every day to France!

I now propose, in conclusion, to deal with the illegal activities attributed by American opinion to the secret agents controlled by the German military authorities, and sent by them to the United States.

As regards the machinations of Franz Rintelen, my first information about him reached me in the late autumn of 1915, and even now I have to rely for most of the details on the American papers. Rintelen, who was a banker by profession, and during the war held a commission as Captain-Lieutenant in the Imperial Naval Reserve, appeared in America in April, 1915, and presented himself to me during one of my periodical visits to New York. He declined at the time to give any information as to his official position in the country, or the nature of his duties; I therefore wired to the Foreign Office for some details about him, but received no reply. Some time afterwards he applied to me for proofs of identity, which I refused to grant him, and as his continued presence in New York was considered undesirable by both von Papen and Boy-Ed, they took steps to have him sent back to Germany. He was captured, however, by the British, on his voyage home. Shortly after this, the affair of Rintelen became a matter of common talk, and the first indications of his mysterious intrigues for the purpose of interfering with the delivery of munitions from the United States to the Allies appeared in the Press; the Foreign Office thereupon instructed me to issue an official *démenti* on the subject. Mr. Lansing, the Secretary of State, however, informed me that, as a matter of fact, Rintelen, while in England, had confessed himself to be an emissary of the German Government. I then heard from Captain Boy-Ed that Rintelen, by representing himself as empowered to purchase large stocks of raw material for Germany in the United States, had obtained a considerable advance from the Embassy's funds. This fact was one of the main reasons for the American Government's request in December, 1915, that Boy-Ed should be recalled. I was never able either in America or Germany to discover the details of Rintelen's intrigues; he himself never allowed anything to leak out about it at the Embassy, and was unable to send any report on the subject to Germany, as he was handed over to the United States by the British after the American declaration of war, and sentenced to some years' penal servitude. The current story in the United States is that he was proved to have been in touch with the Mexican General, Huerta, with the object of bringing about war between the two Republics—an offence of which the famous list of Mr. Bielaski makes no mention. Further, he was supposed to have founded, in conjunction with a member of Congress, and two individuals of evil reputation, a society of workmen in Chicago, with the object of obtaining from Congress an embargo on the export of arms—an undertaking which according to the aforementioned report cost a great deal and proved entirely valueless from the point of view of the German Government. It is not known whether this undertaking brought

Rintelen and his assistants within the reach of the Sherman Act against conspiracies inciting industrial disorders, or whether he had, in addition, made efforts to bring about strikes in munition works. He was certainly suspected of endeavoring to cause trouble among the dockers of New York, in the hope of preventing or delaying the shipment of war material to the Allies; but even Bielaski admitted before the Senate Committee that there was no tangible evidence of this.

As a matter of fact, the real grounds of Rintelen's conviction were apparently that he had prepared, through the agency of a certain German chemist, domiciled in America, named Scheele, a number of incendiary bombs, which were apparently to be secreted by three officers of the German Mercantile Marine on board Allied munition ships, with the object of causing fires on the voyage. After America's entry into the war, Rintelen and his accomplices were sentenced on this count to fairly lengthy terms of imprisonment, and these sentences they are serving at the present moment in the Federal prison at Atlanta.

I have been unable to discover how far Rintelen was actually guilty of the offences imputed to him; but I can only observe that he, and, in so far as he acted under orders, his superiors, gravely compromised the position of the German official representatives in the United States, and afforded our enemies an excellent opportunity of inflaming public opinion against Germany. It is impossible to over-estimate the unfortunate effect produced throughout the world by the discovery of bombs on board a German passenger-steamer, and of their secretion in the holds of Allied munition ships.

Another attempt of a similar kind, which had most unfortunate results from our point of view, was that attributed to a German, Lieutenant Fay, who had likewise come to America in April, 1915, and two other Germans, by name Scholz and Däeche. Their idea was to put Allied munition ships out of action by means of infernal machines, fastened to the rudders, and timed to explode shortly after their departure. My first information concerning these gentlemen was the report in the Press of their arrest, which was apparently effected while they were experimenting with their apparatus under cover of a wood. A telegraphic inquiry elicited from Berlin the reply that Fay was absolutely unknown there; it is possible, however, that he had really come to America on some business of an official nature. He and his accomplices were sentenced in May, 1916, to several years' penal servitude, although no proof was adduced that any real damage could possibly have been caused by their contrivance, which experts informed me was not a practicable one.

Last of all, on Bielaski's list comes the case of the German agent Stermberg, of whom, also, I had never heard. In January, 1915, he was arrested on a charge of having attempted to inoculate horses, purchased for the Allied Armies, with disease germs. As his practical knowledge was not great, his intentions were in excess of his performances. Bielaski, in his evidence before the Senate Committee, at first hesitated to mention this case at all, and was only induced to do so by the insistence of another Government official; it is clear, therefore, that he attached very little importance to it, and, as a matter of fact, the charge was not supported by any witnesses in a court of law, or by any legal attestation.

In a word, during all our period of service in America, as representatives of the German Empire, practically nothing of all that was alleged against us was proved to be true. A few of the stories of illegal activity, however, were based on some foundation of truth, and were popularly but erroneously supposed to further the interests of Germany. By these means we were first brought into discredit, and from that time on, every rumor, or piece of gossip concerning acts of violence on the part of Germans, whether based on fact or not, served only to increase the wide-spread popular suspicion and distrust of everyone and everything German.

CHAPTER VI

THE "LUSITANIA" INCIDENT

On August 6th, 1914, the Government of the United States proposed to all the belligerent Powers that the laws of war at sea, as laid down in the Declaration of London of 1909, should be observed throughout the present war. This reasonable suggestion, which, had it been generally observed, would have saved the world much distress, came to nothing, owing to the refusal of Great Britain to accept it as it stood without reservation. The United States Government thereupon withdrew its proposal on October 24th, and announced that "It was resolved in future to see that the rights and duties of the Government and citizens of the United States should be settled in accordance with the accepted principles of international law and the treaty obligations of the United States, without reference to the provisions of the Declaration of London." Moreover, the American Government drew up protests and demands for compensation, for use in case of any infringement of these rights, or of any interference with their free exercise on the part of the belligerent Powers.

On November 3rd, 1914, Great Britain declared the whole of the North Sea a theatre of war, and thereupon instituted, in flagrant violation of the Law of Nations, a blockade of the adjoining neutral coasts and ports. General disappointment was felt in Germany that the

United States made no attempt to vindicate her rights in this matter, and confined herself to demanding compensation in individual cases of infringement.

Both in Germany and elsewhere it was clearly recognized that England's design was to use this illegal blockade for the purpose of starving out the German people. During a discussion between myself and Mr. Lansing, later Secretary of State, on the matter of assistance to be sent by America to Belgium, he expressed the opinion that nothing would come of the scheme, as Lord Kitchener had adopted the attitude that no food supplies could under any circumstances be sent to territory in German occupation. I answered that I had expected this refusal, as it was England's intention to starve us out, to which Mr. Lansing replied: "Yes, the British frankly admit as much." It will be remembered that, as a matter of fact, Lord Kitchener withdrew his refusal in view of the pressure of English public opinion, which demanded that relief should be sent to Belgium on account of the distress prevalent there, and despite the fact that such a measure was of indirect assistance to us. A subsequent proposal from the American Government for the dispatch of similar relief to Poland was declined in London.

We Germans had hoped that the neutral States would vigorously claim their right to freedom of mutual trade, and would take effective measures, in conjunction with the leadership of the United States, to force the British Government to suspend the oppressive and extra-legal policy. This they failed to do, at any rate, in time to forestall the fateful decision on our part to undertake submarine warfare. It is now impossible to tell whether this policy might not have had more favorable results, had not the growing estrangement between Germany and America caused by the new campaign nipped in the bud any possibility of serious Anglo-American differences. In the other neutral countries this submarine warfare alienated all sympathy for us, and no doubt was one reason why the neutral States, which in previous wars had always attempted to vindicate their rights as against the Power which had command of the sea, now refrained from any concerted action to this end. Such a procedure on their part would have indirectly influenced the situation in favor of Germany, as the weaker Power at sea; it will be remembered that the United States, during their War of Independence against England, drew much advantage from a similar attitude on the part of the European Powers. My knowledge of America leads me to believe that, had we not incurred such odium by our infringement of Belgian neutrality and our adoption of submarine warfare, the action of the Washington Government might have been other than it was; had it even raised a finger to protest against England's methods, the latter must instantly have given way, as had so frequently happened during the last twenty-five years, when the United States took up on any point an attitude hostile to Britain. The contrast between this passive attitude on the part of the President and the traditional forward policy of America vis-à-vis England, goes far to support the contention of Wilson's detractors in Germany—that these two countries were in league and were playing a preconcerted game.

It is impossible to convince one's political foes on any point except by positive proof, and until the time comes when the enemy's archives are published, such proof cannot, of course, be adduced on this particular matter. This time is still far distant. Why should the enemy publish their archives? They have won and have therefore no reason to grumble at the course of events. Thus

I can at present only combat with counter-arguments the contention that I misunderstood the true state of affairs in America. The hypothesis of secret collusion between America and England seems in the present case unnecessary; the attitude of public opinion in America is in itself sufficient explanation of the situation at the time. Sympathy for us from the very first day of the war there was none; but had the general feeling been as strongly for us as it actually was against us, no doubt the Government would have kicked against the English illegalities, and enforced an embargo against her. I still hold to my view that Mr. Wilson made a real effort to maintain the observance of a strict neutrality; but the decisive factor was that he found himself, as a result of his efforts, in increasing measure in conflict with the overwhelming Germanophobe sentiment of the people, and continually exposed to the reproach put forward in the Eastern States that he was a pro-German.

The American public, indifferent as it was to the affairs of Europe and entirely ignorant of its complicated problems, failed to understand the full extent of the peril to the very existence of the German Empire, which compelled its rulers, much against their will and with heavy hearts, to have recourse to the invasion of Belgium. They themselves, living in perfect security and under pleasant conditions, had no means of realizing the perilous position of a comparatively small people, such as the Germans, surrounded by greedy foes, and straitened within narrow frontiers; their judgment, as already remarked, was swayed by their individual sentiments of justice and humanity. The attitude of the Allied and Associated Powers at Versailles might have enlightened the American people as to the peril of dismemberment which threatened a defeated Germany; but such realization, even supposing it to have taken place, has come too late to affect the consequences of the war. I am convinced that they will in a few years be forced to admit that Germany during the course of her struggle was, contrary to the generally accepted view of to-day, quite as much sinned against as sinning.

The German Government, then, decided upon the adoption of submarine warfare, and issued a declaration to this effect. This document, together with explanatory memorandum, was delivered by me on February 4th, 1915, to the Secretary of State, Mr. Bryan; it was to the effect that the territorial waters of Great Britain and Ireland, including the whole of the English Channel, were declared a war area. From February 18th onwards every enemy merchant ship encountered in this area was liable to be sunk, without any guarantee that time could be given for the escape of passengers and crew. Neutral shipping in the war zone was likewise liable to the same dangers, as owing to the misuse of neutral flags resulting from the British Government's order of January 31st, and the chances of naval warfare, the possibility of damage to other shipping as a result of attacks on hostile vessels might sometimes be unavoidable.

I regarded it as my main duty, when handing this document to Mr. Bryan, to recommend to the United States Government that they should warn all American citizens of the danger to the crews, passengers and cargoes of hostile merchant ships moving within the war area from this time onwards. Further, I felt it necessary to draw attention to the advisability of an urgent recommendation that American shipping should keep clear of the danger zone, notwithstanding the express statement in the memorandum that the German naval forces had orders to avoid any interference with neutral vessels clearly recognizable as such.

Mr. Secretary Bryan was at first incredulous; he believed a submarine campaign of this nature to be unthinkable, and my statements to be merely bluff. The American Government therefore resolved to take no measures of precaution, but to dispatch a Note to Berlin on February 12th, summarizing the two conflicting points of view, which remained irreconcilable throughout the whole controversy, on the subject of the submarine war. Germany, on the one hand, defended her course of action as a reprisal justified by the British blockade, which both parties to the discussion agreed to be contrary to the Law of Nations. The United States, for her part, maintained that as long as the blockade of Great Britain was not made effective, neutral shipping had the right to go where it wished unharmed, and that the German submarines were empowered only to hold up merchant ships for search purposes, unless these same ships offered resistance or endeavored to escape.

The chief germ of dissension lay in the fact that the British blockade, which was defended by its authors as being merely an extension of the rights of sea warfare to square with the progress of the modern military machine, was met on America's part only by paper protests, while our own extension of the same rights by means of submarine warfare was treated as a *casus belli*. At a later period of the war the Imperial Government made certain proposals to the United States, who might, by accepting them, have safeguarded all their commercial and shipping interests, not to mention the lives of their citizens, to the fullest possible extent, and yet have allowed us a free field for our submarine warfare. These proposals the United States rejected; thus she set herself to combat with all her strength any continuance of the blockade restrictions through our submarines, while conniving at the similar restrictions exercised by England, although these latter infringed far more seriously the rights of neutral Powers.

The following extract from the American Note of February 12th clearly presaged the conflict to come:

"This Government has carefully noted the explanatory statement issued by the Imperial German Government at the same time with the proclamation of the German Admiralty, and takes this occasion to remind the Imperial German Government very respectfully that the Government of the United States is open to none of the criticisms for unneutral action to which the German Government believe the governments of certain other neutral nations have laid themselves open; that the Government of the United States has not consented or acquiesced in any measures which may have been taken by the other belligerent nations in the present war which operate to restrain neutral trade, but has, on the contrary, taken in all such matters a position which warrants it in holding those governments responsible in the proper way for any untoward effects upon American shipping which the accepted principles of international law do not justify; and that it, therefore, regards itself as free in the present instance to take with a clear conscience and upon accepted principles the position indicated in this Note.

"If the commanders of German vessels of war should act upon the presumption that the flag of the United States was not being used in good faith and should destroy on the high seas an American or the lives of American citizens, it would be difficult for the Government of the United States to view the act in any other light than as an indefensible violation of neutral rights which it would be very hard indeed to reconcile with the friendly relations now so happily subsisting between the two Governments.

"If such a deplorable situation should arise, the Imperial German Government can readily appreciate that the Government of the United States would be constrained to hold the Imperial German Government to a strict accountability for such acts of their naval authorities, and to take any steps it might be necessary to take to safeguard the American lives and property and to secure to American citizens the full enjoyment of their acknowledged rights on the high seas."

The Imperial Government reaffirmed its standpoint in a further Note, dated February 16th, the gist and conclusion of which was as under:

"If the American Government, by reason of that weight which it is able and entitled to cast into the balance which decides the fate of peoples, should succeed even now in removing those causes which make the present action of the German Government an imperious duty; if the American Government, in short, should succeed in inducing the Powers at war with Germany to abide by the terms of the Declaration of London, and to permit the free importation into Germany of foodstuffs and raw material, the Imperial Government would recognize in such action a service of inestimable value, tending to introduce a spirit of greater humanity into the conduct of the war, and would willingly draw its own conclusions from the resulting new situation."

This Note was effective, in that it induced the American Government to dispatch on February 22nd an identical Note to Great Britain and Germany, with the object of arriving at a *modus vivendi* in the matter. Their proposal was as follows: Submarines were not to be employed in any attack on merchant ships of whatever nationality, save in execution of the rights of detention or search; merchant ships, for their part, were not to make use of neutral flags, whether as a *ruse de guerre* or to avoid identification. Great Britain would give free passage to provisions and food supplies consigned to certain agents in Germany, to be named by the United States. These agents would receive all goods thus imported and dispatch them to specially licensed distributing firms, who were to be responsible that they were issued exclusively to the civilian population.

The above project was concurred in by the German Government in a Note of February 28th, which added that "The Imperial Government considered it right that other raw materials, essential to manufacture for peaceful purposes, and also fodder, should also be imported without interference."

The British Government, as was to be expected, rejected the American proposal on somewhat flimsy pretexts, for England's sea supremacy was at stake in this as in her previous wars. "Britannia rules the waves" was, and ever must be, the guiding principle of all her policy, while her world-Empire endures. On this vitally important question England could not be expected ever to yield an inch of her own free will.

Thus the American attempt at mediation died a natural death.

Our adoption of submarine warfare was to be regarded, according to our Note of February 16th, as a measure of reprisal in answer to the English blockade. From a tactical point of view, this contention was unfortunate, as it afforded America the opportunity of agreeing at once, and thus of conceding us a point which benefited us not at all, but merely gave the United States all the more right to renew its protests against the submarine war. It would have been wiser for us to have initiated the submarine campaign simply as a new weapon of war without reference to the English blockade; still better, to put it into operation without declaring a blockade of Great Britain and Ireland, which could never be really effective, and caused constant friction between ourselves and America. Our declaration that the territorial waters of Great Britain were to be regarded as a war area was a legal formality modelled on the earlier English proclamation of the barred zones, and at once antagonized public opinion in the United States. By adopting the point of view we did with regard to reprisals, we laid ourselves open to the charge of illegality, and added to the ill-feeling already excited by the submarine campaign. If the contention of certain naval authorities that the observance of the Declaration of London by our enemies would have brought us no important material advantage is correct, the issue of our Note of February 16th becomes even less comprehensible. Having admitted in this Note that the declaration of the barred zones was caused by the fact that all was not well with us, we could hardly expect England would fall in with the proposal made at our suggestion by Mr. Wilson, and thus allow us so easy a diplomatic triumph. The President, however, after his rebuff from England, was bound, in order to maintain his prestige, to bring all possible pressure to bear on us, in the hope of compensating by diplomatic success in Berlin for his failure in London. My subsequent attitude was laid down, but at the same time made more difficult, by this interchange of Notes; but, generally speaking, my personal action in the matter began with the *Lusitania* incident; previous to this the negotiations had been entirely in the hands of Berlin.

The Washington Government then for the present assumed a waiting attitude, until such time as loss of American lives through our submarine activities should compel its intervention. With regard to damage to property, the standpoint was consistently maintained that claims for compensation for financial loss must be fully met. Every day might see a serious conflict, and this possibility was a source of constant anxiety to us Germans in the United States. The American Government, we thought, still underestimated the dangers of the situation, and failed to take any measures of precaution. In the middle of April I held a meeting in New York, with the representatives of the other German administrative departments, and in view of the great responsibility incumbent on us, we resolved on the motion of Dr. Dernburg to issue a warning to the Press in the form usually adopted for shipping notices. As a rule, these shipping notices were published by the Consulate as a matter of routine. Dr. Dernburg having, however, been unable to come to an agreement with the New York Consulate on the matter, I took upon myself to issue the advertisement as from the German Ambassador. It ran as follows:

"Travellers intending to embark for an Atlantic voyage are reminded that a state of war exists between Germany and her Allies and Great Britain and her Allies; that the zone of war includes the waters adjacent to the British Isles; that, in accordance with the formal notice given by the Imperial German Government, vessels flying the flag of Great Britain or any of her Allies are liable to destruction in those waters; and that travellers sailing in the war zone in ships of Great Britain or her Allies do so at their own risk."

"IMPERIAL GERMAN EMBASSY, Washington.
"*April 22nd*, 1915."

This notice was intended to appear in the Press on April 24th and the two following Saturdays. By one of those fatal coincidences beloved of history, it happened that owing to technical difficulties the *communiqué* was not actually published until May 1st—the very date on which the *Lusitania* left New York harbor. This conjunction was bound to appear intentional rather than fortuitous, and even to-day the majority of Americans believe that I must have known beforehand of the design to torpedo the *Lusitania*.

As the true facts of the matter are not yet clear, and were never explained officially, I have no means of saying whether the destruction of the *Lusitania* was the result of a deliberate purpose on the part of our naval authorities. To the best of my belief technical factors render it impossible for a submarine commander to make any one particular ship the object of his attack, so that the officer responsible for the sinking of the *Lusitania* could not have been certain what vessel he had to deal with. In any case, whether the action of our naval authorities was planned out beforehand or not, we in America had no knowledge of any such plan; indeed, until it actually occurred, I believed the destruction of the *Lusitania* to be unthinkable, not merely for humanitarian reasons, but because it was obviously sound policy to refrain as far as possible from any attack on passenger ships. I did not at the time realize how difficult it was for our naval forces to insure the safety of such vessels without impairing the efficiency of the submarine blockade. Again, I did not believe it possible to torpedo a rapidly-moving ship like the *Lusitania* if she were going at full speed; and, finally, I supposed that a modern liner, if actually struck, would remain afloat long enough to allow of the rescue of her passengers. The captain of the *Lusitania* himself seems to have been quite at ease in his mind on the matter; at all events, he took no precautionary measures to avoid the danger threatening him, or to insure the safety of the people on board in case of need. The rapidity with which the ship went down and the resulting heavy death-roll can only be attributed to the explosion of the masses of ammunition which formed part of the cargo.

Let me once more lay stress on the fact that our notice to the Press had no particular reference to the *Lusitania,* but was simply a general warning, the publication of which was motived simply by humanity and wise policy, and was rendered necessary by the apathetic behavior of the Washington authorities in the matter. We rightly imagined that many Americans had not taken the trouble to read the Notes officially exchanged, and would thus rush blindly into danger. Our failure to achieve any result by our efforts may be appreciated from an extract from the London *Daily Telegraph* of May 3rd, which is before me as I write. The New York correspondent of this paper dealt with our warning in the following headlines:

"GERMAN THREAT TO ATLANTIC LINERS."

"BERLIN'S LATEST BLUFF."

"RIDICULED IN AMERICA."

On May 7th I travelled to New York in the afternoon —a fact in itself sufficient to prove that I was not expecting the disaster to the *Lusitania.* It chanced that Paul Warburg and another American banker were on the same train. I bought an evening paper at Philadelphia, and there read the first news about the sinking of the great liner; I read them to my two travelling companions, both of whom disbelieved the story at the time; but Jacob Schiff met us in New York with the news that it was all too true, and that in the first moment of excitement he had hurried to the station to inform his brother-in-law, Warburg, of what had happened. I had come to New York with the intention of being present at a performance of *The Bat,* given by a German company for the benefit of the German Red Cross; but when I learned on my arrival at the Ritz-Carlton Hotel that over one hundred Americans, including many women and children, had lost their lives in the sinking of the *Lusitania,* I at once gave up all idea of attending the performance. As the hotel was soon surrounded on all sides by newspaper reporters, I remained indoors until my departure on the morrow; I should have returned to Washington at once, but for having to interview certain German gentlemen in New York.

Unfortunately it so happened that Dr. Dernburg was then away at Cleveland, addressing a meeting; he took the opportunity of defending the destruction of the *Lusitania* on the ground that she was carrying munitions of war. This speech aroused a storm of execration throughout the country, which was already indignant enough over the fatal event itself. Even to-day no German seems to realize the full violence of the passion thus aroused; we, accustomed as we have been to daily reports of battles and casualties, were little impressed by the destruction of a solitary passenger ship. America, however, execrated us whole-heartedly as murderers of women and children, oblivious of the fact that the victims of the submarine campaign were far less numerous than the women and children killed by the English blockade, and that death by drowning is no more dreadful than slow starvation. Every one naturally realizes his own misfortunes more vividly than those of others, and the *Lusitania* incident first brought home to the United States the horrors of war, and convinced all her people that a flagrant injury had been done them. On my departure from New York I found myself at once face to face with this immense popular excitement. I left my hotel by a side door, but did not manage to escape notice; several cars filled with reporters followed me to the station, and pressed round me so persistently that I was unable to shake them off. I could only refuse to make any statement, which only increased the excitement of the reporters; but had I said anything at that time, I should but have added fuel to the fire which was already raging in the minds of all. Finally I succeeded in forcing my way through the infuriated and howling mob of pressmen and reaching the train.

For the first few days after my return to Washington I remained in seclusion, so as to avoid any possibility of unpleasant incidents. Those Germans who live in the congenial surroundings of their homes can have little conception of the hostility with which we in America had to contend. We had many true friends, who right up to the final breach between the two countries never deserted us. To them I shall ever feel myself indebted, more particularly in view of their harsh treatment at the hands of their fellow-countrymen and enemy diplomatists, as a result of their staunchness. The pro-Entente elements of the country proposed not only to boycott us socially, but also to terrorize all pro-German Americans. In this connection it is of interest to note that a certain neutral representative was accused by his Government of having taken our part; he was led to believe that this charge had originated in the Russian Embassy, and taxed M. Bakmetieff with the fact. The latter had no better proof of it to adduce than the report that the Dutch Ambassador—for he it was who had been thus attacked—occasionally had breakfast with me at my club, and always stayed at the German headquarters, the Ritz-Carlton

Hotel, whenever he came to New York. The above example is typical of the attitude usually adopted towards us; despite it all, throughout the war I never wanted for true and loyal friends in America, even though, particularly after the *Lusitania* incident, one or other shrank from braving the resulting public odium. Such half-hearted champions we could easily dispense with; the situation at the moment was so strained that we had no use for any save trustworthy and reliable men on our side. I may take this opportunity to place it on record that my relations with all the State Departments remained to the last of the friendliest; I should be doing them an injustice, did I not expressly affirm this.

President Wilson must certainly have under-estimated the spirit of angry hostility towards Germany which then held sway over his people's minds, otherwise he would probably not have gone directly counter to it, as he did in a speech which has now become famous. On May 10th at Philadelphia he gave evidence of his peaceful inclinations in the following words:

"The example of America must be a special example. The example of America must be the example not merely of peace because it will not fight, but of peace because peace is the healing and elevating influence of the world and strife is not. There is such a thing as a man being too proud to fight. There is such a thing as a nation being so right that it does not need to convince others by force that it is right."

This speech did but increase the indignation raging throughout the country, and the phrase "Too proud to fight" became the favorite joke of the Jingo and Entente party against Mr. Wilson. Public opinion with one voice demanded the severance of diplomatic relations with

Germany; and before this powerful pressure the President deemed it advisable to explain away his words.

It may be said, perhaps, in answer to the above, that America was indeed bitterly angry, but still not resolved on war; and that public opinion was indignant, not at Wilson's desire to keep the peace, but at the unfortunate expression "Too proud to fight."

This view was held, for example, by von Tirpitz, and also found expression more than once in the reports of the so-called German Chamber of Commerce in New York, which were regularly transmitted to Germany, and exercised considerable influence on opinion in that country, although their author was a man of no political insight, and the Chamber of Commerce had, as a matter of fact, no actual existence.

They were simply a journalistic device on the part of the paper which published these reports. During the war, and under the influence of the passions which it aroused, there was continually going on in America any amount of mischievous gossip and intrigue concerning which many interesting stories might be told. I have no intention, however, of concerning myself with these unworthy matters now, any more than I allowed them at the time to color my official reports to the home Government; I can only say that if the reports of the Chamber of Commerce had any sort of influence on German opinion, it was much to be regretted. The opinion, therein expressed, that the United States would never, under any circumstances, embark on hostilities against us was unfortunately belied by later events, and the idea that America was at that time compelled to keep the peace by defects in her military equipment, had no foundation in fact. Admittedly, she was in the year 1917 insufficiently equipped for war, and the question of making good her deficiencies had not got beyond the stage of discussion. I should, of course, have been only too pleased if my repeated warnings as to the danger of war with America had proved to be unfounded; in point of fact, after the *Lusitania* incident, America was, for a period of three weeks, on the verge of breaking off diplomatic relations, and panic reigned on the Stock Exchanges throughout the country. The fact that Congress was not sitting at the time prevented a flood of speeches which would only have increased the tension. It will be remembered that by the American Constitution the annual sessions of Congress are short and long alternately; the short session had come to an end on March 4, 1915, and the President had refrained from summoning Congress again, as he wished to avoid discussion on the question of war.

The irresistible strength of the popular indignation may be accurately estimated from the fact that even the German-Americans were terror-stricken by its violence. Not only did our propaganda collapse completely, but even our political friends dared not open their mouths, and only ventured to assert themselves once more after the settlement of the *Arabic* case. Germanism in America may be said to have been absolutely killed by the *Lusitania* incident, and only gradually came to life again.

The first expressions of opinion which I received from the President and Mr. Bryan gave me good grounds for hope that these gentlemen would do everything in their power to preserve peace. I append the two telegrams which I sent to the Foreign Office:

(1). "Washington, May 9th, 1915.

"*Lusitania* incident has caused great excitement, especially in New York, which is most affected, but I hope that no serious consequences will ensue. Mr. Wilson regards matters calmly. I recommend expression of regret for loss of so many American lives, in whatever form may be possible without admission of our responsibility."

(2). "Washington, May 10th, 1915.

"Bryan spoke to me very seriously concerning *Lusitania* incident. His influence will, in any case, be exercised in favor of peace. This influence is great, as Wilson depends on Bryan for his re-election. Roosevelt, on the other hand, is beating the patriotic drum, in order to win over the Jingo elements. It is significant of Bryan's real views that he regrets that we did not support his well-known attempt at mediation; therefore, I again recommend that we should endeavor to bring about an attempt at mediation in some form, in case the position here becomes critical. This would be a good *argumentum ad hominem* in order to avoid war. Another way out, which is recommended, is that we should renew our offer to give up submarine warfare provided that England adheres to the principles of International Law, and gives up her policy of starvation. The position is in any case *very serious;* I hope and believe that we shall find a way out of the present crisis, but in case of any such recurrence, no solution can be guaranteed."

American indignation was directed particularly against Dr. Dernburg, who had defended, in public, the torpedoing of the *Lusitania*. I had, therefore, no other resource but to advise him to leave the country of his own accord. He would probably have been deported in any case, and his continued presence in America could no longer serve any useful purpose, while it was to be hoped that his voluntary departure would appease the popular wrath in some degree, and postpone the imminent rupture of diplomatic relations. The sea was raging and demanded a sacrifice. I sent the following report to Berlin on the subject of Dr. Dernburg's resolve to leave the country:

"Washington, May 17th, 1915.

"As I have already wired to your Excellency, Dr. Dernburg has decided to leave the country of his own free will. I believe that, in so doing, he is rendering a great service to the Fatherland, a service rendered easier by the fact that he could no longer hope to continue in the exercise of his former duties. As I have already reported, he had exposed himself to attack by our enemies by his action in going counter to the present outbreak of hysterical feeling in a speech and an interview which were, unfortunately, not in accordance with your Excellency's instructions, received by me on the following day. So long as Dernburg only wrote articles for the papers, he rendered distinguished and highly appreciated service, but when he commenced to deliver speeches at German-American meetings he trod on very dangerous ground. On this point we are all in agreement here. In any case, in war every possible method must be tried, and if any individual is sacrificed it must be regarded as unfortunately unavoidable.

"When I informed Mr. Bryan that Dr. Dernburg had decided to return home if the American Government would secure him a safe conduct from our enemies, the satisfaction of the Secretary of State was even more pronounced than I had expected. He remarked that Dr. Dernburg's speeches had given rise to the suspicion that the German Government wished to inflame the minds of the American people against President Wilson's administration. It might be possible, now that there were no longer any grounds for this idea, to avoid an immediate rupture of diplomatic relations."

On May 13th the American Government dispatched a strongly worded Note to Berlin, which restated their point of view, as previously given. I reproduce textually the following passage from the Note, which, from the point of view of subsequent events, is of fundamental importance.

"The Government of the United States, therefore, desires to call the attention of the Imperial German Government with the utmost earnestness to the fact that the objection to their present method of attack against the trade of their enemies lies in the practical impossibility of employing submarines in the destruction of commerce without disregarding those rules of fairness, reason, justice, and humanity, which all modern opinion regards as imperative. It is practically impossible for the officers of a submarine to visit a merchantman at sea and examine her papers and cargo. It is practically impossible for them to make a prize of her; and, if they cannot put a prize crew on board of her, they cannot sink her without leaving her crew and all on board of her to the mercy of the sea in her small boats. . . . Manifestly submarines cannot be used against merchantmen, as the last few weeks have shown, without an inevitable violation of many sacred principles of justice and humanity.

"American citizens act within their indisputable rights in taking their ships and in travelling wherever their legitimate business calls them on the high seas, and exercise those rights in what should be the well-justified confidence that their lives will not be endangered by acts done in clear violation of universally acknowledged international obligations, and certainly in the confidence that their own Government will sustain them in the exercise of their rights.

"There was recently published in the newspapers of the United States, I regret to inform the Imperial German Government, a formal warning, purporting to come from the Imperial Germany Embassy at Washington, addressed to the people of the United States, and stating, in effect, that any citizen of the United States who exercised his right of free travel upon the seas, would do so at his peril if his journey should take him within the zone of waters within which the Imperial German Navy was using submarines against the commerce of Great Britain and France, notwithstanding the respectful, but very earnest protests of his Government, the Government of the United States. I do not refer to this for the purpose of calling the attention of the Imperial German Government at this time to the surprising irregularity of a communication from the Imperial Germany Embassy at Washington addressed to the people of the United States through the newspapers, but only for the purpose of pointing out that no warning that an unlawful and inhumane act will be committed can possibly be accepted as an excuse or palliation for that act or as an abatement of the responsibility for its commission.

*   *   *   *   *   *   *   *

"The Government of the United States cannot believe that the commanders of the vessels which committed these acts of lawlessness did so except under a misapprehension of the orders issued by the Imperial German naval authorities. . . . It confidently expects, therefore, that the Imperial German Government will disavow the acts of which the Government of the United States complains, that they will make reparation so far as reparation is possible for injuries which are without measure, and that they will take immediate steps to prevent the recurrence of anything so obviously subversive of the principles of warfare for which the Imperial German

Government have in the past so wisely and firmly contended.

*   *   *   *   *   *   *

"The Imperial German Government will not expect the Government of the United States to omit any word or any act necessary to the performance of its sacred duty of maintaining the rights of the United States and its citizens and of safeguarding their free exercise and enjoyment."

The demands contained in the above Note would have made the continuance of the submarine campaign impossible, and this was, no doubt, the intention of the Union Government. The German answer of May 28th, which defended the torpedoing of the *Lusitania* on the grounds that she should be considered as an auxiliary cruiser and provided with guns, changed the situation in no way. Besides, the *Lusitania* had ammunition and Canadian troops on board; there can be no doubt that the main reason why she sank so rapidly was the exploding of her cargo of ammunition by the torpedo which struck her. With regard to the loss of human life, the German Government had already expressed, to the neutral Powers concerned, its deep regret for the death of their subjects —I had in person conveyed these regrets to the United States Government a few days after the destruction of the *Lusitania*.

After this first exchange of Notes, the gulf between the two points of view appeared fixed, and was bound in face of the prevalent excitement to lead to a severance of diplomatic relations, unless sufficient time were gained to allow the storms of passion to abate. Telegraphic communication between the German Government and the Embassy at Washington was carried out by a circuitous route, which made it extremely slow; thus I was compelled to decide on my own responsibility and take immediate action. I fully realized that the rupture of diplomatic relations would mean war. In America we were face to face with a vigorous hostile propaganda, which had as its sole object to draw the United States into war, and thus bring about a decision by force of arms. From the time of the *Lusitania* incident onwards, the diplomatic struggle between ourselves and the Entente was centred entirely around the question of the future action of the United States. The threatened rupture of relations between that country and Germany would have left the field open for hostile propaganda, by taking from us all chance of combating it. War would thus have been inevitable sooner or later. The first and most urgent necessity was, therefore, the avoidance of such a rupture at whatever cost, and my efforts were now solely directed to this end. As things turned out, it might, perhaps, have been better if the United States had actually gone to war at this moment. Her military pressure, and our consequent defeat, would have come two years earlier, before the German people had been demoralized and exhausted by four years of war and blockade. But at that time I had good hopes of being able to bring about peace through American mediation, and consequently wished to gain time at all costs.

I resolved, without waiting for instructions from Berlin, to make use of my privileged position as Ambassador to demand an audience with the President. I heard later, among other things when I was at Manila, that on this very day, June 2nd, all preparations had been made for breaking off relations, and for the inevitable resulting war. As a result of my interview, however, they were cancelled. I had a long conversation with the President and two of his advisers. Mr. Wilson felt the position acutely, and was animated solely by a desire to preserve peace. We both realized that it was a question of gaining time, and succeeded in coming to an agreement on the measures to be taken to mitigate the crisis. We took the view that the isolation of Germany had given rise to an atmosphere of misunderstanding between her and the United States, and that the establishment of some sort of personal relationship might be expected to ease this tension; I, therefore, proposed, and the President agreed, that Meyer Gerhardt, a member of the Privy Council, who had accompanied Dr. Dernburg to America, and was then acting on behalf of the German Red Cross, should at once go to Germany and report in person to the Government. Mr. Wilson, for his part, undertook that no final decision should be taken until Meyer Gerhardt had reported the results of his mission.

At the end of this interview I was convinced in my own mind that the President would never enter on war with Germany, otherwise I could not conceive why he should have concurred in my proposals instead of breaking off relations at once. He would, had he chosen the latter course, have had American public opinion more decidedly behind him than it was later, at the time of the final breach. Not a voice would have been raised in opposition, except that of the Secretary of State, Mr. Bryan, who, as it was, resigned his office on the ground that the exchange of Notes threatened to involve the United States in war, and could not be reconciled, therefore, with his own pacific intentions.

It is certain that if I had not at this stage of the *Lusitania* crisis had my interview with the President, relations would have been broken off and war between the United States and Germany must inevitably have followed. The view is still held in many quarters that we might safely have disregarded American susceptibilities, as President Wilson was entirely averse to war and would have avoided it by whatever means; then we should have been free to carry on our submarine campaign. This was not the opinion held by myself or any of my colleagues at the Embassy, and later events proved us to have been in the right, as against those Germans and German-Americans, who, in May, 1915, and afterwards, averred that the United States would never declare war on us, and maintained the same view in January and February, 1917. The principles of my later policy were based on the events of this *Lusitania* crisis; I had then gathered the conviction that Mr. Wilson wanted peace but the country wanted war; that the President alone had prevented an immediate rupture, but that as the responsible leader of the American people, he would be compelled to bow eventually to public opinion. When Mr. Wilson had to explain away his unlucky speech at Philadelphia, no action was taken from the German side, and no information given him which might lead him to understand that Germany desired to avoid a *casus belli* at all costs, for fear of giving Mr. Wilson an opportunity to gain a cheap triumph over Germany in a verbal wrangle.

I believe it unjust to Mr. Wilson to suppose that he wished to bluff us into surrender at this time. He had, while fully realizing the danger of war, sought all ways and means to avoid it, and on this hypothesis my whole policy was founded. Moreover the President had then mentioned to me for the first time that he was considering an attempt at mediation between the belligerents.

After my audience at the White House I sent the following wire to the Foreign Office:

CIPHER

"Washington, June 2nd, 1915.

"Seriousness of the present situation here induced me to seek interview with President Wilson. In most cordial exchange of views, in course of which we repeatedly emphasized our mutual desire to find some solution of the present difficulties, Wilson always came back to point that he was concerned purely with humanitarian aspect of matter, and that question of indemnification for loss of American lives in *Lusitania* was only of secondary importance. His main object was complete cessation of submarine warfare, and from point of view of this ultimate aim, smaller concessions on our part could only be regarded as half measures. It behooved us by giving up submarine campaign to appeal to moral sense of world; for issue of the war could never be finally decided by armies but only by peace of understanding. Our voluntary cessation of submarine warfare would inspire Wilson to press for a raising of English hunger blockade. *Reliable reports from London state that present Cabinet would agree to this.* Wilson hopes that this might be first stage in a peace movement on large scale, which he would introduce as head of leading neutral Powers.

"American reply may be expected to lay little stress on purely legal aspect of matter and to dwell rather on question of humanity, emphatically enough, but as Wilson told me, in a sharper form.

"President remarked that on one point at least we should be in agreement, as both Germany and United States of America had always been in favor of freedom of seas.

"Cordiality of conversation must not blind our eyes to seriousness of situation. If our next Note does not tend to tranquillize matters, Wilson is bound to recall his Ambassador. I recommend most earnestly that this should be avoided at all costs, in view of its disastrous moral effect and fact that this result would be immediate increase in export of munitions, and in financial support for our enemies on immense scale. Good prospect exists of success of present movement for forbidding export of arms should understanding be reached; and also movement by Wilson in direction of peace is sure to follow. Decisive factor in result is that our reply should strike correct note from point of view of public opinion, which is decisive factor in balance here. For this essential to leave out legal details and to lift discussion to level of humanitarian standpoint. Meyer Gerhardt leaves tomorrow for Germany as Red Cross representative; he will report fully in Berlin on situation. Beg that our reply be held up till his arrival. Wilson concurs in this.''

Meyer Gerhardt was in a position to give for the first time a full and accurate review of the American situation to the Berlin authorities. I had given him most precise information of my own views and had placed him in full possession of the details of my interview with Mr. Wilson. For the rest I had to content myself with short telegrams by circuitous routes. During our conversation, however, the President offered for the first time to permit me to dispatch a cipher telegram through the State Department, to be sent on by the American Embassy in Berlin. My reports as a matter of fact were somewhat infrequent and always short, as we had to put all our messages into cipher, and this was not always possible. In explanation of the inevitable incompleteness of my communication with the Foreign Office, I may remark that the telegrams of the Wolff and Trans-Ocean Bureaus were regarded as the main sources of information for either side, and that I made use of various arrangements of words, to which the Foreign Office alone had the key, for the purpose of making my own views easily distinguishable in these telegrams.

Meyer Gerhardt, armed with a certificate from Mr. Bryan, to the effect that he was undertaking his journey at the express desire of the American Government, crossed over to Germany with all possible speed. It may be doubted if the English authorities would have taken any notice of this safe conduct, but by good fortune the Norwegian vessel which took him over escaped the attention of their cruisers. His mission was so far successful that the excitement in the United States had time to die down somewhat and the first crisis in German-American relations was thereby tided over satisfactorily. Apart from that, Meyer Gerhardt's mission had no effect on the future course of negotiations. The exchange of Notes between Washington and Berlin continued without an understanding being arrived at; both Governments persisting in their original points of view.

The second American Note, dispatched on June 10th, led to the resignation of Mr. Bryan, the Secretary of State. He considered that American citizens should be forbidden to take passage in vessels bearing the flag of any belligerent nation, and holding these views as he did, declined to make himself responsible for a further exchange of Notes which he believed was bound in the end to result in war.

The resignation of the Secretary of State had another diplomatic prelude of a tragi-comic character. The Austro-Hungarian Ambassador, Dr. Dumba, besought Mr. Bryan to discuss the German-American conflict with him; both gentlemen wished to find some solution to the dispute and hoped that the Ambassadors not directly concerned in it might profitably try to mediate. It was said later, and probably with truth, that there was a mutual misunderstanding on this subject; but whatever be the truth of that, Dr. Dumba took upon himself to send a radiogram to Vienna, by way of Nauen, in which he gave the following résumé of Mr. Bryan's views:

"The United States desire no war. Her Notes, however strongly worded, meant no harm, but had to be written in order to pacify the excited public opinion of America. The Berlin Government therefore need not feel itself injured, but need only make suitable concessions if it desires to put an end to the dispute."

This telegram from Dr. Dumba had just reached the German Foreign Office at the moment when the American Ambassador arrived to inform the Under Secretary of State, Zimmermann, in his customary blunt and abrupt manner, that Germany must yield to America's demands or war would inevitably follow. Zimmermann thereupon, with the object of causing Mr. Gerard to moderate his tone, showed him Dumba's wire, which pointed to the inference that the attitude of the American Ambassador was merely a bluff. Mr. Gerard, as in duty bound, reported the facts to Washington; mutual recriminations ensued and the Press got hold of the story (nothing ever remained a secret for long in the American capital). The general impression there was that Germany, once she were convinced of America's serious intentions to appeal if necessary to arms, would back down; and that now Mr. Bryan was made to appear as a wrecker of the President's policy. His resignation thus became more necessary than ever, and Mr. Lansing, hitherto head of the State Department of Justice, replaced him. American opinion, however, laid the chief blame for what had occurred on Dr. Dumba, who was henceforward regarded as a dangerous intriguer.

Mr. Lansing was a lawyer, not a politician, and looked at everything from the point of view of a lawyer and his position as the President's sole legal adviser. He was, so to speak, Mr. Wilson's legal conscience. My personal relations with him were always extremely cordial.

Mr. Bryan's point of view was in every sense that of a neutral. The only really effective way of safeguarding American interests was, of course, to forbid the use of hostile passenger ships by citizens of the United States, who could perfectly well travel on their own vessels, or those of Holland or Scandinavia. However, the greater part of American public opinion did not accept this strict view of neutrality, and Mr. Wilson, therefore, adapted himself to the predominant opinion. It was useless for us to demand that the President should interpret his neutrality in the manner most convenient to us; we had to accept the fact that his ideas on this subject were neither ours nor Mr. Bryan's, and, on this basis, endeavor to come to an understanding with Mr. Wilson, if we did not intend to bring the United States into the war. It must be remembered that, as I have already said, we had no means of bringing pressure to bear on America, whereas from her point of view war with Germany would be a comparatively simple affair, which would involve no vital risks for her, but would, on the contrary, greatly benefit her from an industrial point of view, besides gratifying the jingoes, by giving them an opportunity of making full use of their long-desired Army, Navy and commercial fleet. There could be considered, as factors tending to the preservation of peace, only the pacific sentiment of the majority of the people working in alliance with the dilatory policy of the President, who still nourished a hope that some favorable turn or other in events, or perhaps the advent of peace, would give him a chance to avoid breaking off relations with Germany.

The diplomatic incident, mentioned above, made such

an impression on Mr. Gerard, as to induce him to make, on his own initiative in Berlin, at the time when the American Note of 10th June had to be answered, a proposal which met with a by no means cordial reception. His suggestion was that a certain number of passenger ships, detailed beforehand for the purpose, and rendered clearly recognizable, should be used for the transport of Americans to England; but though this scheme was embodied in the German Note of 8th July, it was at once rejected at Washington. Any assent to it would no doubt have involved a further departure from the principles laid down by the American Government—principles which it desired should be generally accepted, but which had already been in some measure compromised. The vessels which it was suggested should be employed in this service were to be marked in red, white and blue stripes, and as barbers' shops in the United States are decorated in this manner, they were called "Barber Ships."

On the 21st of July, the final American Note on the *Lusitania* case was dispatched. The Washington Government modified their position to the extent that they recognized the legality of submarine warfare, provided that before the sinking of any merchant ship, the crew and passengers were given a chance to leave in safety; in the main, however, the Note maintained the original American point of view. It read as follows:

"If a belligerent cannot retaliate against an enemy without injuring the lives of neutrals as well as their property, humanity as well as justice and due regard for the dignity of neutral Powers should dictate that the practice be discontinued. If persisted in it would in such circumstances constitute an unpardonable offence against the Sovereignty of the neutral nation affected . . . the Government of the United States cannot believe that the Imperial Government will longer refrain from disavowing the wanton act of its naval commander in sinking the *Lusitania* or offering reparation for the American lives lost, so far as reparation can be made for the needless destruction of human life by that illegal act.

"In the meanwhile the very value which this Government sets upon the long, unbroken friendship between the people and Government of the United States and the people and Government of the German nation, impels it to press most solemnly upon the Imperial German Government the necessity for the scrupulous observance of neutral rights. This is a critical matter. Friendship itself prompts it to say to the Imperial Government that repetition by the commanders of German naval vassels of acts in contravention of those rights must be regarded by the Government of the United States when they affect American citizens as deliberately unfriendly."

The first act of the German-American negotiations on the subject of submarine warfare thus closed with this open threat that war would follow any further action by Germany on the lines of the torpedoing of the *Lusitania*.

I think it well to reproduce here four of my reports, dated from Cedarhurst, a suburb of New York, where the Embassy usually had its headquarters during the hot summer months.

(1) CIPHER

"Cedarhurst, June 9th, 1915.

"The political outlook in America appears at present as calm as a summer's day. The position abroad is perhaps reacting on internal affairs to some extent, as Mr. Wilson, as is usual in this country, considers foreign affairs primarily from the point of view of their influence on the prospects of next year's presidential campaign.

"The tide of anti-German feeling aroused by the *Lusitania* incident is still running pretty high, but it may now be regarded as certain, that neither the President nor the American people want a war with Germany. Mr. Wilson, then, will, I believe, have public opinion on his side, if he can find an honorable solution to his differences with us, and make use of this solution as the basis for a peace movement on a large scale. I am now even more convinced than I was a short time ago, at the time of my long interview with him, that the President's ideas are developing in this direction, and that this is the cause of his suddenly taking up the Mexican question again, as he hopes to find in it a means of diverting public opinion. I am unwilling to give any grounds for exaggerated optimism, but my recent observations incline me to the belief that the President and his Cabinet are more neutral than is commonly supposed. England's influence here is tremendous, permeating as it does through many channels, which we have no means of closing; but the Central Government, none the less, is really trying to maintain a neutral attitude. It is an astonishing thing, no doubt, but well established none the less, that all influential Americans who come from New York, Boston, and Philadelphia, the English headquarters in this country, to Washington, complain about the pro-German feeling there. I feel sure in my own mind that the Government hopes, by reviving the Mexican question, to diminish the export of arms and munitions to Europe. Public opinion, apart from the anti-German clique, would probably welcome such a move, as it is widely felt that the traffic in arms and munitions is hardly consistent with the continual appeals to humanity sent out all over the world from Washington. My general impression, as will be seen from the above, is that Mr. Wilson considers his best chance of re-election lies in bringing peace to Europe and restoring order in Mexico; for the latter purpose he will probably employ General Iturbide, who spent the whole of last winter in New York and Washington. He was at one time governor of the district of Mexico City, where he acquitted himself with courage and credit. He impressed me personally as a man of great ability. He should be able to find sufficient partisans in Mexico to enable him to raise an army, and the bankers of New York would be prepared to advance him the necessary sums. General Iturbide enjoys the full confidence of the present Administration, but only the future can show whether he will succeed in establishing a stable Government in Mexico, without the intervention of the United States."

(2) CIPHER

"Cedarhurst, 12th June, 1915.

"Since the publication of President Wilson's second Note on the *Lusitania* incident, the daily Press has been busy with conjectures as to the real reasons for Mr. Bryan's resignation. It is generally agreed that the Note itself could hardly have been the occasion of the Cabinet crisis; as Bryan had concurred in the first Note, and there was no reason, therefore, why he should not have assented to the second one as well. On the other hand, no one can believe that the controversy with Germany was in reality simply an excuse for a personal trial of strength between Wilson and Bryan, after the manner of the earlier rivalry between Taft and Roosevelt.

"Bryan has now published in the *World* a manifesto addressed to the German-American community defending his attitude in this matter; but it is fortunately couched in terms which are unlikely to find favor in the eyes of those for whose benefit it was written. It would certainly be undesirable from our point of view that Bryan should be regarded as the champion of the German cause in this country; no useful result could follow from such advocacy. We must use all our efforts to come to an understanding with Mr. Wilson, if possible without compromising our present point of view; he is undoubtedly at the moment the most influential man in the country, and if he is antagonized we shall be powerless against him!''

(3) CIPHER

"Cedarhurst, July 2nd, 1915.

"In spite of the English interference with the American mails reported here to-day, I hope that the reports dispatched in the ordinary course of my duty have all reached your Excellency safely. In case they have not done so, I may report that since my audience with Mr. Wilson, the removal of the 'agitator' Dernburg, the mission of Meyer Gerhardt, and the arrival of the Press telegrams from Berlin giving details of the last-named, things have been pretty quiet generally; the situation has reverted to the normal, and will remain normal if our next Note shows a conciliatory disposition. I might even go further, and say that the *Lusitania* incident, taking it all in all, despite the manner in which we dealt with it, has exercised and will exercise in the future a favorable influence on our mutual relations. Of course it has brought us into even greater odium with our avowed enemies; Anglophile 'Society' in New York, Philadelphia and Boston is infuriated, and the Wall Street magnates are little better; but these two cliques have always been inveterate supporters of England. The Government has lost ground for the first time as a result of the *Lusitania* incident, and it now fully realizes the importance of these questions of sea warfare; whereas when I first spoke in February, March and April to various exalted personages about the submarine campaign and kindred matters, no one would listen to me, and the full seriousness of the situation was quite unrealized. Now, however, 'the freedom of the seas' has become the test question of American politics. Every preparation has been made to take energetic measures with regard to England if our answer to the last American Note renders further negotiations possible. Even the New York Press has become more reasonable, and capable of discussing war questions impartially; and this was notably the case over the torpedoing of the *Armenian*. In a word, at no time since the outbreak of war have the omens been so favorable for a rational policy on the part of America."

"Cedarhurst, July 22nd, 1915.

"If we ask what have been the results of our eleven weeks' negotiations over the *Lusitania* incident, and which involved the employment of all our available arts of persuasion, we may well reply that we have, despite our grave difficulties, averted the severance of diplomatic relations, and the inevitable war that must have followed. The former possibility, at all events, was at one time considerably more probable than most people in Germany are aware of.

"There could have been but one opinion among those who saw and felt it as to the popular attitude of mind during the first few weeks following the *Lusitania* incident. In such circumstances we had only one possible resource left to us, to gain time, and hope for the restoration of a more friendly disposition in this country. The continuation of negotiations rendered this contingency possible; and so matters eventually turned out.

"We can hope for further results only if the American

Government decides to institute simultaneous negotia-
tians with Berlin and London, with the object of bringing about a settlement. Our own views and those of
America are radically divergent, and no mere one-sided
discussion between us can bridge the gulf. The American Government went too far in its first Note to allow of
its withdrawing now; although it admits our submarine
campaign to have been a legitimate form of reprisal
against the English hunger blockade, it still persists in
holding us responsible for damage to American lives and
limbs resulting from these reprisals. Put briefly the
demands of the United States are therefore:

"1. A full apology in some form or other, and indemnification for the lives lost in the *Lusitania*.

"2. An undertaking that no passenger ships shall in
future be sunk without preliminary warning.

"The latest Note from America, which is already on
its way to Berlin, will in a sense bring the negotiations
to a conclusion, as the Government want to have a definite basis of agreement which may form the foundation
of their discussions with England. In my conversations
with Mr. Lansing I have been given to understand that
the Government wish to know verbally or in writing
whether we are in a position to incline somewhat to the
American point of view, and whether we can see our way
to assist the present Government to secure by means of
joint conversations with Germany and England the freedom of the seas, which has always been the main object
of Mr. Wilson's endeavors."

Dr. Dernburg returned to Germany in the middle of
June, having been provided, by request of the American
Government, with a safe conduct from the Entente. I

went to New York to take leave of Dr. Dernburg and invited a few friends to dinner in the roof-garden of the Ritz-Carlton Hotel on the eve of his departure. One incident of our gathering may be regarded as typical of the atmosphere of these *Lusitania* days: a party of people for whom the next table to ours had been reserved refused to take it, as they declined to sit down in the neighborhood of Germans.

After Dr. Dernburg's departure I deemed it advisable, in view of the popular hostility towards us, to redistribute the greater part of Dr. Dernburg's duties. I did so, therefore, in agreement with the Foreign Office, and with the assistance of Dernburg's former colleague, Councillor Albert took over, in addition to his former business with the Central Purchasing Company, all financial and economic affairs, and was attached to the Embassy as commercial adviser. Dr. Alexander Fuehr became Chief of the Press Bureau and Captain Hecker took over the duties connected with the German Red Cross. Unfortunately the generosity of many in America, and particularly those of German descent, has not been fully recognized or appreciated by the people of Germany. The total sum remitted to Germany for our Red Cross and other similar societies amounts to over 20,000,000 marks. The disillusion of our people at home when they realized the slight political influence exercised by the German-American element in the United States has led them to overlook their great achievements in the cause of charity, which were inspired by a heartfelt sympathy with the sufferings of the German nation.

CHAPTER VII

THE "ARABIC" INCIDENT

A few days after the dispatch of the last American
Note concerning the *Lusitania* incident, on July 21st,
1915, Mr. Lansing asked me to call on him. He then told
me that the American Government had come to the end
of its resources, and if any further cases occurred of loss
of American lives by the torpedoing of merchant ships,
war must inevitably result. The United States Government intended to write no more Notes, which had been
proved useless, but would request me to undertake further negotiations in person. My action in the *Lusitania*
incident had given proof of my earnest desire to avoid
war, and the American Government were confident that
I should succeed, even under such difficult conditions, in
finding some way out of the present *impasse*.

From this time onwards, Mr. Lansing agreed with me
that, as a regular thing, I should be permitted, whatever
negotiations were going on, to send cipher dispatches to
my Government through the channels of the State Department and the American Embassy in Berlin. It will
be remembered that a similar privilege had been granted
me at the time of the *Lusitania* incident.

My sole ground of hope for success lay in one passage
of the American Note of July 21st, which read as follows:

"The Government of the United States and the Imperial German Government, contending for the same great
object, long stood together in urging the very principles

166

n which the Government of the United States now so
solemnly insists. They are both contending for the freedom of the seas. The Government of the United States
will continue to contend for that freedom from whatever
quarter it is violated, without compromise and at any
cost. It invites the practical co-operation of the Imperial German Government at this time, when co-operation
may accomplish most, and this great common object can
be most strikingly and effectively achieved. The Imperial German Government expresses the hope that this
object may in some measure be accomplished even before
the present war ends. It can be.

"The Government of the United States not only feels
obliged to insist upon it, by whomsoever it is violated or
ignored, in the protection of its own citizens, but it is
also deeply interested in seeing it made practicable between the belligerents themselves. It holds itself ready
at any time to act as a common friend who may be privileged to suggest a way."

It seemed possible to reach some sort of agreement on
the basis of the above request from America that we
should co-operate in endeavoring to restore the freedom
of the seas; but there remained the question of finding
a formula which should serve as a basis for the settlement of the *Lusitania* question and prevent any repetition of such incidents.

I was aware that there were two political counter-cur-
rents in Berlin: the one party desiring at all costs to
prevent war with the United States, the other preferring
to risk war for the sake of continuing the submarine
campaign. I was clearly bound to co-operate with the
first named, as I was convinced that America's participation in the war would certainly result in our eventual
defeat; this view was, I knew, that Von Jagow, Secre-

tary of State for Foreign Affairs, whose opinion on this point was identical with mine. Up to January 31st, 1917, however, I could never ascertain which of these two views was the accepted one in Berlin, although, of course, I always hoped that the party of common sense would eventually prevail, nor was I able to discover what degree of success, if any, Meyer Gerhardt, who had been sent to represent my views to the authorities in Berlin, or Dr. Dernburg, who was working for the same end, had managed to achieve. As will be seen from my account of the subsequent course of events, my information on this point was very insufficient, and I was not even made acquainted with the views of the Berlin Government, on the conduct of the submarine campaign, or on the subsequent peace proposals put forward by the President. I was never informed beforehand as to the real intentions of Berlin, and I cannot understand, even to-day, why I was not told, until after the *Arabic* incident, that the German submarine commanders had been instructed immediately after the torpedoing of the *Lusitania* not to attack liners. A knowledge of this fact at the time would have assisted me greatly in my dealings with Washington. I do not intend to assert that in all this there was any deliberate neglect on the part of the Berlin Government, but neither, on the other hand, can I credit the commonly accepted explanation that the technical difficulties of transmitting reports were insuperable. It should have been possible to give me definite information on these matters by any one of the various channels of communication which were available between the Foreign Office and the Embassy at Washington. No other explanation is possible, except that which is to be found in the conflict of the two parties in Germany. The head of the Foreign Office was well aware that my policy in Washington was the same as his own in Berlin, but he was frequently unable to send me definite and early information because he, himself, could not tell whether his own views could be accepted and acted upon.

At this time I sent the following report to Berlin:

"Cedarhurst, 28th July, 1915.

"I have on more than one occasion respectfully begged your Excellency to be so good as to wait for my report before deciding whether the last American *Lusitania* Note is to be answered, and if a reply is to be sent, in what sense it should be drafted. Neither the Government nor public opinion considers such a reply absolutely necessary, so that there is no danger in delay; but I respectfully request that I may be permitted at all events to undertake further negotiations here, verbally and confidentially, even if my instructions have to be sent by letter. Experience has proved that negotiations, if they are to have any prospect of success with the American Government, must be carried on in Washington. Both President Wilson and Mr. Lansing are now prepared to attempt to reach an agreement by this means. In Germany, where the tone of the American Note must have appeared unnecessarily abrupt, this fact is perhaps not realized; the explanation of course is that Mr. Wilson was carried away by the popular excitement over the *Lusitania* incident, and was, thus, compelled to adopt an intransigeant attitude, from which he cannot now recede, without making his position impossible here. Then besides the resignation of Mr. Bryan, and that unfortunate telegram of Dr. Dumba's, which has become known here, has convinced him that we are not in earnest. Finally, he wishes to come to some kind of settlement with us by means of this exchange of Notes, in order that he may then turn his attention to England; and his well-known pride confirms him in the view that only after he has concluded his negotiations with us, can he take up the matter with her. It should be clearly understood that Mr. Wilson does not want war with us, nor does he wish to side with England, despite all statements to the contrary in the Press of the Eastern States. This Press, in agreement with other powerful and influential circles is Anglophile to a degree and not altogether averse to a war with Germany; but this view is not shared by Mr. Wilson, or the large majority of the American people.

"The great danger of the present situation is that we may be driven to war, either by the efforts of this Press, or by a new *Lusitania* incident. What Mr. Wilson wants is to satisfy public opinion here, by the serious tone of the Note sent to us, and at the same time to induce us to make certain concessions and thus carry out his darling project of the freedom of the seas, by finding some middle course between the German and English views. In his last note, the President has certainly modified his views in our favor by his admission that submarine warfare is legitimate, whereas he formerly maintained that it could not be regarded as permissible from the point of view of international law.

"It is not my business, even were I in possession of all the necessary facts, to say whether it would be better policy from our point of view, to reply to this Note, or to leave it unanswered; I can only describe the situation, as it appears to me at the moment. From that point of view the decision must depend very largely on the results which we expect to follow from the submarine campaign. If this campaign is regarded as an end in itself, and we are justified in believing that it can bring about the overthrow of England, it would be wiser to leave the American note unanswered, and carry on with the submarine campaign and turn a deaf ear to neutral protests. If, on the other hand, this campaign is only a means to an end, the

nd being the removal or slackening of the British blockade restrictions, then I beg respectfully to urge that it
would be worth our while to make some concessions to
President Wilson's convictions, in the hope of achieving
our object through his co-operation. He is reported by a
witness in whom I have complete confidence, to have said:
If I receive a favorable answer from Germany I will see
his thing through with England to the end.'

"Before this report reaches your Excellency, Wilson's
Note will have been delivered to the English Government.
If this is couched in as peremptory a tone as the one
addressed to us, then I urgently recommend that we
should endeavor to come to an agreement with the American Government on the basis of the following draft note.
I hope that your Excellency will send me an authoriza-
tion by wireless—it should be sent in duplicate for greater
safety's sake—to enter into negotiations on this basis; I
believe that I can guarantee to find a satisfactory principle to serve as a weapon for Wilson in his attack on
England. If we show ourselves ready to help him out of
his present difficulties, I am sure he for his part will
energetically prosecute against England his design of
vindicating the validity of international law. 'It can be,'
said the President himself in his last Note. In these three
words may be seen the conviction of Mr. Wilson, that he
can impose his will upon England in this matter.

"As I have already reported, I earnestly hope that it
will be decided to reply to the American note; and a reply
should, to my mind, deal with these three points:

"(1) Settlement of the *Lusitania* incident. In this connection it would be well to state that from the point of
view of reprisals we were entirely justified in attacking
the *Lusitania*. In so doing, however, we had no intention
of taking American lives, and deeply regret that through
a combination of unfortunate circumstances this has

actually occurred. If any distress still exists among th
survivors of the disaster, we should be quite prepared t
leave the amount of financial compensation to be decide
by a later agreement.

"(2) We propose in the future course of the submarin
campaign to abide by the practice recently adopted. A
things stand at present, the arrangement is that no line
is to be torpedoed without warning.

"(3) We should be prepared to support to the utmos
of our power the efforts of President Wilson, to insist o
the observation of the dictates of international law durin
the present conflict, and leave it to his discretion to ente
into conversations to this end with the British Govern
ment. The Declaration of London might serve as a basi
for these conversations, more especially as it was draw
up at the time by the American Government.

"If we act in accordance with these my respectfu
recommendations, the breakdown of the negotiations wit
England is the worst that can happen; and then it woul
be clear for all the world to see that our enemies were t
blame for this breakdown, and Mr. Wilson would com
over to our side. Knowing the President as I do, I hav
not the slightest doubt of this."

I gather from the account in Karl Helfferich's "Worl
War," Vol. II., p. 322, that the Secretary of the Treasur
in Berlin was in favor of this policy, which I held to b
the only possible one. When he stated, as before men
tioned, that his proposal had found no support from th
Foreign Office, I was much astonished.

I was instructed to commence negotiations verbally an
confidentially with Mr. Lansing on these lines, and wa
convinced myself that these would lead to nothing, so lon
as we persisted in carrying on our submarine campaig
on the old lines. Policy should be based on what i

possible; now it was not really possible to unite these two contradictory methods, and to come to an understanding with the United States over the freedom of the seas, and at the same time to bring her to agree to the continuation of submarine warfare on the existing lines. We were bound to decide once for all on the one policy or the other. I supposed that Berlin had decided for the former course of action, as I knew that our submarine commanders had lately been ordered to arrange for the rescue of non-combatants before torpedoing merchantmen, and I was confirmed in my supposition by the very fact that I had been authorized to open conversations with Mr. Lansing.

Scarcely had these conversations begun, when on August 19th the passenger steamer *Arabic* was sunk, and again some American lives were lost. Excitement at once attained a high pitch, and once more we seemed to be on the brink of war.

On August 20th I dispatched by one of my usual routes the following wire (written for reasons of safety in French) to the Foreign Office:

"I fear I cannot prevent rupture this time if our answer in *Arabic* matter is not conciliatory; I advise dispatch of instructions to me at once to negotiate whole question. Situation may thus perhaps be saved."

At the same time, without writing for instructions, I explained both officially and also through the Press that on our side the United States would be given full compensation, if the commander of the *Arabic* should be found to have been treacherously dealt with. It was my first preoccupation to calm the public excitement before it overflowed all bounds; and I succeeded in so calming it. The action I thus took on my own responsibility turned out later to have been well advised, as, although

I did not know this at the time, the submarine commander's instructions had, in fact, been altered as a result of the disaster to the *Lusitania*.

On the 24th of August, in accordance with instructions from Berlin, I wrote to Mr. Lansing the following letter, which was immediately published:

"I have received instructions from my Government to address to you the following observations: Up to the present no reliable information has been received as to the circumstances of the torpedoing of the *Arabic*. The Imperial Government, therefore, trusts that the Government of the United States will refrain from taking any decided steps, so long as it only has before it one-sided reports which my Government believe do not in any way correspond to the facts. The Imperial Government hopes that it may be allowed an opportunity of being heard. It has no desire to call in question the good faith of those eyewitnesses whose stories have been published by the European Press, but it considers that account should be taken of the state of emotion, under the influence of which, this evidence was given, and which might well give rise to false impressions. If American subjects have really lost their lives by the torpedoing of this ship, it was entirely contrary to the intentions of my Government, which has authorized me to express to the Government of the United States their deepest regrets, and their most heartfelt sympathy."

Fortunately, as already mentioned, orders had been given before the torpedoing of the *Arabic*, to all submarine commanders that no liner should be sunk before preliminary warning had been given, and the non-combatants had been placed in safety, unless any ships tried to escape or offered resistance. At the end of August I received an official statement to this effect, intended for my use in the negotiations over the *Lusitania* question. This statement caused the first hitch in these negotiations. The American Government regarded the term "liner" as comprising every steamer plying on recognized routes as distinguished from the so-called "tramp steamer." The German Naval authorities, on the other hand, averred that their reservation only applied to the large ships of the regular passenger services. However, this divergence of opinion only became important at a later date, and was not for the moment an obstacle to our proceedings.

On the other hand, it was certainly unfortunate for us that up to the 31st January, 1917, neither of the two contending parties in Berlin were able to gain complete control in the matter of policy. I, myself, was never in favor of the submarine campaign, because I was convinced that it could not fulfil its avowed object, and would probably involve us in hostilities with the United States; but bad as this policy was, it would have been better to follow it consistently than to halt between two opinions.

The submarine campaign was in the end gradually and unwillingly sacrificed, owing to our desire to placate the United States. If we had made a clean sweep of it, once and for all, after the *Lusitania* incident, or, at any rate, after the sinking of the *Arabic,* as we actually did after the torpedoing of the *Sussex,* considerable advantages would have been gained from the diplomatic point of view. To my mind, there was now only one thing to be done—to abandon our pretensions that the submarine campaign was being conducted in accordance with the recognized principles of cruiser warfare, laid down by international law, and to offer compensation for the loss of the *Lusitania* and the *Arabic.* Having done this, we could then proceed to recall to the American Government their oft-expressed original view of the freedom of the seas. As a matter of fact, immediately after the settlement of the *Arabic* incident, Mr. Lansing sent a peremptory Note to England. But the prospect of any favorable result for ourselves from this exchange of Notes was never fulfilled, as our methods of war at sea always resulted in fresh incidents and fresh conflicts. There was, of course, a second possibility: that is, while persisting in the submarine campaign to recognize that it was inevitably bound to lead to friction with America, and to discount all the ensuing consequences.

Neither of these two courses was consistently followed in our policy. We were for ever trying to square the circle, and to conduct a submarine campaign which should be from a military point of view effective, without at the same time leading to a breach with America. The order that "liners" should not be torpedoed under any circumstances, was regarded simply as a piece of red tape, and not applicable to war conditions, as the submarine was not in a position to distinguish through its periscope between "liners" and other craft. We thus contrived at one and the same time to cripple our submarines, and yet to fail to give satisfaction to America. Probably the German Government did not venture in face of public opinion in the country to desist altogether from the use of submarines.

It has been said that "the freedom of the seas" was an unattainable ideal, a mere phrase, a red herring drawn across our track; but it was in reality none of these things. America attached to this phrase a definite and concrete meaning; namely, the abolition of the law of capture at sea, and I am convinced that after the World War America will yet fall out with England over this question, and will not rest till she has achieved her object. Certainly the original sin of the United States against the spirit of neutrality lay in the fact that she suffered the violation of her admitted rights by England's interference with the reciprocal trade of the neutral States. Messrs. Wilson and House often talked with me about this matter of the law of capture at sea. It would be a complete misconception of American policy to deny that in this phrase, "the freedom of the seas," one of their dearest desires found expression.

When I informed Mr. Lansing confidentially at the end of August of the latest instructions to our submarine commanders, he was much gratified, but explained at once that the fact of its being confidential would deprive the information of all its value; something must, at all costs, be done to reassure public opinion. I could not but admit that the view of the Secretary of State was correct in this respect. The factor of public opinion obviously appeared of less importance in Berlin than in Washington; besides, I knew from experience that no secret could be kept in Washington for long, and that in a few days this, our first sign of yielding, would be common knowledge. I thought it best, therefore, to get the full diplomatic advantage from the new situation, and took it upon myself, on September 1st, to publish my instructions. This exercise of initiative got me a reprimand from Berlin, but I attained my object none the less, in that I avoided any immediate danger of war.

Concerning these negotiations the following correspondence took place with Berlin:

(1) CIPHER

"Cedarhurst, August 30th, 1915.

"I have tried to wire reports to your Excellency by the route placed at our disposal, and inform you as to the progress of the negotiations between myself and Mr. Lansing over the *Arabic* incident. In consequence of the instructions given to me and the information given by your Excellency to the Associated Press in Berlin, the general situation here has taken a turn for the better. The prospect of war is becoming more remote; there are signs of returning confidence on the Stock Exchange, and I have even succeeded in inducing the Press to see things in a more reasonable light.

"Thus up to the present, everything seems to be going well, and a rupture of diplomatic relations appears once more to be indefinitely postponed. None the less, our difficulties are really much greater than at the time of the *Lusitania* incident. The American Government's intentions are undoubtedly peaceful, and the case of the *Arabic*, involving as it did the loss of only two American lives, may be said to be in itself comparatively unimportant. There are other factors, however, to be considered. Both the Government and the people are beginning to have shrewd suspicions, which for reasons of policy they refrain from expressing at present, that we cheated the United States in the matter of the *Lusitania*, that we spun out the discussion as long as possible, and then replied to President Wilson's last and most peremptory Note, by torpedoing the *Arabic*. I am convinced that Mr. Lansing, who is an able lawyer, and as a result of his American training alive to every possible move of an opponent, expects us to follow the same policy over the matter of the *Arabic*. He has thus no great confidence in our good faith, though the President, I am told, is more optimistic, his friend House having informed him that his policy of the 'freedom of the seas' commands general assent in Berlin. The facts of the situation, then, are that the President will not permit any procrastination in the negotiations over the *Arabic* affair, for should no more satisfactory conclusion be reached now than was the case after the *Lusitania* incident, Wilson would forfeit the respect of his countrymen, and would have no other resource but to forego his cherished design with what face he might, or else break off diplomatic relations with Germany. There can be no doubt in the minds of any who are well versed in American affairs that he would elect for the latter course. The Spanish-American War arose out of just such a situation.

"The following conclusions result from the above: I gather from the Berlin reports of the Associated Press that your Excellency has decided to settle the present dispute with the United States on the lines which I have respectfully suggested to you. If this be so I urge the utmost expedition in the matter, that confidence here may be restored, and the way opened for negotiations with England. It is not so much a matter of making apologies or giving explanations, but rather of making a full statement to this Government as to the instructions given to our submarine commanders. If we can prove by this means that after the *Lusitania* incident, orders had been given to attack no passenger ships while negotiations with the United States were going on, or to do so only under certain conditions, all outstanding questions could be solved without difficulty."

(2) CIPHER DISPATCH

"Berlin, September 10th, 1915.

Daily Telegraph of September 2nd publishes what purports to be extract from your aforesaid letter to Mr. Lansing, informing him of instructions issued to submarine commanders. Extract ends as follows:

" 'I have no objection to your making any use you please of the above information.'

"If *Daily Telegraph* has reproduced your letter correctly, above statement is contrary to instructions, which authorized you only to give information confidentially to American Government. Premature publication in American Press places us in difficult position here, especially as no official report of actual contents of your communication to Mr. Lansing has reached us. I beg that you will kindly furnish an explanation.

(Signed) JAGOW."

(3) CIPHER REPORT

"Cedarhurst, October 2nd, 1915.

"Reference your wire No. A 129 of September 10th, I ask your Excellency to be kind enough to pardon me for having taken upon myself to act on my own responsibility over the submarine question. The position at the end of August rendered some action to pacify public opinion imperative, if a breach were to be avoided. Owing to the difficulties of communication with Berlin I could do nothing but acquaint Mr. Lansing with a portion of my instructions concerning the case of the *Lusitania*—the only ones which had then reached me. I at once reported my action to your Excellency in my wireless message, No. 179, and in a previous telegram, No. 165, and requested approval of my action; probably these messages have been delayed in transit, or have not reached Berlin. In further explanation, I may add that in this country, confidential matter, in the European sense, does not exist, and such matter can never be kept a secret from the Press. Sometimes I have been able to come to an agreement with the Government over the wording of their *communiqués* to the Press; that is one of the great advantages of conducting the negotiations on the spot. Had the whole American Press entirely refused to accept our official explanations, nothing further could have been done with the Government."

While my negotiations with Mr. Lansing in Washington for a simultaneous settlement of the *Arabic* and *Lusitania* questions were still in progress, a memorandum was handed to Mr. Gerard, the American Ambassador in Berlin, which purported to justify the action of the offending submarine commanders. Thus the situation once more became acute. The contents of this document were as follows:

"On August 19th a German submarine held up the English steamer *Dunele* about sixty miles south of Kinsale, and having ordered the crew to leave the ship, were about to sink it by gun-fire when the commander observed a large steamer heading directly towards him. This latter, which afterwards proved to be the *Arabic*, bore no ensign, or other marks of neutrality, and was thus obviously an enemy. Approaching nearer, she altered her original course, and again made directly for the submarine, thus leading the commander of the latter to suppose that she was about to attack and ram him. In order to parry this attack, the submarine dived and fired a torpedo, which struck the ship. The submarine commander observed that those on board got away in fifteen boats.

"According to his instructions, the German commander was authorized to attack the *Arabic* without warning, and without allowing time for the rescue of her crew, in case of an attempt at flight or resistance. The action of the *Arabic* undoubtedly gave him good grounds for supposing that an attack on him was intended. He was the more inclined to this belief, by the fact that a few days before, on the 14th, he had been fired at from long range by a large passenger steamer, apparently belonging to the British Royal Mail Steam Packet Company, which he saw in the Irish Sea, but which he had made no attempt to attack or hold up.

"The German Government deeply regrets that loss of life should have resulted from the action of this officer, and it desires that these sentiments should be conveyed more particularly to the Government of the United States, as American citizens were among the missing. No obligation to make compensation for the damage done can, however, be admitted, even on the hypothesis that the submarine commander mistook the intentions of the *Arabic*. In the event of an insoluble difference arising on this point between the German and American Governments, the German Government suggests that the matter in dispute should be referred to the Hague Tribunal as a question of international law, in accordance with Article 38 of the Hague convention for the peaceful solution of differences between nations; but it can do so only with this reservation, that the arbitrator's award shall not have the validity of a general decision as to the international legality or otherwise of the German submarine warfare."

The following three reports or telegrams dispatched by me to the Imperial Chancellor describe the situation in Washington at this juncture:

(1) CIPHER

"Washington, September 14th, 1915.

"Lansing has given me permission to wire you by this route, without the messages being seen by him; he will also forward your Excellency's reply, and from this it appears to be the Government's view, that any further exchange of Notes, the subsequent publication of which, in both countries, would merely involve further misunderstandings, is bound to lead to a breach. It considers the present system of confidential negotiations with me as the only promising method of arriving at an agreement. The memorandum on the *Arabic* is not understood here, and in so far as it is understood, is considered to be a manifestation of German bad faith—a sign that we may perhaps give way in principle, but will always in practice seek to evade our obligations thus incurred.

"Lest this telegram should, by its length, give offence to the British, Mr. Lansing is forwarding the evidence in the *Arabic* case to Mr. Gerard for transmission to your Excellency; he is himself quite convinced that the submarine commander was not compelled in self-defense to torpedo the Arabic, and that his action in so doing was therefore unjustified. He hopes that your Excellency will, after study of the evidence, agree with him in this.

"To obtain full and complete agreement it is first of all necessary that I should be empowered to publish in full those instructions given to our submarine commanders in so far as these were not given in my previous summaries on the matter. If we still consider ourselves bound to maintain that the officer concerned in the *Arabic* case was only obeying orders, we can never hope to come to an agreement, for no one can possibly feel any confidence in the sincerity of our intentions. In the meantime I shall try to reach a settlement on the matters now in dispute by means of arbitration. Finally, the question of compensation must, in accordance with my instructions for the *Lusitania* case, be referred to the Hague Tribunal.

"I am quite certain that if we fail to reach an agreement, severance of diplomatic relations cannot but follow.

"Lansing will not reply to the *Arabic* memorandum, and, as I said before, will conduct the diplomatic exchanges on this matter only through me. He considers this as the only possible course on the ground that Wilson and I are alike committed to the policy of 'the freedom of the seas.'

"Finally, I may observe that everyone here would be much gratified if we could see our way to extend the scope of our latest instructions to our submarines so as to include all merchant shipping. It is argued that these vessels are slow moving and could easily be warned; the advantage of acting without warning is only of importance in the case of swift passenger ships, which we have, none the less, undertaken not to attack without notice. The suggested proposal, therefore, could not harm us; it would, on the other hand, make us very popular here and give the United States a very strong position in her negotiations with England. Of course, I may be able to effect an agreement without this. The main point in dispute is the verdict on the action of the commander in the *Arabic* case, because this involves the whole question of our good faith. Anyway, there is no doubt whatever that a second *Arabic* case is bound to result in war."

(2) CIPHER TELEGRAM

"Cedarhurst, September 22nd, 1915.

"As position is still very difficult, I am carrying on conversations in strict confidence through personal friend of Wilson's. Request, therefore, that no directions be sent as regards question of responsibility for *Arabic* incident, till your Excellency hears again from me. Lansing at present gone on leave. Personally I do not believe that I shall manage to secure International Commission of Inquiry. According to present view, main point of dispute is question of disavowing action of submarine commander. I hope, however, that after reviewing American evidence, your Excellency will be able to find formula for such disavowal, agreeable to both Governments, especially if I can get concurrence of Wilson before press gets hold of it. Request, therefore, that American correspondents in Germany be told nothing more than that American evidence being carefully gone into in Berlin."

(3) Cipher Report

"Cedarhurst, September 28th, 1915.

"The negotiations about the submarine campaign are at a standstill at present. From the fact that Lansing has not been recalled from leave and that President Wilson does not seem over-eager to give an opinion on the proposals which I have put forward for his consideration, I consider myself justified in concluding that the Americans do not consider the situation to be any longer critical. Even the Press is no longer agitated, as in all recent cases of attack by German submarines. Their commanders have acted quite in accordance with our assurances. Under these circumstances Mr. Wilson may possibly fall in with our proposal that the particular case of the *Arabic* should be dealt with by an International Commission of Inquiry. In any case, some means must be found of finishing once for all with the *Arabic* and *Lusitania* incidents; only then shall we be in a position to see whether President Wilson will keep his word, and take energetic measures *vis à vis* England.

"The Anglo-French Loan Commission, assisted by their agency, the Morgan group, are working at high pressure. Stories of Allied victories in Europe are sedulously spread abroad in order to enlist the support of public opinion. Despite these efforts the commission found Chicago so invincibly hostile that they were compelled to proceed there in person, but they will probably, in any case, manage to raise a loan, as the Morgan group are quite strong enough for the purpose. The rate of interest they are demanding is very high, as up till now they have financed all English purchases here. By these means, they are, no doubt, making considerable profits, but in order to secure them, they will, of course, consolidate their floating debt and unload it on to the public. The only question is to what extent they will be able to do this. Opinion varies as to the size of England's present debt; a prominent banker here, in close touch with the Morgan group, estimated the total to 500,000,000 dollars; if this estimate is correct, a loan of 500,000,000 dollars would only just cover the liabilities hitherto existing.

"The Morgan group certainly had to make two great concessions: first, that the proceeds of the new loan shall not be employed for the purchase of munitions, and second, that Russia shall be excluded from the loan; only by these means could they overcome the opposition of the German-Americans and the Jews. Our Jewish friends here are in no easy position. Their action, or rather inaction, takes the form of what is commonly known as 'egg-dancing,' or 'pussyfooting'; they wish to stand well with all sides, but have not the courage of their convictions, and are very anxious to make money. All this is very easily understood, when one remembers the ambiguous position of these gentlemen. A regular devil's dance around the 'Golden calf' is now going on here. All the European Governments are coming to buy in the American market, and usually paying double for their goods, as they only purchase what they urgently need. *One lesson* we may learn for future reference from the present state of affairs, and that is that we must not allow ourselves again to be left to the tender mercies of the German-Jew bankers here. After the war, we must have branches of our large banks in New York just as we have in London. All evidence goes to show that New York will then be the center of world-finance, and we should, therefore, take all steps to act on this assumption as soon as possible."

The Foreign Office in Berlin, who naturally wished to avoid a rupture with the United States, accordingly dispatched to me the following telegraphic instructions:

"We have no doubt that in this instance submarine commander believed *Arabic* intended to ram and had every reason for such belief. However, German Government prepared to give credence to sworn evidence of English officers of *Arabic* and agree that in reality no such intention existed.

"Attack of submarine thus was unfortunately not in accordance with instructions; communication to this effect will be made to commander. German Government is for sake of final settlement by friendly agreement prepared without admission of responsibility from point of view of international law, to give indemnification for death of American citizens. Your Excellency is empowered to notify American Government of above, and to negotiate with them in case of acceptance concerning amount of compensation, subject to our concurrence. Confidently expect that incident will thus be finally liquidated, as above is limit of possible concessions."

The American Government during verbal negotiations with me on this matter considered it essential that a phrase expressing Germany's disapproval of the commander's action should be incorporated in the explanation which I proposed to publish. I was not sure whether I was really authorized by the above instructions to comply with this condition, but in view of the fact that it was the only hope of avoiding a breach and further delay in the negotiations would profit us nothing, as we were bound to make some sort of reply to the American demand within a certain definite time, I acted once more on my own responsibility and gave the following explanation to Mr. Lansing:

"The Government of his Majesty the Kaiser, in its orders with which I previously made you acquainted, has so framed its instructions to its submarine commanders as to avoid any repetition of incidents such as that of the *Arabic*. According to the report of the officer who sank the *Arabic* and his sworn evidence, together with that of his crew, this commander believed that the *Arabic* intended to ram the submarine. On the other hand, the Imperial Government does not desire to call in question the good faith of the English officers of the *Arabic*, who have given evidence on oath that the *Arabic* had no intention of ramming. The action of the submarine was therefore contrary to orders, and the Imperial Government both disapproves of it and regrets it. A communication to this effect has been made to the officer in question. Under these circumstances my Government is prepared to give compensation for the lives of American subjects drowned, to their great regret, in the *Arabic*. I am empowered to discuss with you the amount of this compensation."

The above explanation finally resolved the second crisis. The German naval authorities naturally complained of my action, as the "disapproval" stuck in their throats, and I was once more taken to task—a matter which weighed little with me. For I felt that my interpretation of the instructions from the Foreign Office was the only one which could have saved us from war, and that now the road was open for the final settlement of the

Lusitania incident and the discussion of the great question of "the freedom of the seas." The outlook for us was most promising. Opinion in America as a result of the solution of the *Arabic* question was once more favorable to us. A leading American paper, the *New York Sun,* said at this time in its leading article:

"The successful issue of the conversations with Germany over the submarine campaign cannot fail to be of benefit to all nations, as a proof of the possibilities of diplomacy as against war. It has been a personal triumph for both the participants, President Wilson and Count Bernstorff."

The position of both men has been much strengthened thereby, and what they have already achieved is no doubt only a presage of still greater results in the future.

The following four reports to the Foreign Office deal with the settlement of the *Arabic* case:

(1) CIPHER
"Cedarhurst, October 6th, 1915.

"The settlement of the *Arabic* case reported to your Excellency in my wire, has caused great satisfaction in all circles here. Of course a few avowedly Anglophile papers, such as the *New York Herald* and the *New York Tribune,* reveal the cloven hoof, and are clearly disappointed that a rupture of diplomatic relations between America and Germany has been averted; for the rest, at no time since the outbreak of war have we had such a good Press as at this moment.

"History alone will be in a position to say whether the settlement of the *Arabic* case really prevented a war with the United States or not; but your Excellency knows my views that without this settlement a conflict must eventually have become inevitable. I respectfully submit that the preservation of peace alone was a sufficient motive to induce us to come to terms; but you also know that this was by no means my sole object. I wished also to induce the Government of the United States to take energetic proceedings against England, with the object of translating into fact its idea of the freedom of the seas. I trust we shall not be disappointed in this regard, and I shall, certainly, leave no stone unturned to keep Mr. Wilson on the right path. Whatever may be one's personal opinion of the President, whether one believes him to be really neutrally-minded, or not, his great services to the cause of peace cannot be denied. A Republican President would certainly not have stood up, as he has done, against the united forces of anti-Germanism represented by Wall Street, the Press, and so-called Society.

"At the present moment it looks as if the American Government are ready to let the *Lusitania* matter drop altogether, provided we agree to refer the question of compensation to the Hague Tribunal after the war. The general belief here is that judicial proceedings are out of the question during the continuance of hostilities. At least I gather as much, indirectly, of course, from one of the President's friends."

(2) CIPHER

"Cedarhurst, October 15th, 1915.

"I much regret that owing to a mistake on the part of the State Department, your Excellency was not earlier informed of the settlement of the submarine question. Mr. Lansing left my letter, which should have accompanied the telegram, in his writing-table by mistake, for which oversight he afterwards apologized to me. The Imperial Embassy was in no way to blame.

"The importance attached by the President, from the very first, to those main points on which we were unable to make concessions rendered the task of arriving at an agreement by no means an easy one. Thus on three of the most important points no agreement has been reached, and over these we must, for the present, draw the veil. Only a few of the most rabid of the pro-English papers venture openly to reproach President Wilson with having achieved nothing but the security of passenger-ships, but all Americans are prepared to admit in confidence that the Government has completely departed from its original position.

"The three important questions still in dispute, as mentioned above, are the following:

"(1) The German Government's responsibility for American lives lost in the torpedoing of British ships.

"(2) The responsibility for the payment of compensation for the American lives so lost.

"(3) The American demand that *all* merchant ships should be warned by our submarines before being attacked.

"This demand was at first so worded as to imply that submarines, like other warships, had only the right of search.

"The Government, realizing that we could not make concessions on the above three points, had to be content with our admission that the case of the *Arabic* should be regarded as exceptional. This very fact rendered it impossible to reach a similar settlement in the case of the *Lusitania,* in which no error on the part of the submarine commander concerned could be adduced. However, the Government seemed to be only too satisfied to have come so well out of their difficulties, and have no wish to raise any further obstacles because of the *Lusitania* incident. This matter, as I have already had the honor to report, may now well be left to drag on indefinitely, and can be referred in the end to the Hague Tribunal after the war. Our Press should, therefore, be warned that further discussion of the controversy between Germany and America over the submarine campaign is undesirable "

(3) CIPHER

"Cedarhurst, October 20th, 1915.

"Your Excellency's last wireless requested me to render a report on the settlement of the *Arabic* question. I have already complied with these instructions, and the documents are now on their way to you, and should have reached you. However, it may be advisable to explain briefly the more important points of the matter.

"From the date of the sinking of the *Lusitania,* America has always been on the verge of breaking off diplomatic relations with us. The German people, I am convinced, have no idea of the full danger of the situation, at least, if one may judge from our Press. On two occasions we were compelled to sacrifice individuals in order to avoid a breach, Dernburg and Dumba being our scapegoats. Their mistakes would under normal circumstances have been overlooked, but their removal was at the time necessary in order to give the American Government the opportunity of showing its strength without breaking off diplomatic relations with us.

"As I have more than once explained in my reports, no solution of the *Lusitania* question, agreeable to the Americans, could be found, so long as we were not prepared to admit the responsibility of the Imperial Government for the disaster, or its obligation to make reparation, and so long as our views on the principles of submarine warfare differed from those held by the American Government.

"By dint of drawing out the negotiations as long as possible, and by the employment of all my persuasive powers, I succeeded in tiding over the moment of *acute* tension. Then came the incident of the *Arabic.* My laboriously constructed diplomatic edifice came tumbling about my ears, and things looked blacker than ever. The American Government regarded the *Arabic* incident most seriously, believing as they did that it was typical of the whole German policy *vis-à-vis* America. They argued that either the whole affair had been prearranged as a manifestation of our intention to have our own way in the matter of submarine warfare, or else it was a blunder which could be dealt with in the ordinary course of diplomacy. Negotiation became possible when your Excellency notified this Government that satisfaction would be given in the event of the submarine commander being proved to have acted contrary to his instructions. Further negotiations followed on this basis, and it was finally agreed that we should admit the exceptional nature of the *Arabic* case, without yielding our ground on the main points. Such agreement would have been impossible had President Wilson adhered to his previous position, but he wished to have done with the whole business, and could only do so by throwing dust in the eyes of the American public. He hoped by these means to get rid of the *Lusitania* incident unostentatiously, and told me, through one of his personal friends, 'to let it drift.' The idea at the back of his mind is that it shall be left to an international tribunal sitting after the war, to decide whether we shall pay compensation or not.

"The only really important question as regards the settlement of the *Arabic* case, is whether it is worth while for us to risk a rupture of relations with the United

States, for the sake of this affair. I still persist in my opinion, that it would infallibly have led us into a new war.''

(4) Cipher

"Washington, 1st November, 1915.

"Your Excellency's last wire on the matter of the submarine campaign raises two points of the highest importance.

"First, as to Wilson's policy of the 'freedom of the seas;' this has been the idea underlying all our recent negotiations over the submarine warfare. Our agreement with this policy has been constantly emphasized in all my conversations with leading men here; but it is of course necessary carefully to choose our moment for the public declaration of our agreement with Wilson's point of view, as people here naturally fear that if England believes us to be behind any agitation for the freedom of the seas she will resist it all the more firmly. I respectfully recommend, therefore, that we should leave Mr. Wilson to carry on his present controversy with England, for the present at all events, unaided. We shall lose nothing by so doing, and if an opportunity comes for our participation, we can make use of it.

"After this expression of opinion, let me pass on to the second point I have always clearly stated here, that we reserve to ourselves full liberty of decision, if England refuses to receive our advances. At present, now that the *Arabic* case has been recognized as exceptional, this 'freedom' is only being encroached upon from one direction as we have undertaken not to sink passenger ships without warning, etc. By this undertaking we must abide, unless we wish to go to war with the United States of America. Any future destruction of passenger ships with Americans on board, especially if such took place without warning, and with the approval of the Imperial Government, would inevitably cause a rupture."

The political sky in the United States was thus becoming more propitious day by day; but our enemies' exertions for the purpose of undermining the present friendly relations, redoubled in proportion. The German Embassy became the chief object of attack, owing to the fact being clearly realized by our foes, that so long as its influence in Washington political circles remained unimpaired, no rupture of diplomatic relations could be hoped for. Entente diplomacy left no stone unturned which could be of service against us; lies, robbery, personal defamation, gossip, were all used to discredit us.

The conduct of a British officer on duty in Washington affords a good example of the unscrupulous policy of our foes. According to the evidence of Dr. Fuehr, this gentleman, now holding a high position in London, attempted in the early months of 1916 to corrupt a messenger of our Press Bureau in New York, one Alfred Hoff, whose daily duty it was to take newspaper cuttings to Councillor Albert's office. Two of his people stopped this boy in the street and invited him to the British Consular offices; here he was received by the Captain himself, who showed him a bag filled with bank notes, and promised him a liberal reward, if he would undertake to obtain some letters from Dr. Fuehr's desk. Hoff pretended to fall in with this suggestion, but at once informed his employer of the incident. The Captain then made a second effort to bribe Hoff by the promise of a money reward for every document from the Press Bureau, and also a ride in a motor for the letters which it was his duty to take from the Bureau to the German Embassy at Cedarhurst, during the coming summer. One of the British agents told Hoff that he would be well paid if he handed over the letters of Dr. Fuehr, which he often used to seal and frank, and also certain other documents of a specially confidential nature. Dr. Fuehr finally put an end to this unsavory episode, which had been fully investigated by private detectives, by publishing a detailed account of the whole affair in the Hearst papers. At the same time he brought the matter before the Public Prosecutor, who, however, was unwilling to interfere in the matter unless it should be further discussed in the Press. This limited comprehension of duty Dr. Fuehr could hardly be expected to agree with.

During my encounters at this time with the Entente, I entirely lost any respect I may previously have felt for their moral character, which was reputed to be so high. I came then to realize that we could expect nothing better from them in the hour of our defeat, than a Peace of Versailles, which would make of no account all their earlier loftier professions. We, in Washington, were therefore, in duty bound, to strain every nerve to avert such a catastrophe to our country. Unfortunately the activities of the agents dispatched from home invariably deranged our plans in a most unfortunate manner, and, while affording our foes the desired opportunities for damaging our cause, achieved nothing of advantage in compensation. The English Secret Police, and all the detective agencies of the United States which were in their pay, were always at our heels, endeavoring to establish some collusion on the part of the German Embassy in these isolated cases of sabotage. However, all this subterranean plotting and counter-plotting was but so much lost labor. It was the decision on the policy of continuing or not continuing the submarine campaign which finally turned the scale.

At the beginning of August one of these agents managed to steal a portfolio of documents from Councillor Albert while he was traveling on the New York elevated railway, and its contents were published in the *World* from the 15th of August onwards. We always thought the perpetrator of this theft was an Entente agent, but it now appears from Senator Frelinghuysen's evidence before the Senate Committee of Enquiry on 13th July, 1919, that the guilty individual was really a member of the American Secret Police. It would certainly have been an unheard-of thing for an American agent to have robbed a member of the diplomatic corps and sold the proceeds of his deed to the Press. Probably what really happened was that the man was in the pay of the Entente. The investigations at the Senate Committee disclosed a number of cases of corruption and theft which the agents of the Entente did not scruple to use in their efforts to compromise and discredit the German Embassy; so this supposition is in itself by no means improbable. The affair was merely a storm in a tea-cup; the papers as published afforded no evidence of any action either illegal or dishonorable; otherwise the American Government would certainly have demanded the recall of Albert as they did later in other cases. The Press manufactured a considerable sensation out of the contents of the port-folio, but generally speaking the efforts of the Entente in this affair proved completely without effect.

The Entente agents, however, were more successful in their next attack, to which the Austro-Hungarian Ambassador fell a victim. Dumba had already in the winter of 1914-15 recommended to me the American war correspondent James Archibald, who had been at the Austro-Hungarian Front, as having German sympathies. Thereupon I also recommended this gentleman in Berlin, where he was granted all facilities. In the summer of 1915 Archibald returned to America, to lecture on his experiences. As he was anti-Entente, these lectures brought us financial profit, and therefore we paid Archibald's travel-

ing expenses. At the beginning of September, 1915, he
went once more to Europe, and dined on the eve of his
departure with Dumba and myself on the roof-garden of
the Ritz-Carlton Hotel in New York. By this means our
personal connection with Archibald was openly recognized. The Austro-Hungarian Ambassador, confiding in
his character and his American nationality, gave him
certain political reports which were not even in cipher, to
take to Vienna. Archibald had also offered to take
papers to Berlin for me. I, however, declined with
thanks, as I scented danger, and I would have warned
Dumba also, if I had known that he intended to entrust
dispatches to Archibald. The English seized the latter
in Kirkwall and took away all his papers.

Since then I have never set eyes on Archibald, and I
could not help suspecting that there was something un-
canny about the case. By arresting Archibald the English undoubtedly thought they would compromise me. I
cannot prove that there was anything wrong with Archibald, but in all the circumstances he could easily have
destroyed the papers, had he wished to do so. In the
meanwhile a report was found among the dispatches of
the Austro-Hungarian Ambassador transmitting to his
Government a memorandum from the Hungarian journalist, Warm. In this note Warm recommended propaganda to induce a strike among the Hungarian workers
in arms and munitions factories, and demanded money
for this object.

The statement of Dumba's report that the Ambassador
had shown the suggestion to Captain von Papen, who had
thought it very valuable, was very compromising for us.

The German Military Attaché was therefore placed in
an awkward position; the letter contained several other
blazing indiscretions. Thus, for instance, in one paper
Dumba described President Wilson as self-willed, and

von Papen in a letter to his wife spoke of the "imbecile Yankees."

As I previously mentioned, the position of the Austro-Hungarian Ambassador was much shaken by the Dumba-Bryan episode. His defence, that he had only forwarded the note of an Hungarian journalist, without identifying himself with it, was not favorably received by the American Government. A few days later his passport was presented to him; at the same time the Entente granted him a safe conduct.

Previous to his departure from New York similar scenes took place to those which followed the sinking of the *Lusitania*.

The Hotel St. Regis, in which the Austro-Hungarian Ambassador lived, was surrounded day and night by innumerable reporters.

When I called on him there to take leave of him, I had to make use of a back entrance to the hotel in order to avoid numerous impertinent questions. Dumba himself was followed at every step by reporters, who among other things often chased him for hours on end in motor-cars.

In the meanwhile Rintelen (mentioned in the fifth chapter) had been taken prisoner in England. Further, the case of Fay led to a disagreeable discussion in public, and lastly action was taken against the Hamburg-Amerika Line for supplying our squadron of cruisers with coal and provisions. Thus it was easy for the Entente agents to establish connection between these offenders and the Military and Naval Attachés of the German Embassy. How far these gentlemen were really implicated I did not know at the time, nor do I now. In this they must plead their own case. As far as I am concerned both gentlemen always denied that they in any way transgressed against the American law. It cannot, however, be denied that they were, in fact, compromised by their relations with these guilty parties; I do not think that anything beyond this can be authenticated.

Captain von Papen's reputation, therefore, suffered from the time of the Dumba-Archibald incident; both he and Captain Boy-Ed were constantly attacked in the anti-German Press, and accused of being behind every fire and every strike in any munition factory in the United States. The *New York Herald* and the *Providence Journal* took the leading parts in this business. At the same time a campaign was begun against the German-Americans, who were accused of being practically without exception disloyal citizens of the United States. All the various incidents, accusations, so-called conspiracies, etc., were grist to the Entente's mill, and were exploited to the full. Congress was about to assemble, and it was therefore to be expected that the Government would take steps to strengthen its position.

Mr. Lansing asked me on 1st December to call on him and informed me that the American Government had requested that von Papen and Boy-Ed should be recalled, as they were no longer *personæ gratæ!*

To my inquiry as to the reasons for this action, Lansing refused to reply; he merely remarked that any Government was within its rights in simply stating that a member of a diplomatic corps was not *persona grata*. In the course of further conversation, however, I discovered one thing at least, that Capt. Boy-Ed was supposed to have been conspiring with the Mexican General Huerta—an obviously baseless charge, considering that Boy-Ed had never made the acquaintance of the ex-President. It is true, however, that Rintelen had had dealings with Huerta, and it was known that Rintelen had received from Boy-Ed the sum of half a million dollars previously mentioned.

My first message—written in English—to Berlin on his affair ran as follows:

CIPHER MESSAGE

"Washington, 4th December, 1915.

"In an official Note of to-day's date American Government, as stated in previous conversations with me, request immediate recall of Military and Naval Attachés, on the ground of various facts brought to notice of Government, particularly implication of these Attachés in llegal and doubtful activities of certain individuals within United States. Government deeply regrets necessity for this step, and trusts Imperial Government will understand that no other course seems to them to be compatible with the interests of the two Governments and their reciprocal friendly relations."

I also telegraphed as follows to my Government on September 5th:

"Explanations of von Papen and Boy-Ed herewith as requested by Military and Naval Authorities:

"'State Department request my recall. Reasons for his given to Ambassador. Case of Stegler and my two upposed meetings with Huerta. Stegler case settled ince March. Stegler in matter of his pass proved a liar. Had nothing to do with his transactions; not the least roof that I ever had; see my report No. 4605, March 20th, and others. I have never in my life met Huerta; have never concerned myself with Mexican affairs in any way; I have never to my knowledge acted contrary o the interests or laws of the United States. Conjectures and absurd newspaper stories about me result of English influence and money. Must therefore request my recall be considered unjustifiable.

" 'BOY-ED.'

" 'No illegal action can be laid to my charge; demand for recall unjustified. Importance of military interests of our enemies here renders necessary effective representation of Central Powers, so long as America officially neutral. Therefore it should be insisted on that American Government secure safe-conduct for my successor.

" 'PAPEN.' "

In view of the approaching session of Congress, the Government, on December 5th, published the fact that they had demanded the recall of the Attachés. This fact, with slight foundation for the American Government's suspicions, made a bad impression in Berlin; I went, therefore, to see Mr. Lansing on December 8th, and obtained from him this letter:

"As I have already stated, the demand for recall of the two Attachés of your Embassy was made as a result of the careful investigation of a number of facts and circumstances, which convinced this Government that they could no longer consider these two officers as *personæ gratæ*, and that their continued residence in the United States was, therefore, no longer compatible with diplomatic propriety. This being the considered and deliberate view of this Government, it would seem that the mere fact of Captains von Papen and Boy-Ed being no longer acceptable, should have been sufficient justification for their immediate recall by the German Government without further discussion. The expectations of the United States Government, in this respect, were in accordance with all diplomatic precedent in cases where such requests have been made, and there seemed to be, therefore, no reason why this demand should have been kept a secret. It is regretted that the Imperial Government should have regarded the publication of the American request as an act of discourtesy towards itself. The United States Government does not share this view of its action, and, therefore, cannot be expected to express its regret for having acted as it has done.

"This Government is surprised that the Imperial Government should not have complied at once with its request for the recall of the two Attachés, who are no longer *personæ gratæ* here. It seems to me obvious that whatever may have been the reasons for such request, it is for this Government, and not for the German Government, to say whether the charges alleged against the members of a German diplomatic mission appear sufficiently well-founded to justify action such as that now taken. In other words, the causes of the demand are legitimate and sufficient, as being based on suppositions or suspicions of undesirable activities on the part of these two officers.

"In any case, the fact remains, that Boy-Ed and von Papen are no longer acceptable to this Government.

"As I already apprised you by word of mouth, and in my letter of 4th of this month, the relations of the two Attachés with individuals who participated in illegal and questionable activities, are established. The names of von Wedell, Rintelen, Stegler, Buröde, Archibald and Fay may be mentioned as some of those who have transgressed against our laws. I could also name other men and cite other examples of their activities, but as these are at present the object of an official inquiry, I, by this means, should only prevent the arrest of those who violated our laws and still continue to violate them.

"Although I have already said that this Government

does not want to do anything further than to request the recall of Boy-Ed and von Papen, since they are no longer *personæ gratæ,* I, nevertheless, do not desire to go beyond the above declaration; so that your Government may be in a position to institute an inquiry into the manner of dealing with your Attachés, should it wish to do so. If I should go into further details on this matter I might interfere with the inquiry which is now being taken up by this Government, dry up very valuable sources of information, and thus hinder the course of justice. On the other hand there might thus be raised other grounds for suspicion, serving rather to disturb than to improve the present friendly relations between the two countries. I need not tell your Excellency, that it is the sincere wish of this Government to avoid difficulties of this kind, so far as may be consistent with its dignity and its responsibilities."

Besides dispatching a copy of the above letter, I wired to Berlin on 8th December, as follows:

CIPHER

"Convinced that Rintelen is the main cause of the Attachés' recall. Immediate categorical disavowal is absolutely necessary. Only possible connection with us is matter of 500,000 dollars, received from the Naval Attaché and demanded for the exportation of goods."

Thereupon I received the following wireless message in English:

CIPHER

"You are empowered to disclaim connection with Rintelen, who had no orders to do anything whatsoever, which was an offence against the American law.

"JAGOW."

The peculiar relations of the Naval and Military Attachés with the Embassy had, even in times of peace, often led to diplomatic difficulties. For instance, it has often happened to us and to other countries to have to recall Military or Naval Attachés for spying. The diplomatic standing of the head of the Mission would not generally be affected thereby, but, in view of the passions of wartime, and the general tension of nerves, I realized that I might be compromised by the demand for the recall of the Attachés. I questioned Lansing outright on this point, and added that I should immediately hand in to my Government my resignation, if I was considered to be myself "tarred with the same brush." The Secretary of State assured me that I was by no means involved, and that I should not on any account give up my post, since I had to carry on the momentous negotiations now in course, and the American Government had full confidence in me. Under the circumstances I saw no reason why the enforced recall of the Attachés should have any further results, and I was confirmed in this view a few days later when House repeated to me Lansing's assurance with even greater emphasis. His exact words were as follows:

"You must not dream of going home before peace is declared. You are the one tie that still binds us to Germany. If this tie should break, war would be inevitable."

Both Attachés returned to Berlin under safe-conduct from the Entente at the end of December, 1915. Their offices were taken over by their representatives, but only for the purpose of settling up any outstanding matters.

At the beginning of 1916, there was in the United States no single German organization which merited the name of "propaganda." Thus no activities which could compromise us in any way ensued henceforward.

The political situation had become so serene that we had no need for propaganda. The pacifist elements in the United States did this work for us. The only question was as to whether we would remain really at one with them, or whether we meant to persist in submarine warfare, which must inevitably lead us into war.

President Wilson opened Congress on 7th December, 1915, with a message, in which he set forth the new programme for national defence. "Preparedness" became the order of the day in the United States. The message demanded that the Army and Navy should be increased, and added:

"The urgent question of our mercantile and passenger shipping is closely connected with the problem of national supply. The full development of our national industries, which is of such vital importance to the nation, pressingly calls for a large commercial fleet. It is high time to make good our deficiencies on this head and to restore the independence of our commerce on the high seas."

In this message may be recognized the second important point in the Presidential programme for the next election. "Peace and Preparedness" was to be the battle-cry of the Democratic Party. The Mexican imbroglio of 1913-14 had proved that the armed forces of the United States were unequal even to the demands of a comparatively small campaign; and the American Government, for lack of means, had been unable to impose its will on Mexico. Now the European War stirred all imaginations and offered a favorable occasion for overcoming the prejudices of the pacifist section against military armaments. It was not so long since the song "I didn't raise my boy to be a soldier," was sung with fervor all the land over; but now events had too clearly proved the powerlessness of any but well-armed nations even to follow their own lines of policy; and the necessity of a mercantile marine of their own grew daily clearer to the people of the United States. Hitherto the Americans had always found enough of foreign vessels for the transport of their goods, had found it cheaper to make use of these facilities than to supply their own under the conditions existing in the States. Now, however, the shortage of merchant tonnage was acute, and American goods were piled roof high in all the warehouses of New York harbor. It was clear that now or never was the time to seize the chance afforded by the war of persuading Congress to sanction the provision of a strong Army and Fleet.

The Presidential message also touched on the "conspiracies," but without any mention of the German Embassy's supposed share in them. The period of these so-called "conspiracies" thus closed with a sharp reprimand addressed by Mr. Wilson to the German-Americans, and with my official recommendation to the Germans in the United States to abstain from all forms of illegal action. The after-effects of this period, however, may be traced in the subsequent lengthy trials of the various offenders. I cannot be sure that since the beginning of 1916, not one single incident which could be comprised under the term "conspiracy" came to light; but these trials and Entente propaganda kept the recollection of such affairs alive, and the American war propaganda service had no difficulty subsequently in retelling the old tales which, but for the entry of the United States into the war, would have passed into oblivion.

The paragraphs of the message dealing with this subject ran as follows:

"We are at peace with all the nations of the world, and there is reason to hope that no question in controversy between this and other Governments will lead to any serious breach of amicable relations, grave as some differences of attitude and policy have been and may yet turn out to be. I am sorry to say that the gravest threats against our national peace and safety have been uttered within our own borders. There are citizens of the United States, I blush to admit, born under other flags, but welcomed under our generous naturalization laws to the full freedom and opportunity of America, who have poured the poison of disloyalty into the very arteries of our national life; who have sought to bring the authority and good name of our Government into contempt, to destroy our industries wherever they thought it effective for their vindictive purposes to strike at them, and to debase our politics to the uses of foreign intrigue. Their number is not great as compared with the whole number of those sturdy hosts by which our nation has been enriched in recent generations out of virile foreign stocks; but it is great enough to have brought deep disgrace upon us and to have made it necessary that we should promptly make use of processes of law by which we may be purged of their corrupt distempers.

"But the ugly and incredible thing has actually come about and we are without adequate federal laws to deal with it. I urge you to enact such laws at the earliest possible moment, and feel that in doing so I am urging you to do nothing less than save the honor and self-respect of the nation. Such creatures of passion, disloyalty and anarchy must be crushed out. They are not many, but they are infinitely malignant, and the hand of our power should close over them at once. They have formed plots to destroy property, they have entered into conspiracies against the neutrality of the Government, they have sought to pry into every confidential transaction of the Government in order to serve interests alien to our own.

It is possible to deal with these things very effectually. I need not suggest the terms in which they may be dealt with."

The message, up to a point, maintained an impartial attitude, for it not only blamed the German-Americans but continued in the following words, aimed solely at the many Americans in London and Paris who disapproved of Wilson's policy of peace and neutrality:

"I wish that it could be said that only a few men, misled by mistaken sentiments of allegiance to the governments under which they were born, had been guilty of disturbing the self-possession and misrepresenting the temper and principles of the country during these days of terrible war, when it would seem that every man who was truly an American would instinctively make it his duty and his pride to keep the scales of judgment even and prove himself a partisan of no nation but his own. But it cannot. There are some men among us, and many resident abroad who, though born and bred in the United States and calling themselves Americans, have so forgotten themselves and their honor as citizens as to put their passionate sympathy with one or the other side in the great European conflict above their regard for the peace and dignity of the United States. They also preach and practise disloyalty. No laws, I suppose, can reach corruptions of the mind and heart; but I should not speak of others without also speaking of these and expressing the even deeper humiliation and scorn which every self-possessed and thoughtfully patriotic American must feel when he thinks of them and of the discredit they are daily bringing upon us."

About the turn of the year 1915-16, the severance of diplomatic relations between the American and Austro-

Hungarian Governments had become imminent. The Italian liner *Ancona* was torpedoed on November 7th in the Mediterranean Sea by an Austro-Hungarian submarine, and went down before all the passengers could succeed in escaping; many lives were lost, American citizens being among them. In consequence, the Washington Government dispatched to Vienna a Note couched in far stronger terms than any it had yet sent; demanding that the action should be admitted to be unlawful and inexcusable, that compensation should be made, and that the officer responsible should be punished for his deed, which would be branded by the whole world as inhuman and barbarous, and would incur the abhorrence of all civilized nations.

The Austro-Hungarian representative, Baron Zwiedeneck von Suedenhorst, found himself in an extremely difficult position. Owing to the fact that he only ranked as chargé d'affaires, and that his appointment only dated from Dr. Dumba's departure, he was not empowered to enter into negotiations. He had always proved himself a very loyal colleague and acted in close co-operation with me, but in this instance, as the matter was one solely for Vienna's decision, I could be of little service to him. I counselled him to telegraph frankly to his Government, that if the American demands were not conceded, a breach was to be expected. I was myself inclined to believe that, as in the case of our Naval and Military Attachés, Mr. Wilson's real purpose was to give the lie to those accusations of weakness which the Entente party was constantly casting in his teeth, and this, I thought, accounted for the unwonted sternness of the American Note, which seemed absolutely to challenge a rupture. It was not conceivable that the Austrian Government could swallow this bitter pill, while from the point of view of the American Government, the breaking-off of relations would be a real diplomatic victory; for on the one hand the political situation would remain unchanged so long as the German Embassy was in Washington, and on the other hand, Mr. Wilson would have achieved his object and shown the Berlin Government that his threats of war were seriously meant.

However, the Austro-Hungarian Government, after a short further exchange of Notes, complied under protest with the American demands. I learned after my return home that in so doing, they acted under pressure from the German Foreign Office. Thus, this crisis also blew over, not, however, without a serious loss of prestige for the Central Powers, who had been compelled to yield to demands generally regarded as utterly unacceptable. Nothing could be more fatal to our position in the world than this alternation of defiance and submission, which served no diplomatic object and merely betrayed infirmity of purpose.

CHAPTER VIII

THE SECOND "LUSITANIA" CRISIS

In Germany, and particularly before the Committee of the National Assembly, the American Government has been reproached with *mala fides* for having unnecessarily reopened the *Lusitania* question. The line of argument is approximately as follows:

After the settlement of the *Arabic* case one can suspect the obstinate harping on the *Lusitania* affair, which had really died down, as a sign of *mala fides*. Did the Americans want to secure a fresh diplomatic success against us? They had already carried their principle with the settlement of the *Arabic* case; was their object now to make a still greater splash? The continued possibility of a conflict with Germany—which was quite within practical politics if nothing intervened—made a very favorable background to make clear to American public opinion, in conjunction with a campaign on the same lines by Wilson himself, the following point: "We must get ourselves out of this situation pregnant with war by vindicating our right with both sides."

Apart from the fact that the negotiations on the *Lusitania* question had been allowed to hang fire for about six weeks I believe that in this case we have again underestimated the significance of hostile public opinion in America. The best way of making clear the situation in the United States will probably be for me to reproduce here the telegrams and reports in which I informed Berlin of the reopening of the *Lusitania* negotiations.

1. Report in Cipher

Washington, 23rd November, 1915.

Secretary of State Lansing after long hesitation took up the *Lusitania* question again with me. At the beginning of October I had handed to him a draft of a letter which contained what I thought myself able to write to him within the scope of my instructions. This draft was merely intended to serve as a basis for more detailed negotiations and was only to be regarded as official in case the American Government should regard the whole incident as satisfactorily settled. There was nothing to be gained by stirring up public opinion again here by publishing documents which were regarded from the beginning as unsatisfactory.

As I have several times had the honor to report, there is, in my opinion, no hope of settling the *Lusitania* question, as the American Government does not think that it can agree to refer it to a court of arbitration *now*. They are, however, counting here on a decision at a later date by such a court, which would be sure to award the Americans an indemnity, because the Hague court of arbitration from its very nature is obliged to stand for the protection of neutral non-combatants. Consequently, Mr. Lansing cannot understand why we do not pay the indemnity of our own accord and so settle the whole matter, especially as, in view of our pledge for the future, it is of no practical importance to us. Mr. Lansing is primarily concerned with the indemnity, whereas President Wilson now, as formerly, lays the chief weight on the pledge for the future and the humanitarian aspect of the question. Mr. Wilson always keeps his eye fixed on the two closely connected goals: the development of international law with regard to the freedom of the seas and the restoration of peace.

Mr. Lansing now reopens the *Lusitania* question for the following reasons, part of which he has himself openly stated, and the rest have become known to me through other channels. In the first place the Government is afraid of attacks in the impending Congress. It was, therefore, eminently desirable that it should be able to inform Congress that something had been done in the *Lusitania* affair. Even if nothing comes of it they could answer that they are waiting for a reply from Germany. President Wilson himself does not believe in the possibility of the question being solved, and hopes to keep the matter in the air until the conclusion of peace, provided that public opinion does not become restive or new eventualities occur. The *Ancona* affair has had an unfavorable effect in this respect. Even though it has not aroused any great excitement, it has caused the whole question to be reopened, and everyone on this side lays at our door the responsibility for the Austrian act; for they base their reasoning on the assumption that the war is directed entirely from Berlin. Whenever mention is made of the *Ancona* incident it recalls the fact that the *Lusitania* question still remains unsettled.

It is a well known fact that we are faced here with an anti-German ring of great influence. I have repeatedly pointed this out in my reports. This ring is trying to exploit the *Ancona* and *Lusitania* questions with a view to driving into the background the American Note to England and the British infringements of international law. The Government is treating this anti-German ring with the same weakness as are the majority of American private citizens. They are submitting patiently to terrorization as well as continual baiting and sneering. The recluse at the White House has, indeed, great plans, but his freedom of decision is seriously compromised by his anxiety to be re-elected. He refuses to allow himself to be drawn into too serious extravagances; and so he certainly deserves the credit for having prevented war with Germany, but he allows himself, nevertheless, to be influenced by the anti-German ring and hampered in the pursuit of his plans.

2. TELEGRAM IN CIPHER

"Washington, 2nd December, 1915.

"The Government here have lost their nerve as a result of the impending Congress, the Hapag case, the *Ancona* incident, and the explosions and fires in munition and powder works, and like all private individuals here are allowing themselves to be terrorized by the anti-German ring. Hence the anxiety for the recall of Papen and Boy-Ed. The Government fear that Congress will take the above questions, as well as the *Lusitania* affair, into their own hands, and deal with them in more radical fashion than the Government. This is the reason for the present demand for the recall—which is intended to serve as a safety-valve—lest Congress should break off diplomatic relations with us. Whether there is any real danger of this happening it is difficult to say. Lansing thinks there is. In any case everything is possible in the present state of public feeling. They have not the courage to swim against the stream. Perhaps the recall of the attachés will still the storm for a time, as was the case with Dernburg and Dumba; meanwhile everything turns on the attitude of Congress, who, it is to be hoped, will not be anxious to declare war on us. Colonel House, who is a good reader of the barometer here, sees no danger. I, personally, also do not believe that Congress will decide to resort to extremes on one side,—*i.e.*, without attacking England—for the breaking-off of diplomatic relations would certainly be quickly followed by war.

"In any case it is my sacred duty to inform your Excellency that Congress may produce unpleasant surprises, and that we must, therefore, be prepared to do *something* with regard to the Lusitania question. How far we can approach the Lansing draft it is difficult to judge from here. It depends in the first place on the state of public opinion in Germany, for the matter has no further practical importance since we have pledged ourselves to spare passenger-ships.

"Hitherto my personal relations with the American Government have been so good that it was always possible to prevent the worst happening. Lansing volunteered yesterday to send this telegram. But if the matter once gets into the hands of Congress it will be much more difficult to exert influence, especially as nothing can be kept secret here. It is not yet possible to say when Congress will ask for the *Lusitania* documents, but it will probably be in a few weeks' time, provided that no diplomatic understanding can be reached meanwhile."

3. REPORT IN CIPHER

"Washington, 7th December, 1915.

"The action that *Congress* will take with regard to the *Lusitania question* is of primary importance for us. It is my opinion that President Wilson, when he asked for the recall of our two attachés, had the thought in the back of his mind that Congress would let the *Lusitania* question rest for a time, because relations with Germany are already sufficiently strained and only the rabid pro-English want war. One cannot, however, count on anything now, because the anti-German ring are seeking to terrorize all who do not agree with them. The senators and members of Congress from the west are certainly more difficult to influence, as their constituents have only a slight economic interest in the cause of our enemies. It is also probable that the senators from the south will all stand by us, because they are very much embittered against England on account of the cotton question. Nevertheless, we must, as I have already pointed out by telegram, be fully prepared for further negotiations on the subject of the *Lusitania*. If we refuse to give way at all, the breaking of diplomatic relations, followed by war, is inevitable. In my opinion it is out of the question to find a formula that will satisfy public opinion on both sides. It may, however, be possible to find a formula that will skim over the points of contention, as was done in the *Arabic* case. In spite of all the outcry over here there is no doubt that the American Government and the greater part of public opinion would be only too delighted if we could find a graceful way of settling the *Lusitania* question without a conflict. What is required in the first place is:

"1. A declaration on our side that the attack on the *Lusitania* should be regarded as an act of reprisal and, therefore, not within the scope of existing international law.

"2. The payment of an indemnity, which in my opinion could be made without committing ourselves on the question of responsibility.

"President Wilson had hoped that the whole question could be shelved until after the end of the war. Now the war still drags on, and Mr. Wilson is afraid of radical intervention on the part of Congress. Over here it is quite impossible to prophesy. The unexpected is the only thing that consistently recurs. No one can say what Congress will do. Meanwhile, it is my duty to describe the situation as I see it to-day. Whether the *Lusitania* question is of sufficient practical importance to allow it to bring upon us the breaking-off of diplomatic relations and war with the United States I must leave it to the exalted judgment of your Excellency to decide.''

* * * * * *

The American Government had established a basis for the negotiations with regard to the *Lusitania* and "the Freedom of the Seas" which was in our favor when, on the 21st October, they sent a very circumstantial Note to London in which they demonstrated that the English blockade was a breach of international law and definitely stated that this blockade was neither effective, legal nor defensible.   Further, that the United States could not, therefore, submit to an infringement of her rights as a neutral through measures which were admittedly reprisals, and, consequently, contrary to international law. That she could not with equanimity allow her rights to be subordinated to the plea that the peculiar geographical position of the enemies of Great Britain justified measures contrary to international law.

The conclusion of the Note read as follows:

"It is of the highest importance to neutrals not only of the present day, but of the future, that the principles of international right be maintained unimpaired.

"This task of championing the integrity of neutral rights, which have received the sanction of the civilized world against the lawless conduct of belligerents arising out of the bitterness of the great conflict which is now wasting the countries of Europe, the United States unhesitatingly assumes, and to the accomplishment of that task it will devote its energies, exercising always that impartiality which from the outbreak of the war it has sought to exercise in its relations with the warring nations."

The above programme was in accordance with the proposal of the American Note of 21st July, which had touched on the subject of co-operation in realizing the "Freedom of the Seas." It was, however, clear to me, apart from anything else, that the United States would not expend energy in championing the rights of neutrals so long as a conflict with Germany threatened. The settlement of the *Arabic* question gave grounds for hope that the views of the two Governments on the question of submarine warfare would coincide. This appeared to me to be the most important point; the American Government, however, insisted on the settlement of the *Lusitania* incident, which I foresaw was going to prove a very difficult problem. Even in the *Arabic* affair it was only by my own independent action that it was possible to avoid a break. The *Lusitania* question, however, was much more unfavorable to us because at that time the old instructions to submarine captains were still in force. I should, therefore, have been glad to avoid negotiations on the *Lusitania* question, but Mr. Lansing insisted on a settlement before he spoke on the future "Freedom of the Seas." The reason for this attitude of the Secretary of State, as appears in my reports reproduced above, lay in the state of public opinion. It was unfortunately impossible for the American Government to carry through the policy they had adopted in respect to England so long as the *Lusitania* question was brought forward daily in the American Press.

The negotiations should have been carried through orally and confidentially between Mr. Lansing and myself. Unfortunately, however, it was impossible to keep anything confidential in Washington, particularly as, very

much against my wishes, the conversations were protracted for weeks. The state department was continually
besieged by journalists, who reported in their papers a
medley of truth and fiction about each of my visits. In
this way they provoked denials, and so ended by getting
a good idea of how the situation stood. In addition to
this, authoritative persons in Berlin gave interviews to
American journalists, who reported to the United States
papers everything that they did not already know. Consequently, the negotiations did not progress in the way
Mr. Lansing and I had expected. We wanted to arrive
quickly at a formula and make it known at once. Public opinion in both countries would then have been set at
rest, and the past would have been buried so long as no
fresh differences of opinion and conflict arose out of the
submarine war. The formula, however, was not so easy
to arrive at. The wording of the Memorandum which I
was to present to the American Government had to be
repeatedly cabled to Berlin, where each time some altera-
tion was required in the text that Mr. Lansing wanted.

The American Government held to the point of view
which they had formulated in the Note of the 21st July,
as follows:

". . . for a belligerent act of retaliation is *per se* an
act beyond the law and the defense of an act as retalia-
tory is an admission that it is illegal."

The standpoint of the American Note of the 21st July,
1915, shows clearly the mistake of treating the submarine
war as reprisals. It shows how every surrender of a
position compromises the next.

The German Government, on the other hand, refused
under any circumstances to admit the illegality of the
submarine warfare within the war-zone, because they
regarded the right to make reprisals as a recognized part

of the existing international law. Further, the American demand was regarded in Germany as a deliberate humiliation, as well as an attempt to coerce us unconditionally to renounce unrestricted submarine warfare once and for all. To have admitted that the submarine war was a breach of international law would have involved us in the same unpleasant consequences to which now, after our defeat, we are compelled to submit. If we admitted the illegality of the submarine campaign we should have been obliged, on the conclusion of peace, to meet all the demands for damages arising out of it.

For the third time, then, the word "illegal" brought us face to face with a crisis which was within an ace of causing a rupture of diplomatic relations. The last days of the negotiations turned out very unfortunately for us. Mr. Lansing and I had agreed upon a formula in which the word "illegal" did not occur, because my instructions categorically prohibited its use. In Berlin it was not yet known that we had arrived at the desired agreement, and it was there thought necessary to call public attention to the danger of the situation, and explain the seriousness of the position in the hope that by this means the American Government might be moved to adopt a more conciliatory attitude.

On 5th February, Under-Secretary of State Zimmermann gave an interview to the Associated Press in which he said he did not wish to conceal the seriousness of the position. That Germany could under no circumstances admit the illegality of the submarine campaign within the war-zone. The whole crisis arose from the new demand of America that Germany should admit the sinking of the *Lusitania* to be an act infringing the law of nations. Germany could not renounce the submarine as a weapon. If the United States insisted on bringing about a break Germany could do nothing further to avoid it. The

Imperial Chancellor confirmed these statements in a conversation with the Berlin correspondent of *The World*.

These interviews compromised once more the settlement of the negotiations, because the American Government were doubtful as to whether they could allow the word "illegal" to be omitted, after the sharp difference of opinion between the two Governments had become public property. The agreement which had been reached voluntarily now looked like a weak surrender before a German threat. In the end, however, a compromise was arrived at. I handed to Mr. Lansing in writing a declaration amounting to an admission that reprisals were admissible, but that they should not be allowed to injure neutrals, and that therefore the German Government regretted the incident and were prepared to offer satisfaction and compensation. The American Government were willing to confirm the receipt of this Memorandum and declare themselves satisfied. Fate, however, had decreed that I should play the rôle of Sisyphus at Washington. Scarcely were the negotiations terminated when the German Government, on the 8th February, declared the so-called "ruthless submarine war," *i.e.* announced to the sea powers their intention of sinking armed merchantmen without warning and without regard to crew or passengers. In view of this the American Government refused to complete the exchange of letters on the subject of the *Lusitania*. Instead of this there began a new controversy on the question of "armed merchantmen." My hope of settling the *Lusitania* question and then passing on to the discussion of "Freedom of the Seas" was shattered. This hit me all the harder as I was convinced that the conversations on the latter question would have developed into peace negotiations.

The opinion has been expressed in Germany that the

breaking-off of diplomatic relations at this stage was regarded, even in America, as precipitate, since no really acute provocation had been given. That it was a shamelessly engineered break after we had in principle yielded on every point. That the Americans had apparently been bluffing and continually increasing their demands with a view of enhancing their own prestige by scoring further diplomatic successes against us which, in view of the previous course of events, they could regard as certain.

In this case I do not myself believe that the American Government were really thinking seriously of breaking off diplomatic relations. They only wanted to pacify public opinion by a settlement of the *Lusitania* question, which was essential before passing on to negotiations with regard to the "Freedom of the Seas" or to steps for peace. Threats of war arose only because the negotiations were protracted for weeks, and the word "illegal" was discussed in the Press in every possible tone. It was a misfortune that these negotiations were not carried on—like the subsequent conversations with regard to peace—in secret. I had actually persuaded the American Government to give way on the word "illegal," which had become much more difficult for them owing to the publicity that was given to the negotiations. Had it not been for the ruthless submarine campaign the *Lusitania* question would have been finally buried and the negotiations could have been continued in a friendly spirit. Moreover, the so-called ruthless submarine campaign was, according to the opinion of Admiral von Tirpitz, who was at that time still in office, although he was not consulted until the decision was taken, a military farce. He declared the order to be technically nonsense, and the pompous way in which it was issued as unnecessarily provocative and a challenge. The whole thing was neither "fish nor flesh."

The controversy over the "armed merchantmen" had a prologue which could only be described as a comedy of errors, were the matter not so serious. It is well known that the constitution of the United States allows the President the right of independent political action. He alone is responsible, and his Secretary of State and the other Ministers are only his assistants, without personal responsibility. Mr. Wilson has made much greater use of his rights in this respect than even Mr. Roosevelt. From the very beginning his administration was a one-man Government.

In general terms the development of democracy in America amounts to this, that the electors vest unlimited rights in one man for a short time, and after that they re-elect or replace him according to whether he has won or lost their confidence.

Thus arises a sort of temporary autocracy which combines the advantages of a monarchy and a democracy. Whether this historically developed system really coincides with our idea of formal democracy is another question.

However this may be, the political life of a nation is not to be ruled by catch-words. History is the only builder of state organisms. No one can foretell in what direction our young democracy will develop. In view of the indifference of the German people to politics it may be assumed, however, that it will develop on similar lines to that of America when we have once accepted the principle of the election of the President by the people. Such a President will always possess great power and authority in his relation to other bodies, while it is probable that the German people will be willing to leave political affairs in the hands of the man they have elected, and will even give him charge of their economic affairs. The German President of the future will certainly find himself involved in the same differences with the Ministers responsible to the majority in the Reichstag as the American President has had so frequently with the Senate. In such cases the American people nearly always support the President, directly chosen by them, and so bring corresponding pressure to bear on the Senate.

The brief constitutional diversion from the question of "armed merchantmen" was to give an opportunity for announcing the surprising catastrophes which had occurred in the course of the development of this question. About the end of the year 1915 Mr. Wilson had married for the second time and was absent for a time from Washington. Consequently the President seems not to have exerted the same close control as usual over the political actions of his Ministers. In any case he had not read, or only hastily glanced through, a Memorandum on the submarine campaign which Mr. Lansing had handed on the 18th January, 1916, to the representatives of the Entente, and had not therefore realized its far-reaching importance. This Memorandum only came to the knowledge of the Central Powers at a later date, through the medium of the Press, which had got to know of it from one of the Entente representatives or through some indiscretion.

The Memorandum went even further than the Note of the 21st July, 1915, and recognized that the use of submarines could not be prohibited to the combatants after they had proved their value in attacking enemy commerce. It laid down, however, that the submarine campaign must, without interfering with its effectiveness, be brought into harmony with the general provisions of international law and with the principles of humanity. It was, therefore, necessary on the one side that the submarines should be instructed to conduct their campaign within the limits laid down for cruiser-warfare against merchant shipping, *i.e.*, they must not sink without first stopping and examining the ship and giving the passengers and crew a chance to save themselves. On the other side, the merchant ships were not to carry arms, since, owing to the nature of the submarines, it would be impossible for them to conduct their operations on the lines of cruiser-warfare if the merchantmen were even lightly armed, as had hitherto been permitted by the principles of international law for purposes of defense. Under the prevailing circumstances any arming of a merchant ship would have an offensive character.

The Memorandum concluded as follows:

"I should add that my Government is impressed with the reasonableness of the argument that a merchant vessel carrying an armament of any sort, in view of the character of submarine warfare and the defensive weakness of undersea craft, should be held to be an auxiliary cruiser and so treated by a neutral as well as by a belligerent Government, and is seriously considering instructing its officials accordingly."

Although this Memorandum bears no historical weight I deal with it in detail here because it played a leading part before the Committee of the National Assembly as a proof that no confidence could be placed in Mr. Wilson as a peace mediator.

I have no doubt that the Memorandum was intended to carry on the policy of the American Notes of the 21st July and 21st October, 1915, which had given rise to the American struggle for the "Freedom of the Seas." It was not, however, in keeping with Mr. Wilson's usual methods to make such a sharp thrust at the Entente as the concluding paragraph of the Memorandum represented, so long as the negotiations with me on the subject of the *Lusitania* incident were not yet concluded and so long as it was not absolutely sure of the support of public opinion. Just as the Note of the 21st October, 1915, was not sent to London until the President thought he had cleared the way with respect to us by the settlement of the *Arabic* question, so in January, 1916, he wanted to keep his hands free until the chance of a conflict with us was past. The popular saying in America is that Wilson has a single-line brain and only deals with one matter at a time. Moreover, out of regard for the state of public feeling in the country the President wanted to take each political step without being openly coerced by us. It is not my intention to defend Mr. Wilson's conception of neutrality to-day, after I have opposed it for years, but I will only attempt, without any personal ill-will, to contribute to Klio's work of discovering the real truth. To me personally the matter of paramount interest to-day, as at that time, is not what Mr. Wilson did or did not do, but the question what we ought to have done in the interest of Germany.

I shall often have to return to the developments which, after the 31st January, 1917, made the President our open enemy. If we wish to be lovers of truth we must distinguish sharply between the two periods before and after the 31st January, 1917. It is certain that Mr. Wilson was never even near to being pro-German. By descent, education and training he was unconsciously much too much under the English influence already mentioned. But until the 31st January, 1917, the President had striven to be neutral. All his speeches testify to this. No un-neutral remark of Mr. Wilson, even in private, has ever reached my ears. He always resisted the pressure of the Entente party, in spite of the fact that he was almost entirely surrounded by anti-Germans. The only one I could mention whose advice to the President was always definitely neutral was Mr. House. For the rest, in the east of the United States we found ourselves morally in an enemy country. Every neutral step taken by Mr. Wilson was immediately hailed as "pro-German." For instance, I am convinced that the President could never have carried out the threat contained in the final clause of the Memorandum of the 18th January. Gradually all the Entente merchantmen were armed. If these were to be treated in American ports as auxiliary cruisers the whole of American commerce would of necessity have come to a standstill, for it was already suffering seriously from lack of freight space. The Entente knew exactly how much value all Americans placed on their commerce, and could therefore reject the proposal of the United States with equanimity.

Nevertheless, it is well worthy of notice that in the Memorandum of the 18th January, 1916, the legally trained and legally minded Secretary of State Lansing, as well as Mr. Bryan, brought forward or attempted to bring forward a different kind of neutrality from that of the President. The only question is whether Mr. Wilson could at that time have carried through the Lansing policy. I do not think so. This does not in itself relieve the President of the responsibility of not wishing to make such a sharp thrust against the Entente as was represented by the Memorandum so long as the negotiations on the *Lusitania* affair still remained unsettled. Yet throughout the whole war Holland has never followed the regulations of the Memorandum. This fact remains. Mr. Wilson did not enforce the Memorandum because he could not do so without prejudicing the interests of American commerce. In this case Mr. Lansing was the neutral advocate and the President the American politician, whose decisions on foreign questions, as usually happens in the United States, were actuated by domestic politics.

After the issue of Mr. Wilson's protest against the English blockade, and in view of the turn that the Lansing action against armed merchantmen had taken, it can be understood that the German Imperial Government henceforward was suspicious of the good-will and power of the President as a peace mediator. Meanwhile there came a change in the domestic situation, and this, as I have already mentioned, is always the decisive factor in the United States in all questions of foreign policy.

It would have been a good move on our part to wait for the result of the *Lusitania* negotiations, and then to give Mr. Wilson time to take in hand his policy with regard to the "Freedom of the Seas" on his own initiative. Berlin, however, was always in a hurry to bring in the new measures of submarine warfare, although the disadvantages that this would cause us always outweighed the advantages. However, the Americans themselves will perhaps some day have occasion to regret that they did not seize the opportunity of the war to insure the "Freedom of the Seas." If during the five years of war —from the mobilization to the peace offer and the armistice—we Germans were always in too great a hurry with our decisions, the American Government, on the other hand, lost through hesitation many an opportunity of keeping out of the war. There could be no doubt that the United States could, as a neutral power, have brought about a better peace than they have done as the decisive combatant power.

In January, 1916, there occurred an unfortunate misunderstanding, which must have strengthened the German Government in their intention of declaring the unrestricted submarine war. The Austrian representative had an interview with Mr. Lansing with reference to the

Ancona incident, in which he understood the Secretary of State to say that it would be agreeable to the American Government if the Central Powers in future regarded armed enemy merchantmen as auxiliary cruisers. Baron Zwiedineck sent a wireless report of this interview to his Government via Nauen. As has already been mentioned, all our wireless messages were read by the American Government departments, and it had often occurred that objection had been raised. As this message of Baron Zwiedineck was sent without protest I assumed that Mr. Lansing had agreed to its contents. Later a confidential discussion took place between the Secretary of State, Baron Zwiedineck and myself, on the subject of this incident. Mr. Lansing said that he had not read the wireless message, as such messages were only examined by the censor, with a view to seeing that they did not compromise the neutrality of the United States. Further, he maintained, that Baron Zwiedineck must have misunderstood him, as he had not made the statement imputed to him in the message. We did not treat the conversation as official, in order not to put any greater difficulties in Mr. Lansing's way than he already had to face as a result of his Memorandum of 18th January.

The German Memorandum of 8th February, 1915, proclaiming the unrestricted submarine campaign, was handed to Mr. Gerard in Berlin. I had for the moment no further negotiations to conduct, as the *Lusitania* question was never again reopened and the question of the "Freedom of the Seas" had been quashed by the unrestricted submarine campaign.

Meanwhile Colonel House had gone for a second time to Europe, this time as the official representative of the President. He was in Berlin just at the time when the second *Lusitania* crisis reached its apogee.

I had announced his visit to Berlin, and prepared

everything so that he might have every opportunity for conversation with the authoritative political personages.

When Colonel House returned to America, he told me that the time had not yet come for the mediation of the United States. He had, however, had the opportunity to state his views in London, Paris and Berlin, and had met with the greatest opposition in Paris, because France had suffered so seriously in the war that she had little more to lose by prolonging it.

In Berlin, on the other hand, he had found a disposition to agree to mediation by Mr. Wilson when a favorable opportunity occurred.

In accordance with the wish of the President, I had discussed the peace question exclusively with Colonel House since his second visit to Europe. This made it possible for the conversations to be kept strictly confidential. I could call on Colonel House at his private residence in New York at any time without attracting attention, whereas the State Dpartment and the White House were always besieged by journalists, as I have already mentioned. As a rule, I took the night train to New York and called on Colonel House in the morning, before the Press were aware that I had left Washington.

On the 8th March, according to my instructions, I handed to the American Government a further Memorandum, which set out in concise terms the German standpoint.

After recapitulating the various phases of the negotiations which are already known to the reader, it defined the existing situation with regard to the war at sea as follows:

England was making it impossible for the submarines to carry on their campaign against commerce in accordance with the provisions of international law by arming practically all merchantmen, and ordering the use of their guns for offence. Photographs of the English orders had been sent to the neutral Governments, with the Memorandum of the 8th February, 1916. These orders are directly contrary to the declarations of the English Ambassador in Washington on the 25th August, 1914. The Imperial German Government had hoped that these facts would prompt the neutral Governments to carry out the disarmament of merchant vessels on the lines of the proposals for disarmament made by the United States Government on 23rd January, 1916. Actually, however, the arming of these ships with guns provided by our enemies has been energetically pursued.

Advantage was taken by England and her Allies of the American Government's decision not to keep her citizens off enemy merchant ships to arm merchantmen for attack. This makes it easy for merchantmen to destroy the submarines, and, in case of the failure of their attack, to count themselves secure owing to the presence on board of American citizens.

The order as to the use of arms was supplemented by instructions given to the masters of the merchant vessels to fly false colors and to ram the submarines. The news that prize-money was paid to successful captains of merchant ships and honors conferred upon them increased the effectiveness of these orders. The Allies have associated themselves with these English measures.

Germany now finds herself faced with the following facts:

(a) That for a year a blockade contrary to international law has kept neutral commerce away from German ports and made export from Germany impossible.

(b) That for six months an extension, contrary to international law, of the laws of contraband has hampered the maritime commerce of neutral neighbors in respect of Germany.

(c) That interference with the post, contrary to international law, is striving to cut Germany off from all communication with the outside world.

(d) That systematically increased coercion of neutrals, on the principle that "Might is right," is stopping trade with Germany across the land frontiers, with a view to completing the starvation blockade of the non-combatant population of the Central Powers.

(e) That Germans who are found at sea by our enemies are robbed of their liberty regardless of whether they are combatants or non-combatants.

(f) That our enemies have armed their merchant ships for attack, and have thus made impossible the use of submarines in accordance with the principles of the Declaration of London.

The English White Book, of the 5th January, 1916, with regard to the restriction of German commerce, boasts that through these measures Germany's export trade has been almost completely stopped, and that her imports have been made dependent on the good-will of England.

The Imperial Government may hope that, in view of the friendly relations that have existed between the two countries for a hundred years, the standpoint herein laid down will meet with the sympathy of the people of the United States, in spite of the increased difficulty of mutual understanding brought about by the conduct of our enemies.

The last words of this Memorandum were vigorously commented on by the American Press as a proof that we wished to appeal, not to the American Government, but to the American people, as a result of the movement which had been set on foot in Congress, and especially in the Senate, that American citizens should be prohibited from travelling on the armed merchant vessels of combatant States.

The struggle which was at that time being waged in Congress has been greatly exaggerated in Germany. At home it was thought that the weight of opinion in Congress in favor of the warning of passengers was very great. On the pro-German side in New York it was thought that Congress was anxious to avert danger of a conflict. If this could have happened through a yielding on the part of Germany, it would, of course, have made things much easier for the Americans; if, however, Germany refused to give way, they thought the United States would have found a more conciliatory formula, as the country was seeking before all things to avert war. They believed that the re-election of 1916 had been largely won through the battle-cry, "He kept us out of the war," which showed that Congress, with its love of freedom, reflected the general opinion. It was, moreover, doubted in the same quarter whether Wilson, as a pacifist candidate for the Presidency, could declare war at that time, when there was as yet no definite provocation—as, for example, the Mexico Dispatch. The theory of this small pro-German group in New York was that Congress would at that time have done anything to avoid war, and that they had only accepted the Gore resolution in order to humiliate the President in the eyes of the world as no head of a State had ever been disavowed before.

In the same quarter—as also happened before the Committee of the German National Assembly—the whole question aroused indignation. It was said that when the Germans read that it had been pompously brought forward as a point of honor whether a few Americans should travel by enemy armed vessels, they bristled with anger. It looked to them as though the alternatives were whether these few Americans should travel in the war-zone on neutral ships, or whether a great civilized nation like Germany should go under! The matter developed from the "too proud to fight" attitude—when Wilson really believed there was a danger of war, and so drew back—to the tone of February, 1916—when he no longer believed in the possibility of war, but felt sure that he could subdue us with hard words. They thought it strange, moreover, to hear Wilson speaking of the gradual breakdown of the delicate structure of international law. That had resulted from England's attitude, and in 1812 America had declared war on the English because of an illegal blockade.

Politics are not to be carried on by indignation, but only with a cool head and a clear vision for political realities. We could not alter the American situation, but must strive to conduct ourselves in such a way as to prejudice the position of the United States as little as possible.

I had from the beginning little doubt that Mr. Wilson would make his will prevail, because the domestic position in the United States made any other issue impossible. The presidential election was imminent, and the Democratic party had no likely candidate apart from Mr. Wilson. If a split occurred within the party the Republicans would be bound to win. Senators Stone and Gore were the leaders of the Democratic Opposition, while the Republicans in this case supported the policy of the President, partly because they were on the side of the Entente, partly because they wanted to assure the interests of American commerce. As has already been mentioned, Senator Stone had always maintained a neutral attitude to the last, chiefly because he was one of the two representatives of Missouri, and could not ignore the large number of Germans among his constituents. For this reason he was called by the pro-Entente Press, like the *New York Herald*, "pro-German Mr. Stone." Senator Gore was a Pacifist on principle, and thought that the resolution for which he was responsible, to prohibit Americans from travelling on armed merchantmen, would avert the danger of war.

The whole Congress story can only be read as a domestic party skirmish, with a view to the approaching Presidential election; one section of the Democratic party wanted a candidate other than Wilson. Just as it was at that time a mistake to expect any advantage from the Congress Opposition, so to-day a similar mistake is made in Germany, when it is assumed that the struggle in the Senate over the ratification of the Peace Treaty has a pro-German background.

The debate in Congress was not in any way connected with an acute German-American situation. It seems necessary to give here a short survey of the negotiations, as they appeared from my point of view. Our first concession occurred after the *Arabic* incident, our second later, after the *Sussex* incident. Between these two there was never any concession to America on the part of Germany, for the shelving of the second *Lusitania* crisis constituted a compromise. Between February, 1915, and the *Lusitania* incident we were conducting an unrestricted submarine campaign, subsequently a limited one, though this was not known to America until after the sinking of the *Arabic;* after February, 1916, the unrestricted campaign was renewed until the *Sussex* incident, after which cruiser warfare was begun. This is all that concerned me in this connection. Internal differences of opinion within the German Government, such as occurred after February, 1915, did not make their way across the Atlantic; for instance, the resumption of the unrestricted submarine campaign in February, 1916, was discussed with me as little as it was with the American Government itself.

From these facts it is evident that the action of Congress was of no practical importance for us, for when, after this debate, the *Sussex* incident occurred—when, moreover, it was a question of an unarmed ship—Mr. Wilson was free to issue his ultimatum, and could also have broken off diplomatic relations, if we had refused to give way. The American Government had then no thought of a complete defeat of Germany, such as later occurred, for otherwise they could easily have found an excuse for coming into the war. At that time Mr. Wilson was convinced that the war would end in a peace without victory, for which he intended to use his influence. The whole question was merely whether we realized these facts and would avail ourselves of them or not. Our one asset in America was the disinclination of the majority of the people for war, for otherwise—as appeared later—it would have been only too easy for the United States to make war upon us with success.

The President wanted to continue the policy he had adopted hitherto, by standing firm to the point of view that the submarine war must be conducted according to the principles of international law, and, further, was waiting to see whether the unrestricted submarine campaign would give rise to any further incidents.

In a letter written to Senator Stone, on the 24th February, the President defined his policy in the following terms:

"You are right in assuming that I shall do everything in my power to keep the United States out of the war. I think the country will feel no anxiety about my line of action in this respect. I have devoted many anxious months to this task under much greater difficulties than appeared on the surface, and so far with success. The course which the Central Powers intend to adopt in future with regard to submarine warfare, as shown by their Memorandum, seems at the moment to raise insuperable difficulties; but its contents are at first sight so difficult to reconcile with the specific assurances which the Central Powers have recently given us as to the treatment of merchant shipping on the high seas, that I think that explanations will shortly be forthcoming which will throw a different light on the matter. We have in the past had no reason to doubt their good faith, or the sincerity of their promises, and I, for my part, am confident that we shall have none in the future.

"But in any event our duty is clear. No nation, no group of nations, has the right, while war is in progress, to alter or disregard the principles which all nations have agreed upon in mitigation of the horrors and sufferings of war; and if the clear rights of American citizens should ever unhappily be abridged or denied by any such action, we should, it seems to me, have in honor no choice as to what our own course should be.

"For my own part, I cannot consent to any abridgment of the rights of American citizens in any respect. The honor and self-respect of the Nation is involved. We covet peace, and shall preserve it at any cost but the loss of honor.

"To forbid our people to exercise their rights for fear we might be called upon to vindicate them would be a deep humiliation indeed. It would be an implicit, all but an explicit, acquiescence in the violation of the rights of mankind everywhere and of whatever nation or allegiance. It would be a deliberate abdication of our hitherto proud position as spokesmen, even amid the turmoil of war, for the law and the right. It would make everything this Government has attempted and everything that it has accomplished during this terrible struggle of nations meaningless and futile.

"It is important to reflect that if in this instance we allowed expediency to take the place of principle the door would inevitably be opened to still further concessions. Once accept a single abatement of right, and many other humiliations would certainly follow, and the whole fine fabric of international law might crumble under our hands piece by piece. What we are contending for in this matter is of the very essence of the things that have made America a sovereign nation. She cannot yield them without conceding her own impotency as a Nation and making virtual surrender of her independent position among the nations of the world."

Soon afterwards—on the 3rd March—the Senate decided by 68 votes to 14 to postpone the discussion of the Gore resolution *sine die*. The struggle had then already ended in a victory for Mr. Wilson when I handed over the above-mentioned Memorandum.

Regarded from our own point of view, the declaration of the "unrestricted submarine war" was a serious political mistake, which was not even justified by the results of the measure. The least we could have done was to wait for the settlement of the *Lusitania* question and the subsequent action of Mr. Wilson. The "unrestricted submarine war" was not the right way to improve our situation, but was bound inevitably to lead to a new conflict with America. It was absolutely impossible for the submarine captains to ascertain with certainty through the periscope whether an enemy merchant ship was armed or not. Mistakes, therefore, were sure to arise sooner or later. On the other hand, the Americans would not refrain from travelling on enemy passenger ships, as their business took them mostly to England and France, and there were not enough of their own or neutral ships at their disposal.

The one hope for the continued avoidance of a conflict was that the Imperial Government should not withdraw the concessions they had made on the 5th October, 1915, with regard to "liners," and that enemy passenger ships should not be unarmed out of regard for their neutral passengers.

There were, as a rule, no Americans on cargo ships, for there were at that time few sailors in the United States. From the above-mentioned letter of Mr. Wilson to Mr. Stone, however, it appeared that the American Government regarded our concessions as applying to all merchant vessels, while, as I have already stated, the German naval authorities had only intended to include passenger steamers.

This misunderstanding might now give rise to a fresh conflict, even if mistakes on the part of submarine captains were by special good fortune avoided.

CHAPTER IX

THE "SUSSEX" INCIDENT

ON the 24th March the unarmed passenger-ship *Sussex* was torpedoed without warning, and several Americans lost their lives. The first information about this incident was so vague that the matter was at first treated in a dilatory fashion in Washington. At the time I sent the following report to Berlin:

REPORT IN CIPHER

"Washington, 4th April, 1916.

"During the fourteen months that have passed since the opening of the submarine campaign there have been intermittent periods in which the American Government have shown themselves aggressive towards us, and others in which the now proverbial expression 'watchful waiting' formed the *Leit-motif* of their attitude. The past month belonged to the second category until the sinking of the *Sussex* and other similar incidents stirred American public opinion to fresh excitement. Officially I have, during the last four weeks, heard nothing further from the American side on the subject of the submarine campaign. During this time Mr. Lansing even allowed himself a fortnight's holiday for recuperation. On my side there was no occasion to reopen the submarine question as a complete understanding with the American Government cannot be attained,* and in my opinion it is advisable to avoid as far as possible any new crisis in our

*i.e., Without instructions from Berlin.

relations with the United States. I therefore contented myself with keeping in touch with Colonel House so that I should not be taken by surprise by any *volte-face* on the part of the American Government. As soon as a new crisis arises Mr. Wilson will, as usual, be in a fearful hurry and bring us to the brink of war. Whether such a crisis will be precipitated by the *Sussex* incident, and whether the President in that case will shrink from war at the last moment, it is difficult to foretell, as this question—like all others at the present moment—will be viewed exclusively from the standpoint of the approaching presidential election.

"Except for the surprises that are usual over here, things are at present quite calm. This is due, in the first place, to the desire for peace shown by the population, who are not anxious to be disturbed in their congenial occupation of money-making, and secondly, to the development of the Mexican question. This latter question stands in the forefront of public interest, and it seems to be increasingly probable that the punitive expedition against Villa will lead to a full-dress intervention. A few days ago it was reported that Villa was defeated, then wounded, and finally even a prisoner. All this good news proved later to be false and now Villa is said to have escaped south and won over fresh supporters. So long as the Mexican question holds the stage here we are, I believe, safe from an act of aggression on the part of the American Government.

"On the other hand it looks as though Mr. Wilson were looking for a fresh way out of the *impasse* into which his attitude on the question of the submarine campaign has led him. As I have already had the honor to cable, Colonel House holds out the prospect of an early move towards peace by the President. The view is entertained here, and strengthened by the impressions gathered from

Colonel House, that gradually the stress of circumstances will force all the neutral Powers into the war. If this happens there will be no further prospect of the conclusion of peace, as there will be no one available to set the ball rolling. It is therefore essential that the foundations of peace should be laid before the world conflagration spreads any further and finally destroys the prosperity of every nation. This view may sound like pure theory, but it gains substance from the fact that it can very well be made to harmonize with Mr. Wilson's election campaign. In his capacity of founder of peace in Europe, and peace-maker—i.e., indirectly conqueror—of Mexico, it would be difficult, if not impossible, to vanquish Mr. Wilson in the election. Mr. Theodore Roosevelt would then shout himself hoarse to no purpose and Mr. Charles Hughes, the strongest Republican candidate, would perhaps not even go so far as nomination if his position seemed hopeless.

In that report I announced for the first time that Mr. Wilson had so far changed his policy as now to put peace mediation in the foreground and to give the question of the 'Freedom of the Seas' second place. I shall return later to this political development.

When news reached Washington which left no doubt that the *Sussex* had been torpedoed by a German submarine, I immediately cabled to Berlin for instructions in order to be in a position to give an official disavowal of the act. It required nothing further to convince me that it was now a question of bend or break. I had no means of knowing whether the supporters of the submarine campaign or the partisans of an understanding with the United States would win the day. In the former case war was inevitable. To provide for the second alternative I recommended in my cablegram that there should be no question of an official exchange of Notes, because I was anxious that our withdrawal should not be accompanied by a humiliation. If our Government were prepared to give way I regarded as the most appropriate *modus procedenti* the immediate issue of instructions to me, empowering me to offer the American Government satisfaction and compensation for this fresh incident. There was no hope of purchasing immunity from a break with any less concession than a pledge to carry on the submarine campaign for the future in accordance with the principles laid down by international law for cruiser warfare. I recommended, however, a provisional cessation of the submarine war on the basis of an oral agreement with the American Government. If this proposal had been acted on, the American Government would have been obliged to follow suit and there would have been no sharp exchange of Notes, which still further prejudiced the position on both sides. If, after such a pause in the submarine war and the establishment of a really clear diplomatic situation, Mr. Wilson failed us and made no positive progress either with regard to his programme for the 'Freedom of the Seas' or the conclusion of peace, we should have held quite a different position from which —if we really thought it desirable—to reopen unrestricted submarine warfare. We had always made the mistake of dealing in half-hearted concessions. In my opinion it was essential for us to strive for a complete understanding with America if we were not prepared to carry on the submarine campaign without regard to consequences.

No attention was paid to my suggestion in Berlin at the time. Admiral von Tirpitz had just resigned and the decision had been taken against the continuance of unrestricted submarine warfare. I do not know why the dispatch of an official Note was preferred to the oral negotiations I had suggested, but I think that the deciding factor was consideration for public opinion in Germany.

A few days later I cabled the following to Berlin:

TELEGRAM IN CIPHER

"Washington, 8th April, 1916.

"House gave me a very gloomy view of the position with regard to the *Sussex*. At the White House the situation is regarded as hopeless because the view is held that, in spite of Tirpitz's resignation, the German Government, with the best will in the world, cannot curb the submarine campaign. It has hitherto been merely due to good luck that no American has lost his life and any moment might precipitate a crisis which would be bound to lead to a break. The American Government are convinced that the Sussex was torpedoed by a German submarine. A repetition of such mistakes would be bound to drive the United States of America into war with us, which Wilson would greatly regret, as he is anxious— as I have already reported—to lay the foundations of peace in a few months. If the United States were drawn into the war all hope of an early peace would be at an end.

"I request to be furnished with instructions on the basis of which I can pacify the Government here, which now has doubts of our *bona fides*."

After Mr. Gerard, apart from other questions concerning doubtful cases of torpedoing, had also submitted a similar inquiry to the Foreign Office on the subject of the *Sussex* incident, an official reply was handed to him on the 10th April which read in the following terms:

"A decision as to whether the Channel steamer *Sussex* was damaged by a German submarine or not is made extraordinarily difficult owing to the fact that no exact information is known as to the place, time and accompanying circumstances of the sinking, and moreover a picture of this ship could not be obtained until the 6th April. Consequently the inquiry has had to be extended to all submarine enterprises which took place on the day in question, 24th March, in the Channel anywhere on the course between Folkestone and Dieppe.

"In this area on the 24th March, in the middle of the English Channel, a long, black vessel, flying no flags, with a gray funnel, small gray superstructure and two high masts was hit by a German submarine. The German captain was definitely convinced that she was a ship of war, and indeed a mine-layer of the newly-built English *Arabic* class. He was led to this conviction:

"1. By the flush deck of the ship.

"2. By the shape of the stern, which sloped outwards.

"3. By the paintwork, which was that of a ship of war.

"4. By the high speed of about eighteen knots which the ship developed.

"5. By the fact that the ship was not steering the course north of the light buoys between Dungeness and Beachy Head within which frequent observation had led the German submarines to keep a look out for merchant shipping, but was in mid-Channel, heading almost for Le Havre.

"Consequently, the submarine fired a torepdo at 3.55 p.m. Central European time, 1½ knots southeast of the Bull Rock. The torpedo struck, and so heavy an explosion occurred that the whole of the ship forward of the bridge broke away. The unusually heavy explosion leaves no doubt that there were large stores of ammunition on board.

"The German captain has prepared a sketch of the ship he attacked, of which two copies are sent herewith. The two copies of pictures of the *Sussex,* also enclosed, were photographed from the English newspaper *The Daily Graphic,* of the 27th inst. A comparison of the sketches and the photograph shows that the vessel attacked is not identical with the *Sussex;* particularly striking is the difference in the position of the funnel and the shape of the stern. No other attack was made by a German submarine on the course between Folkestone and Dieppe at the time of the *Sussex* incident.

"From this the German Government are obliged to assume that the sinking of the *Sussex* is to be set down to other causes than attack by a German submarine. Some light may be thrown on the incident by the fact that on the 1st and 2nd April alone no less than twenty-six English mines were destroyed in the Channel by German naval forces. In general the whole of that area is rendered dangerous by drifting mines and not torpedoes. Off the English coast the Channel is also made increasingly dangerous by German mines which have been laid for the enemy naval forces.

"If the American Government should have at their disposal any further data that may help to elucidate the *Sussex* incident, the German Government beg that it may be communicated to them so that they may subject it to examination. In the event of differences of opinion arising between the two Governments the German Government now declare themselves ready to submit the whole incident to an International Commission in accordance with the third clause of the 'Hague Convention for the Pacific Settlement of International Disputes of the 18th October, 1907.'"

I have reproduced this Note in full because its influence was quite particularly fateful and because it was probably the most unfortunate document that ever passed from Berlin to Washington. Mr. Wilson thought he detected a direct untruth, and the mixture of an uneasy conscience and clumsiness which the German Note appeared to betray prompted the sharp tone of the President's reply. For the sake of his prestige Mr. Wilson was now compelled by the recent course of events to take action, although the excitement of public opinion was this time undoubtedly less than was the case after the torpedoing of the *Lusitania* and the *Arabic*. The American Government, therefore, couched the Note which they dispatched on the 18th April in the terms of an ultimatum. In the meantime, the discovery in the hull of the *Sussex* of a piece of a German torpedo placed the matter beyond all doubt. Additional importance was given to the ultimatum by the fact that before dispatching it Mr. Wilson laid it personally before Congress at a special sitting.

It is my firm conviction that had it not been for this ultimatum diplomatic relations would not have been broken off immediately, even in 1917. In the increased tension of the situation resulting from the exchange of Notes on the subject of the *Sussex* I see, therefore, one of the immediate germs of the war with America. After this exchange of Notes a challenge in the form of our formal declaration of the 31st January, 1917, could no longer be tolerated. The clumsiness of such formal declarations was, as I have said, only surpassed by the regrettable impression of a juristic argument produced by our first *Lusitania* Note.

As the American ultimatum later formed the basis on which the American Government, immediately after the declaration of unrestricted submarine warfare, broke off diplomatic relations, I here give the vital contents of the American Note of the 18th April verbatim:

"Again and again the Imperial Government has given its solemn assurances to the Government of the United

States that at least passenger ships would not be dealt thus with, and yet it has repeatedly permitted its undersea commanders to disregard those assurances with entire impunity. As recently as February last it gave notice that it would regard all armed merchantmen owned by its enemies as part of the armed naval forces of its adversaries, and deal with them as with men-of-war, thus, at least by implication, pledging itself to give warning to vessels which were not armed and to accord security of life to their passengers and crews; but even this limitation their submarine commanders have recklessly ignored.

"The Government of the United States has been very patient. At every stage of this distressing experience of tragedy after tragedy it has sought to be governed by the most thoughtful consideration of the extraordinary circumstances of an unprecedented war, and to be guided by sentiments of very genuine friendship for the people and Government of Germany. It has accepted the successive explanations and assurances of the Imperial Government as of course given in entire sincerity and good faith, and has hoped, even against hope, that it would prove to be possible for the Imperial Government so to order and control the acts of its naval commanders as to square its policy with the recognized principles of humanity as embodied in the law of nations. It has made every allowance for unprecedented conditions and has been willing to wait until the facts became unmistakable and were susceptible of only one interpretation.

"If it is still the purpose of the Imperial Government to prosecute an indiscriminate warfare against vessels of commerce by the use of submarines without regard to what the Government of the United States must consider the sacred and indisputable rules of international law and the universally recognized dictates of humanity, the

Government of the United States is at last forced to the conclusion that there is but one course to pursue. Unless the Imperial Government should now immediately declare and effect an abandonment of its present methods of submarine warfare against passenger and freight-carrying vessels, the Government of the United States can have no choice but to sever diplomatic relations with the German Empire altogether. This action the Government of the United States contemplates with the greatest reluctance, but feels constrained to take in behalf of humanity and the rights of neutral nations."

After this Note it is obvious that there was no longer any doubt in Berlin, that persistence in the point of view they had hitherto adopted would bring about a break with the United States, for I received instructions to make all preparations for German merchant ships lying in American ports to be rendered useless by the destruction of their engines.

I also received orders to arrange that Mr. Gerard, who had not been informed of the minimum demands of the American Government, should be instructed accordingly.

My reply was as follows:

CABLEGRAM IN CIPHER

"Washington, 1st May, 1916.

"House has informed me that at his request Gerard has already been informed of the minimum demands of the American Government. Wilson is strongly influenced by peace votes. Even the anti-German ring desires the end of the war, as otherwise they fear financial loss. My suggestions are based on the view that submarine warfare, according to international law, is valueless, and in any case, the opening of peace negotiations is more important. It would be advisable in the Note of reply to touch only on the principal points, to talk much of international law and humanity, and to leave details to be settled at a later date. I fear that the continuance of the submarine campaign, on the lines of cruiser warfare, only means the postponement of the rupture as fresh incidents are bound to occur."

On the 4th May followed the German reply, which averted the fourth serious crisis, by declaring that the submarine campaign would return to the recognized laws of cruiser-warfare. The Note began by opposing, in strong terms, the American view, and concluded with the following sentences:

"The German Government feel themselves justified in declaring that it would be impossible to answer to humanity and history, if, after twenty-one months of war the contention over the submarine war were allowed to develop into a serious menace to peace between the German and American peoples. Such a development the German Government will do everything in their power to prevent. They desire, at the same time, to make a final contribution towards confining—so long as the war lasts —the war to the present combatant Powers, an aim which includes the freedom of the seas, and in which the German Government believe themselves still to be in agreement with the Government of the United States.

"On this assumption the German Government beg to inform the Government of the United States that instructions have been issued to the German naval forces to observe the general principles of international law, with regard to the holding up, searching and destruction of merchant vessels, and not to sink any merchant vessel, even within the war zone, without warning and rescue of the passengers and crew, unless they attempt to escape or offer resistance.

"The German Government hope and expect that these

new instructions to the naval forces will also remove in
the eyes of the United States Government every obstacle
that might stand in the way of the realization of the offer
of co-operation contained in the Note of the 23rd July,
1915, towards restoring the freedom of the seas during
the war, and they do not doubt that the United States
Government will now insist with all possible emphasis
on the immediate observation by the British Government
of those international rules which were universally accepted before the war, and which are specifically stated in
the Notes of the American Government to the British
Government of the 28th December, 1914, and the 5th
November, 1915. Should it happen that the steps taken
by the Government of the United States do not meet with
the desired result of insuring recognition of the laws of
humanity by all the combatant nations, the German Government would consider themselves faced by a new situation, for which they must reserve for themselves full
freedom of decision."

The German Note reached the German Embassy piece-
meal, and while the first part was being deciphered, its
harsh tone produced in an increasing degree the impression: "Then it is war," which was not relieved until
we came to the conclusion of the text.

The attempt made by the Imperial Government to
reserve to themselves the right to resume the submarine
campaign at a later date was not accepted by Mr. Wilson,
and so the difference of opinion remained, which was
bound to become a *casus belli* if we reverted to unrestricted submarine warfare. This reservation led to a
further Note from Washington, which I give here:

"The Note of the Imperial German Government under
date of May 4th, 1916, has received careful consideration
by the Government of the United States. It is especially

noted, as indicating the purpose of the Imperial Government as to the future, and that it 'is prepared to do its utmost to confine the operations of the war for the rest of its duration to the fighting forces of the belligerents,' and that it is determined to impose on all its commanders at sea the limitations of the recognized rules of international law upon which the Government of the United States has insisted. Throughout the months which have elapsed since the Imperial Government announced on February 4th, 1915, its submarine policy, now happily abandoned, the Government of the United States has been constantly guided and restrained by motives of friendship in its patient efforts to bring to an amicable settlement the critical questions arising from that policy. Accepting the Imperial Government's declaration of its abandonment of the policy which has so seriously menaced the good relations between the two countries, the Government of the United States will rely upon a scrupulous execution henceforth of the now altered policy of the Imperial Government, such as will remove the principal danger to an interruption of the good relations existing between the United States and Germany.

"The Government of the United States feels it necessary to state that it takes it for granted that the Imperial German Government does not intend to imply that the maintenance of its newly-announced policy is in any way contingent upon the course or result of diplomatic negotiations between the Government of the United States and any other belligerent Government, notwithstanding the fact that certain passages in the Imperial Government's Note of the 4th instant might appear to be susceptible of that construction. In order, however, to avoid any possible misunderstanding, the Government of the United States notifies the Imperial Government that it cannot for a moment entertain, much less discuss, a suggestion that respect by German naval authorities for the rights of citizens of the United States upon the high seas should in any way or in the slightest degree be made contingent upon the conduct of any other Government affecting the rights of neutrals and non-combatants. Responsibility in such matters is single, not joint; absolute, not relative."

This American Note, however, in no way affected the peaceful conclusion of the negotiations.

As a direct result of the *Sussex* incident, a step forward was taken in the question of American peace mediation. When I called on Colonel House, during the last days of the crisis, we had a long conversation on this question. As always, Colonel House had used his influence on the side of peace with regard to the *Sussex* incident. He took this opportunity to convey to me the pleasing news contained in a cablegram from Mr. Gerard, that the German Government were now ready to agree to American mediation.

This cablegram was the outcome of the following facts: Mr. Gerard, on account of his anti-German tendency, was not popular in Berlin. He regarded it as a personal slight that the most important negotiations should have been carried on partly in Washington, and partly by Colonel House in Berlin. The Ambassador wanted, therefore, to use the opportunity of the *Sussex* incident to assert himself, and expressed a desire to visit G.H.Q. and explain the American point of view in person to the Emperor. On the 1st May, Mr. Gerard was received by the Emperor, in the presence of the Imperial Chancellor, on which occasion he received the assurance contained in his telegram. Karl Helfferich's account in *Weltkrieg* gives the impression that the question of American mediation was mentioned for the first time on the 1st

May. The two journeys of Colonel House, which were of far greater importance than Mr. Gerard's visit to G.H.Q., are not mentioned in the Helfferich account. For the rest I have to rely for my information about events in Germany on this and other publications, in addition to the evidence given before the Commission of the National Assembly. In any case, Colonel House regarded the telegram from Berlin as the sequel of his own negotiations there, which point was placed beyond all doubt by the text of the information he communicated to me. In order to inform myself on my side also as to the attitude of our Government, I sent the following telegram to Berlin, to ascertain whether the information from the American Ambassador was in accordance with the facts:

TELEGRAM IN CIPHER
"Washington, No. 26, 4th May.

"House informs me that Gerard has cabled that we would agree to the President's mediation, and that a visit from House to Berlin, with this object, would be welcomed. Nothing known here about solution of *Lusitania* question. Mediation naturally depends on this running smoothly, which would be most easily assured by cessation of submarine campaign during negotiations."

I received the following reply from the Imperial Chancellor:

TELEGRAM IN CIPHER
"Berlin, 6th May, 1916.
"Reply to telegram No. 26.
"For Your Excellency's information.

"We hope that our Note and great concession finally removes cause of mistrust, and opens era of greater mutual confidence. Animosity of public opinion here against Wilson, as result of tone and contents of his Note and impression of *parti pris* against us, however, so great that he must take open and unmistakable action with regard to England before he would be accepted as unbiassed mediator by German people. To this extent Gerard's telegram is premature. If Wilson neglects to take such action, there is danger that the animosity may become irremediable and possibility of mediation driven into distant future. Smoothing the way for peace, of course, always desired. Action against England, however, seems necessary to encourage conciliatory attitude there, if a peace exclusively favorable to England is to be avoided.

"If it is found impossible to induce England to discuss peace with us, even though unofficially perhaps at first, we shall, as England refuses to return to the provisions of the Declaration of London, be placed in an absolutely free position with regard to our great concession amounting to abandonment of submarine campaign. A visit from House very welcome here at any time.

"BETHMANN-HOLLWEG."

Karl Helfferich's account confirms the view I held at that time, that our concessions in respect of the submarine campaign were essentially prompted by the hope of mediation by Mr. Wilson. The following words of the Emperor make this plain:

"In politics it is necessary, before all things, to know the other party's point of view; for politics are a question of give and take. Gerard's utterances had made it clear that Wilson was seeking a ladder for re-election. It was better, then, that we should offer him the ladder of peace than the ladder of war, which will eventually fall on our own heads."

Moreover, Herr von Bethmann-Hollweg has declared before the Commission of the National Assembly that he had expressed to Mr. Gerard the hope that the President would now take steps to bring about the restoration of peace.

When, at that time, Colonel House was discussing with me the German reservation in the Note of the 4th May, in connection with the questions of the "Freedom of the Seas" and peace, he said that the circumstances were then such that the President no longer possessed the power to compel England to observe international law. England would only give way before the menace of war. In view, however, of the state of natural feeling in the United States, and the development of trade relations between America and the Entente, war with England was out of the question. On the other hand, Mr. Wilson possessed the power to bring about peace, because on this question he could rely on the support of the majority of the American nation. When the time was ripe, the President would take the desired steps, but a neutral act of this nature would be cried down by the very active Entente party in the United States as pro-German, and could only be carried through if the national feeling towards Germany took a more friendly turn. It was, therefore, necessary that there should be a period of lull, during which Germany should possibly not be discussed at all. The approaching hot season and the usual exodus of political personages from Washington to the country would offer a favorable opportunity to let all negotiations rest, especially as, after the settlement of the *Sussex* question, no new incidents were to be expected. Colonel House's remarks accurately reflected the actual position in the United States at the time. I could not but express my agreement, and felt no doubt that the American mediation would begin in the late summer. After our giving way on the submarine question, in order to avoid a break with the United States, I regarded it as certain that we would not directly bring about the rupture which had just been averted with such difficulty by reopening the unrestricted submarine campaign, for in view of the American ultimatum of the 18th April, 1916, there was no alternative.

I should like to take this opportunity of making clear that I always regarded American mediation as the only possible way out of the war. I had no faith in the submarine campaign as likely to save the situation, because the entry of the United States into the war would more than outweigh all the advantages that the submarines could bring us. On the other hand, I was convinced that, if the American Government established a peace conference, this would be sure to lead to peace itself. It could not be imagined that, in view of the nations' need of peace, such a conference could break up without having reached any result. Moreover, after the meeting of a conference, the United States would no longer be in a position to enter the war, because American public opinion would not have allowed it. But without the help of the United States, the Entente could not win. It resolved itself, therefore, into a question of the skill of our negotiators to ensure a tolerable peace for us, as the result of the conference. Diplomatic negotiations have a way of ending owing to general weariness, in which case the party which holds the best cards secures the greatest advantages. If this happened, we should have the advantage of the position as our military gains would give us a strong lever in the negotiations.

Here I may touch on another question which was engaging my attention at that time. Since the *Lusitania* catastrophe I had adopted the principle, and put it into practice as far as possible, of leaving the propaganda to our American friends, who were in a position to get an earlier hearing than we, and in any case understood the psychology of the Americans better than the Imperial German agents. Indeed, the words "German propagandist" had already become a term of abuse in America. We were reproached there with being too indulgent, while in Germany the opposite criticism was levelled at us. In spite of the difficulty of the situation, however, there were Americans of German and other origin, who had the courage openly to champion our cause and to swim against the stream. Among others, a "Citizens' Committee for Food Shipments" was formed, whose activities spread through the whole country, and were avowedly pro-German. A special function of the committee with Dr. von Mach as executive chief, was a month of propaganda throughout the country, with the object of obtaining the means to supply the children of Germany with milk. The English control of the post even led to the bold plan of building a submarine to run the milk through the English blockade. The propaganda was very vigorously attacked by the greater part of the American Press, but pursued its course unafraid, collected money, submitted protests to the State Department against the attitude of the Entente, and so on.

Dr. von Mach succeeded in bringing the matter to the notice of the President who actively interested himself in it, and promised to see that the milk should pass the English blockade and reach Germany in safety. Accordingly, the State Department instructed the American Embassy in Berlin to issue a statement. Meanwhile, the well-known American journalist, McClure, returned from a tour of investigation in Germany, where he had been supported in every way by the German Government departments. He gave a very favorable account of the milk question, as of the feeding of infants in general, and this gave rise to the first disagreeable controversy. Mr. McClure took up an unyielding attitude. Unfortunately, however, the State Department then published an equally favorable report, which, coming from the American Embassy and published with the approval of the Foreign Office in Berlin, caused the complete collapse of Dr. von Mach. This incident made a very painful impression in America, and led to a series of bitter attacks on Dr. von Mach and the whole movement, which was thus exposed in a most unfortunate light. The favorable report on the milk question was drawn up by a Dr. E. A. Taylor, and definitely confirmed, and, indeed, inspired, by the German authorities.

I mention this incident to show that our propaganda was not by any means made easier by Germany, although our Press Bureau repeatedly brought up this very question in Berlin. This movement was particularly dear to us, because the Americans are most easily won over when an appeal is made to their humanity. Moreover, the favorable reports on the question of supplies in Germany did not coincide in any way with our defence of the submarine campaign as an act of reprisal. This method of propaganda from home lost us our best argument. Even to-day the majority of Americans certainly have no idea how many children have been murdered by the blockade.

At the time of which I am speaking occurred also the much discussed Bolo affair. It is quite astonishing how many lies were told before the commission of inquiry of the American Senate with regard to this affair. Among others, hotel servants, chauffeurs, etc., were sworn, and gave evidence that I had met Bolo in the apartments of Mr. Hearst. True, I have often visited Mr. Hearst, which goes without saying, as he was the only important newspaper proprietor who maintained a neutral attitude throughout the war. I did not, however, meet Bolo, either there or anywhere else; I have never made his acquaintance, or even seen him in the distance. I heard his name for the first time when he was brought up for trial in Paris.

If the statements made before the commission of inquiry are to be relied on in any point at all, it is to be assumed that Bolo first came to America to arrange a combine between the *Journal* and the Hearst Press. This combine was to support the cause of Pacifism after the war. Who Bolo's principal was I do not know, but so much seems to be established, that he was connected with the *Journal*. Apparently, Bolo wanted to sell shares in this paper to Mr. Hearst, in order to acquire funds for the Pacifist agitation. This theory seems justified since Bolo, on the voyage to America, got into touch with Mr. Bartelli, Hearst's representative in Paris. The latter did fall in with Bolo's ideas.

Later—whether intentionally or not I do not know—Bolo met the co-proprietor of the firm Amsinck and Co., Herr Pavenstedt, who was one of the most respected, if not *the* most respected, Imperial German in New York, and intimately acquainted with all the members of the Embassy. Herr Pavenstedt, who as a private citizen was not in a position to accept Bolo's suggestions, then travelled to Washington to lay the matter before me. He gave me to understand that a French acquaintance of long standing, for whose good faith he could vouch, had come to America to raise funds for a Pacifist agitation in France. He said that national feeling in that country had reached a point which promised success for such a movement, if the prospect could be held out of a peace by negotiation. Herr Pavenstedt said that he could not, under any circumstances, disclose the gentleman's name. As the plans of the Frenchman recommended by Herr Pavenstedt coincided with my policy for bringing about a peace by negotiation, and I had absolute confidence in Herr Pavenstedt, I communicated the matter to Berlin, where the necessary money was granted. Later, the breaking off of diplomatic relations with the United States interrupted the policy I had initiated, and also put an end to any prospect of effecting a change of feeling in France, where the hope of American assistance revived enthusiasm for the war.

I do not know how Bolo's enterprise came to the knowledge of the French Government. In any case this cannot have been due to the deciphering of my telegrams to Berlin, as I did not know Bolo's name. Owing to this ignorance on my part it was arranged between Herr Pavenstedt and myself, at a second interview, that the anonymous Frenchman should at a given time address further communications on the progress of the movement to our Embassy at Bern under the pseudonym "St. Regis."

At the time of the *Sussex* crisis a further awkward incident occurred which took us back to the days of conspiracies. In consequence of the Welland Canal case the American secret police came down upon Herr von Igel, the representative of the Military Attaché, in his New York office, for alleged complicity, arrested him by force and seized papers which were found on his table. I immediately laid a protest before the State Department, whereupon Herr von Igel was set at liberty and a long international controversy arose which had not come to an end when Herr von Igel returned with me to Germany. The American Law Department maintained that Herr von Igel was suspected of complicity in a legal offence, that he could not therefore plead extra-territoriality, and must stand his trial before an American Court. The State Department, it is true, had doubts as to whether an office in New York could be recognized as extra-territorial, but for the rest maintained a correct attitude and refused to agree to the opening of proceedings against Herr von Igel.

The seized documents were handed over to the State Department, where they probably still lie. The State Department declared to me their readiness to hand back the papers if I wished to declare them Embassy documents. I, however, thought that an attempt might be made later to use such a declaration against me as a trap and I rejected the offer to return the papers on these conditions, as they were of no further importance to us. If there was among them material which could be used against the former Attachés it might be assumed that the Law Department would long ago have had the documents copied.

The Igel affair had no definite political result, as the American Government dropped all controversies when they began to take up the question of mediation.

To return to the settlement of the *Sussex* incident, it should be mentioned that our surrender on the submarine question was widely resented in Germany. Further, it caused a check in submarine construction. At least, Secretary of State von Capelle has declared before the Commission of the National Assembly that an extensive submarine construction programme had to be abandoned because it would have been too sharp a contrast with Germany's attitude after the settlement of the *Sussex* affair. As a matter of fact, submarine construction was never carried on with full vigor after 1916, as has been pointed out by Messrs. Struve, Gothein and Co. In the light of this the gravity of the decision in 1917 to resort to unrestricted submarine warfare is doubled. It will be seen clearly here how our divided policy on the one hand permanently crippled the submarine policy and on the other that of mediation.

To conclude the *Sussex* question, I will add one more telegram which I sent to the Foreign Office after Secretary of State Lansing had publicly mentioned an Anglo-American agreement—a remark which in Berlin was taken to mean that America had formed an alliance with England. It is well known that during the war such a statement has frequently been made.

TELEGRAM IN CIPHER

"Washington, 21st May, 1916.

"I am working confidentially in co-operation with House for the settlement of such still unsettled questions as the *Lusitania* and the Igel cases, so as to clear the air completely. Feeling here now more favorable owing to the influence of the Irish executions. Wilson regards conflict with us as a thing of the past and desires to let things rest and soon to lay the foundations of peace. Lansing's speech as to Anglo-American agreement refers to the Bryan agreement. He desired to make clear that war with England because of the blockade is out of the question, and therefore there is no means of bringing pressure to bear. The speech coincides with the American view I have already reported that it would be easier to bring the war to an end than to force England to raise the blockade."

Hitherto I have not mentioned the different German vessels which visited United States ports during the war. Besides their history is well known. I will therefore only describe their psychological influence and my own experiences.

The auxiliary cruisers *Kronprinz Friedrich Wilhelm* and *Eitel Friedrich* were the first German ships to enter Hampton Roads, there to be interned.

Much more interest was aroused by the arrival on the 15th February, 1916, of the *Appam,* because it was then a long time since the German flag had been seen on the American side of the Atlantic. The facts are familiar to German readers from Count Dohna's *Möve* book. Lieutenant Berg's exploit met with general appreciation in the United States, especially as his conduct was completely in accord with the American conception of international law. Even to-day I can hear the tone of absolute conviction in which Secretary of State Lansing told me at the Metropolitan Club that the voyage of the *Appam* was a "marvellous achievement."

In the far-off future, students of international law will quote the *Appam* case as a classic. At the German Embassy in Washington volumes were filled with the opinions of eminent lawyers, for the incident was not treated politically by the American Government, but submitted to the courts. Meanwhile the *Appam* remained interned in Hampton Roads as a prize. The case was not settled until after the breaking-off of diplomatic relations, when it was no longer of any importance to us.

The interest roused by the *Appam* shrank into nothing before the excitement caused by the arrival of the submarine *Deutschland* on the 8th July, 1916. Apart from those that followed the agreement on the *Arabic* incident, the few days after the arrival of the *Deutschland* were the pleasantest I experienced in America during the war. Feeling on all sides was openly friendly, and Captain König was the most popular man in the United States. If we had sent ten such merchant submarines to America and for the rest had carried on the submarine campaign according to the principles laid down for cruiser warfare,

we should have attained far greater political results than
has been the case.

The arrival of the submarine *Deutschland* at Baltimore
and Captain König's first visit to the town resembled a
triumphal procession. I had intended to go there at once
to welcome the hero of the day and his bold seamen, but
thought it better to wait and see what would be the American attitude towards the protests of the English and
French Ambassadors, who had both claimed that the
Deutschland, as a submarine, should be regarded without
hesitation as a ship of war. On the 13th July a most
minute inspection of the *Deutschland* was made by an
American Government Commission consisting of three
naval officers, and she was recognized as a genuine merchant vessel. In consequence the *Deutschland* had a right
to lie at Baltimore as long as was necessary to take a
cargo on board for the return journey. It was now
possible for me to pay an official visit to Baltimore and
to view the *Deutschland.* The Mayor of the town accompanied me and went down with me, in spite of the terrific
heat of about 40° centigrade, into the lowest parts of the
submarine, which cost the stoutly-built gentleman considerable effort and a good deal of perspiration. In the
evening the Mayor gave a banquet which passed off as
in the good days before the war. The rooms were decorated with German and American flags, the band played
the "Wacht am Rhein," and many speeches were made
on the good relations between the two countries.

Again on her second visit, which took place in October
in New London (Connecticut), the *Deutschland* met with
a very friendly reception, even though the atmosphere
was appreciably cooler. Feeling in the New England
state has always been particularly unfavorable to us.
But there, too, I passed a very pleasant day with Captain
König.

In contrast to the moral gain of the visit of the *Deutschland* was the generally unfavorable impression created by the visit at the same time of the U53. Quite unexpectedly I received the news that a German submarine had arrived at Newport, the captain of which had reported himself to the American commandant and had handed him a letter addressed to me. The letter attracted a good deal of attention in the Press, but it actually contained nothing further than the introduction of the captain. The episode of the U53 was, from a political point of view, most undesirable and of no military value. When, moreover, a few days later the news arrived that the U53 had sunk several ships off the American coast—always, it is true, according to international law—the incident assumed a fairly serious aspect. Meanwhile I travelled direct to Shadow Lawn, the President's beautiful summer residence on the New Jersey coast, to hand to Mr. Wilson a letter from the Emperor. The President had appealed to the Heads of all the combatant States to urge them to permit relief to starving Poland, as had been done for Belgium. As was to be expected, the Entente rejected the proposal while the Central Powers agreed to it. The Emperor's approval was contained in the letter which I brought to Mr. Wilson.

The President took this opportunity to speak to me very seriously on the cruise of the U53, and urged me to see to it that this incident was not repeated. Otherwise he could not be responsible for public feeling in the United States, which might again become very bitter. The affair was very disagreeable to me personally, because I was building hopes on Mr. Wilson's mediation and because I feared that the cruise of the U53 would be interpreted as an attempt on our part to put difficulties in the way of the President's re-election. It might be assumed that his Republican opponents would say that

Germany could now do what she liked, as Mr. Wilson had never adopted energetic measures.

On the subject of this conversation with Mr. Wilson I sent the following telegram to the foreign office:

Telegram in Cipher
"Washington, 11th October, 1916.

"I had a conversation with Mr. Wilson on the occasion of handing over the Emperor's autograph letter with regard to Polish relief. The President is anxious to carry the matter further and asked me how this could best be done. I replied that the difficulties lay exclusively on the English side.

"The cruiser warfare undertaken by our submarines off the American coast is naturally regarded by Mr. Wilson with anxiety, because all his hopes of re-election are based exclusively on the fact that according to the opinion held over here he has kept the United States out of the war and in spite of that has put an end to our so-called illegal attacks on American lives. His whole position falls to pieces if American lives are lost now, or if indignation is aroused by a submarine campaign off the American coast. So far this has not occurred. The exploit of U53 is even hailed as a sporting achievement. This view will, however, be changed if the incident is repeated. For this reason Wilson spoke plainly about a continuance of the submarine campaign off the American coast. He regarded as particularly serious the fact that two neutral ships were sunk, as well as a Canadian passenger vessel making for the United States. He said that such incidents could not be understood by the American public."

To this telegram I received from the Imperial Chancellor the following reply:

TELEGRAM IN CIPHER
"Berlin, 4th October, 1916.

"England entirely responsible for difficulties with regard to Polish relief. For Your Excellency's exclusive information it is not intended to continue submarine campaign off American coast. Final decision as to activity of U53 not possible until she returns. Our concessions to America are being strictly observed and will be until explicitly revoked.

"BETHMANN-HOLLWEG."

CHAPTER X

AMERICAN MEDIATION

At midsummer, 1916, the political lull desired by Colonel House actually set in. The Colonel betook himself to one of the beautiful lakes of New Hampshire, in the far north of the United States, where in the ordinary way I could only reach him by letter or telegram. How secret we kept our communications is shown by the fact that, according to agreement, I wrote and telegraphed to Colonel House under the pseudonym "Martin." This caution proved to be fully justified, as the inquiry by the Senate Committee has shown that the letters from the Embassy were frequently opened by agents of the Entente propaganda, whether with or without the connivance of the American secret police I will not definitely say. I have already had occasion to mention this question in connection with the robbing of Mr. Albert. There are in the secret police of all countries men of doubtful honor. It might be taken as certain that there were such men in the pay of the Entente agents.

Soon after the settlement of the *Sussex* incident—on 27th May—Mr. Wilson made public, for the first time, his plan for the League of Nations. This idea was to constitute the foundation-stone of his mediation and fulfil all the hopes of the American pacifists for a compulsory court of arbitration in international disputes and general disarmament. Before the war many shrewd men in the United States thought that the arbitration system initiated by the American Government would exclude the possibility of great wars. The outbreak of the World War showed that this was an illusion, and the question arose what precautions could be taken to prevent a recurrence of the world catastrophe. Mr. Wilson was one of the first in whom the idea matured that the scheme, hitherto regarded as utopian, of a league binding all civilized nations to a peaceful settlement of their disputes was capable of being made a practical proposition if backed, as a means of compulsion, by a commercial boycott, similar to that which the Entente, in contravention of international law, employed with such terrible results against Germany.

The most important sentences of the speech which the President addressed to the American peace league ran as follows:

"When the invitation for me to be here to-night came to me, I was glad to accept,—not because it offered me an opportunity to discuss the programme of the League, —that you will, I am sure, not expect of me,—but because the desire of the whole world now turns eagerly towards the hope of peace, and there is just reason why we should take our part in counsel upon this great theme. . . .

"With its causes and its objects we are not concerned. The obscure fountains from which its stupendous flood has burst forth we are not interested to search for or explore. . . .

"And the lesson which the shock of being taken by surprise in a matter so deeply vital to all the nations of the world has made poignantly clear is, that the peace of the world must henceforth depend upon a new and more wholesome diplomacy. Only when the great nations of the world have reached some sort of agreement as to what they hold to be fundamental to their common interest, and as to some feasible method of acting in concert when any nation or group of nations seek to disturb those fundamental things, can we feel that civilization is at least in a way of justifying its existence and claiming to be finally established. It is clear that nations must in future be governed by the same high code of honor that we demand of individuals. . . .

"Repeated utterances of the leading statesmen of most of the great nations now engaged in the war have made it plain that their thought has come to this, that the principle of the public right must henceforth take precedence over the individual interests of particular nations, and that the nations of the world must in some way band themselves together to see that right prevails as against any sort of selfish aggression; that henceforth alliance must not be set up against alliance, understanding against understanding, but that there must be a common agreement for a common object, and that at the heart of that common object must lie the inviolable rights of peoples and mankind. . . .

"This is undoubtedly the thought of America. This is what we ourselves will say when there comes a proper occasion to say it. . . .

"We believe these fundamental things: First, that every people has a right to choose the sovereignty under which they shall live. Like other nations, we have ourselves no doubt once and again offended that principle when for a little while controlled by selfish passion, as our franker historians have been honorable enough to admit; but it has become more and more our rule of life and action. Second, that the small States of the world have a right to enjoy the same respect for their sovereignty and for their territorial integrity that great and powerful nations expect and insist upon. And, third, that the world has a right to be free from every disturbance of its peace that has its origin in aggression and disregard of the rights of peoples and nations.

"So sincerely do we believe in these things that I am sure that I speak the mind and wish of the people of America when I say that the United States is willing to become a partner in any feasible association of nations formed in order to realize these objects and make them secure against violation. . . .

"But I did not come here, let me repeat, to discuss a programme. I came only to avow a creed and give expression to the confidence I feel that the world is even now upon the eve of a great consummation, when some common force will be brought into existence which shall safeguard right as the first and most fundamental interests of all peoples and all governments, where coercion shall be summoned, not to the service of political ambition or selfish hostility, but to the service of a common order, a common justice, and a common peace. God grant that the dawn of that day of frank dealing and of settled peace, concord, and co-operation may be near at hand!"

This speech displayed all the characteristics of Mr. Wilson's oratory: brilliant command of the English language, dazzling wealth of vocabulary and nebulous sentence construction which made the purpose clear only to the initiated. Nevertheless, the vital points of the speech could not be misunderstood. It prepared the world for American mediation by strong emphasis of the League of Nations idea.

The political lull of midsummer brought an important improvement in public feeling towards us. This change for the better was reflected with special clearness in the reception given to the merchant submarine *Deutschland*, as I have already described.

At the time of this speech of Mr. Wilson's, I sent the following report:

REPORT IN CIPHER

"Washington, 28th May, 1916.

"The placation of American public opinion is progressing. Hardly any mention is now made in the Press of German-American relations. Only two persons are still wavering. The American Government are delaying the publication of my letter on the subject of the *Lusitania* settlement, because they think that it will not satisfy public opinion here. It may be assumed that its publication will take place at the beginning of June, during the Republican National Convention, so that it may pass as far as possible unnoticed in the general excitement about domestic politics. The American Government's delay in this matter shows clearly how great the opposition has been. While we thought to have made important concessions, the American Government here consider that they have not attained the objective prescribed for them by public opinion.

"Further, the Igel incident is not yet settled. On this question there is a difference of opinion between the State and Law Departments. The former confirming our standpoint that the seizure of the papers was illegitimate and that they must be returned. The Law Department, on the other hand, holds that Herr von Igel has been guilty of a legal offence and so has forfeited his diplomatic privileges. Consequently I get no further, and the case is continually deferred. It is to be hoped that the State Department will soon bestir itself to make a decision which will, however, in any case, necessitate the recall of Herr Igel.

"Mr. Wilson's peace plans are becoming more and more tangible. The only question is whether he possesses

sufficient authority to force our enemies to agree to negotiations. Colonel House is convinced that Mr. Wilson
will succeed. The President is considering the plan of
calling together a conference at the Hague, in which the
neutrals will only participate so far as the 'Freedom of
the Seas' is concerned. If the project materializes,
Colonel House is sure to take part in the conference, even
though he may not be the official American representative.
His influence, however, would be sure to be great, for no
one else is so completely in touch with Mr. Wilson's
views. The latter is still of the opinion that the United
States should under no circumstances take part in the
actual settlement of the peace conditions. He and his
alter ego are meanwhile very much afraid that our
enemies might remain obdurate, since they are under the
impression, or are trying to spread the impression, that
the President, in opening the peace negotiations, is acting for Germany. Certainly England continually drags
this idea into the discussion. At one time it is said that
Prince Bülow is coming here to submit the German peace
conditions to Mr. Wilson; at another, that Germany is
on the brink of starvation and must therefore sue for
peace. We ought as far as possible to counteract this
propaganda of our enemies. It is to be hoped that it will
not do serious harm, because the peace vote in America
continues to grow and Mr. Wilson can count with certainty on re-election if he establishes a peace conference.
We shall therefore daily gain ground here so long as we
appear to be ready to encourage the American peace
movement, while our enemies adopt an unfavorable attitude. The American people is now pacifically minded.
It becomes clearer every day how difficult it is to arouse
enthusiasm for war preparedness, etc. No one who has
lived here for any length of time can help coming to the
conclusion that peaceful money-making is the Americans'

chief interest in life. Only when they think that their rights have been seriously infringed do they lash themselves into an hysterical war-fever. Why should war passion smoulder in the hearts of a people whose boundaries are so secure that no enemy has ever been seen inside them, nor in all human probability ever will be?''

After the settlement of the *Sussex* incident the Imperial Government naturally hoped that Mr. Wilson would take steps to justify our concessions with regard to the submarine question. Accordingly I received the following general instructions:

"Berlin, 7th June, 1916.

"Order A. 56.

"Confidential.

"More than a month has passed since our last Note to the United States without President Wilson making up his mind to approach the English Government on the question of the blockade. True I do not expect that England would allow herself to be influenced by the United States to abandon her infringement of international law; nor do I imagine that a rejection of the American demands by England would lead to a serious disturbance of the relations between these two countries. The existing arbitration treaty, which makes it possible in extreme cases to delay the settlement of the points of contention indefinitely, rules this out. But the complete passivity of Mr. Wilson, which could be understood so long as he wished to avoid giving the impression that he was acting under German coercion, but which cannot continue to be justified on these grounds, is bound to re-act very unfavorably on public opinion here and puts the Imperial Government in an extremely difficult position.

"From the information which has reached you, Your Excellency will already realize that our surrender to America on the submarine question has met with approval in wide and influential circles in Germany. If President Wilson persists in his passive attitude towards England, it is to be feared that the section of German public opinion whose attitude has so far been favorable to the Government will ally themselves with the opponents of the Government policy, and that the whole of public opinion in Germany will clamor for the resumption of the submarine campaign on the old lines. In that case, the Imperial Government would be all the less in a position to resist this demand for any length of time, as all the military authorities have always been unanimous in regarding and urging unrestricted submarine warfare as the only effective means to bring about the defeat of England. Moreover, as we have received secret information that the Entente have decided on a drastic tightening of the blockade, and at the same time have agreed in future to meet the protests of the neutrals, and particularly America, with the argument that only in this way can the end of the war, which is also in the interests of the neutral countries, be brought about. Your Excellency will therefore bring to the notice of President Wilson and Mr. House the serious dangers which his passivity towards England involves.

"With regard to Mr. Wilson's plans for mediation, they are meanwhile meeting with vigorous opposition in England. If they are rejected by England, the result cannot but be favorable to us, for we are naturally sceptical of mediation on the part of a statesman so partial to England, and at the same time so naïve as President Wilson. This necessarily follows on the consideration that the President would primarily be concerned to construct peace on the basis of the *status quo ante*, and par-

ticularly in respect of Belgium. Although there is to-day
little on which to form an estimate as to how far we shall
be in a position to bring about a solution in conformity
with our own interests to the Belgian question, which is
the direct result of the war, so much is certain, that if
the war continues in our favor, a peace on the basis of
the absolute *status quo ante* would not be acceptable to
us. So, as the President interprets his rôle as the chosen
champion of all that, in his opinion, is right and just, it
is to be feared that a refusal on our part to make peace
on this basis might induce him to go over openly to the
enemy's camp. It is not, however, out of the question
that public opinion in England may in time again turn to
Mr. Wilson and his desire for mediation. As soon, therefore, as Mr. Wilson's mediation plans threaten to assume
a more concrete form and there is evidence of an inclination on the part of England to fall in with them, it will
be Your Excellency's duty to prevent President Wilson
from approaching us with a positive proposal of mediation. The choice of means for attaining this object without endangering our relations with the United States I
think I may leave to Your Excellency's diplomatic skill,
as from here I am not in a position to get a clear insight
into the position of affairs in America.

"VON JAGOW."

I have already mentioned that Mr. Wilson had for some
time past subordinated the question of the "Freedom of
the Seas," i.e., in this concrete instance the English
blockade, to his desire for mediation. Regarded from his
point of view, this new ordering of his plans was based
on an entirely correct political train of thought. The
President gave first place to the attainable, with a view
to taking up later what was for the time being unattainable. In view of the fact that we could bring no pressure

to bear to change Mr. Wilson's point of view, it only remained for us to exploit his plans as far as possible in the interests of German policy.

As my instructions on the most important point—the question of mediation—did not appear to me sufficiently clear, I asked in the following report, dated from the summer quarters of the Embassy, for a more detailed explanation:

REPORT IN CIPHER

"In reply to Order A. 56,
"Rye, 13th July, 1916.

"The inactivity of Mr. Wilson, who has only one thought, re-election, is due in the first place to the fact that no pressure is being put upon him by American public opinion to take action with regard to England. It is obvious that conditions here are not favorable to such action. Those American circles which are suffering financial losses as a result of the English blockade, have no weight in face of the tremendous stream of gold which our enemies have poured lavishly over this country, not haggling over details, and conniving at 'graft.' For the rest, Mr. Wilson's train of thought with regard to action in respect of England practically coincides with that expressed by Your Excellency. He does not think at present that it is likely to meet with any success, as he has no means of bringing pressure to bear. No one would take him seriously if he threatened England with war.

"The position is quite different with the President's well-known anxiety to bring about peace in Europe. In this matter he now has the whole of American public opinion behind him. He also believes that, after the expected failure of their present offensives, our enemies will be ready to open peace negotiations. If this assumption proves unfounded, and our enemies reject an American invitation on these lines, the main question dealt with in Your Excellency's instructions to me will be settled. Meanwhile, he is sure to make an attempt to negotiate peace, if only for election purposes. I therefore venture to request Your Excellency to cable me further brief instructions as to how I am to interpret the words 'more concrete form of mediation plans,' and 'positive proposal of mediation.' I am assuming that the main part of my respectful reports will only reach Your Excellency at the same time as this. Therefore, Mr. Gerard, when Your Excellency spoke with him at the beginning of May, on the question of mediation, would not have received detailed instructions as to the President's intentions. In any case, he was mistaken as to the attitude Your Excellency should adopt with regard to an American peace-movement. On the strength of a telegram received at that time from Mr. Gerard, Mr. Wilson believed that the Imperial Government was ready to accept his mediation, and I accordingly contradicted this assumption as instructed. As far as I know, Mr. Wilson refuses definitely to take any part in the discussion of territorial questions, but confines his interest to 'disarmament' and 'Freedom of the Seas.' His idea is that there should be a conference at the Hague, in which the United States and other neutral Powers would only take part in so far as these two questions are concerned. 'Disarmament' may certainly be very undesirable for us, but, on the other hand, the 'Freedom of the Seas,' ought, without a doubt, to bring us on the side of the United States. If it once comes to peace negotiations between the combatants, I regard it as out of the question—even were they to fail—that the United States would enter the war against us. American public feeling in favor of peace is too strong for that. It required the hysterical excitement roused by the *Lusitania* question, and the incidents connected with it, to produce a state of mind among Americans which at times made war seem inevitable. In the absence of similar incidents, such a state of public feeling could not be aroused. The admiration with which the cruise of the submarine *Deutschland* was regarded showed plainly which way the wind blows now.

"I made the above mentioned request because I consider it out of the question to prevent Mr. Wilson from taking action with regard to peace. I am in doubt, however, whether by a 'positive proposal of mediation' your Excellency means such a proposal as that made by Mr. Roosevelt after the Russo-Japanese War. On that occasion it is well known that the negotiations were carried on under direct American influence. This, as I have already said, is not what Mr. Wilson wants. He only wants to play the part of peace-instigator; he would like to deserve the credit for having brought the combatants to negotiate one with the other. Such a success would, in view of the state of feeling here, probably assure his re-election.

"I am therefore convinced that within the next few weeks the President will institute proceedings with regard to peace, provided that the enemy offensive continues to prove abortive. Mr. Wilson will then tell England that he has been obliged on the grounds of domestic politics to make a sharp protest against the blockade, provided that peace negotiations have not been opened. For me the question now arises whether I am to try to stand in the way of these proceedings. Of course I could exert strong influence on Colonel House. Wilson, however, would immediately suspect that we were attempting to deal with his successor, and to give Mr. Hughes the honor of instigating peace proceedings.

"As far as I can judge from here, there seem to be three possibilities:

"1. That the Wilson peace movement should fail in consequence of the obduracy of our enemies. In that case, if we were to reopen the submarine campaign to bring England to her knees, the situation would at least be more favorable to us than before.

"2. That the peace movement should fail through us, and that we should resume the submarine war.

"3. That the peace movement should be accepted by both sides.

"In the first case, I consider war with the United States probable; in the second, certain. This is the reason for my request for more definite instructions as to whether I am to impede a peace movement, or only a positive proposal that would bind us in respect of territorial conditions."

To this report I received the following reply, containing quite clear instructions, emphatically to encourage Mr. Wilson in whatever course he might take:

TELEGRAM IN CIPHER

"Berlin, 18th August, 1916.

"In reply to report A. 350 of the 13th inst.

"Mediation by the President intended lead to the opening of peace negotiations between the combatants we are gladly ready to accept. Please encourage emphatically the President's efforts in this direction. Naturally it must not be imagined that in accepting such mediation we bind ourselves to any concrete peace conditions. A general peace conference with participation of neutrals only tolerable on the lines of previous successful peace-negotiations between combatants with

regard to general and international questions of Freedom
of the Seas and Disarmament.

"BETHMANN-HOLLWEG."

In close connection with the above exchange of letters
with Berlin, stood an interchange of telegrams dealing
with the eventual reopening of the unrestricted submarine campaign. I received the following telegrams:

TELEGRAM IN CIPHER

"(Strictly confidential.)
"Berlin, 12th June, 1916.

"The Army and Navy are again urging submarine
warfare as the only weapon against England, and particularly against her blockade, to which President Wilson
has never, nor can very well, take exception.

"It now remains to be decided:

"1. Whether after his nomination Wilson would still
be prepared to press matters as far as a rupture and
war, even if we spare human life in the new submarine
war?

"2. What attitude the Republican candidate would
adopt on this matter?

"Public opinion in England is opposed to mediation
by Wilson, which is also not wanted on principle here,
because too unpopular.

"VON JAGOW."

I dispatched as quickly as possible to Berlin the following telegram:

TELEGRAM IN CIPHER

"Washington, 19th June, 1916.

"Assuming that it is intended that the resumption of
the submarine campaign be accompanied by the official

or clandestine withdrawal of the concessions granted in our Note of the 4th May, such a withdrawal or modification of our concessions would in my opinion lead to a rupture and America's entry into the war. By condoning such a move Wilson would forfeit all hope of being re-elected and Hughes, who is already suspected of being the German candidate, could not afford to recommend a surrender. With regard to mediation and blockade I am in constant communication with House. The former to be expected in course of summer, for election reasons; probably Wilson will inform our enemies that he will have to resort to sharp measures if peace is not attained."

From the orders and telegrams here reproduced I gathered that the political situation was, as far as I was concerned, to be regarded as a kind of race between the unrestricted submarine campaign on the one hand and the American peace mediation on the other. There was apparently no third possibility.

On the 1st September I saw Colonel House again. In order that this visit should not attract notice I went to stay with other friends in New Hampshire for the customary American September holidays (Labor Day). From there I motored to New London, where Colonel House had been spending the summer. The conversation brought out that the President considered a postponement of mediation unavoidable, because the Entente were now filled with hopes of victory in consequence of Rumania's entry into the war. In all my conversations with Colonel House we both proceeded from the assumption that an attempt to bring about American mediation could only succeed provided that the Entente had given up hope of victory without the entry into the war of the United States. For this reason Colonel House repeated

his advice that there should be less public talk in Berlin
of an early peace than had hitherto been the case, since
in this way we were betraying weakness and making
America's task more difficult.

Colonel House also said that the President now intended to await the further development of the war, and,
if he should be re-elected, immediately to take steps towards mediation. Before the presidential election the
time was too short for any action, for the Entente
would pay no heed to the mediation of a problematical
candidate.

Looking back, I am still convinced even to-day that
Colonel House's estimate of the situation with regard to
the President was entirely correct from the American
point of view. Mr. Wilson could only afford to offer his
mediation provided that he was sure of success. For us
the position was in my opinion different. For Germany
American mediation would have been welcome at any
time. It would either succeed and bring about an acceptable peace, or the Entente would reject Wilson's proposal after we had accepted it. In the latter case we
should score a diplomatic success in Washington which
would make it very difficult for the American Government to enter the war. The third possibility, that the
German Government, after all that had passed, might
refuse Mr. Wilson's mediation, I did not even consider.

Immediately after my return from New Hampshire I
telegraphed the following to the Foreign Office:

TELEGRAM IN CIPHER No. 100

"Rye, 6th September, 1916.

"Wilson's mediation postponed until further notice
because for the moment out of question, owing to Rumania's entry into war and consequent renewed prospect

of victory for our enemies. Wilson thinks he cannot now mediate before the election, because England might pay little attention to him until after the election, and if he were not elected would have nothing further to do with him. If, however, Wilson wins at the polls, for which the prospect is at present favorable, and if the war meanwhile remains at a standstill, the President will at once take steps towards mediation. He thinks in that case to be strong enough to compel a peace conference.

"Wilson regards it as in the interest of America that neither of the combatants should gain a decisive victory."

This telegraphic report of my conversation with Colonel House reached Berlin when they were beginning to grow impatient of the delay in the peace movement. According to Karl Helfferich's account the question was discussed at the time between himself, the Imperial Chancellor and Herr von Jagow. Thereupon, according to General Ludendorff's "War Memories," "the Chancellor proposed to His Majesty that instructions should be given to Ambassador Count Bernstorff to induce the President at the earliest possible moment, and in any case before the presidential election, to make a peace offer to the Powers." Herr Helfferich then goes on to report that the Chancellor cabled to me to question me quite personally as to my opinion of Wilson as a peace mediator. The accounts of both these gentlemen are doubtless accurate, but they do not mention that the inquiry addressed to me did not, nor was intended to, create a new situation, but had as its sole object to obtain my opinion as to the prospects of a movement which had long been set on foot. In the inquiry, as Herr Helfferich also reports, I was informed that we would evacuate Belgium. This was of course a necessary preliminary to Mr. Wilson's mediation, which otherwise, in view of the feeling prevailing in America, would have been entirely out of the question.

The Chancellor's inquiry read as follows:

TELEGRAM IN CIPHER No. 74

"Berlin, 2nd September, 1916.

"*Confidential.*

"Our West Front stands firm. East Front naturally threatened somewhat by Rumania's declaration of war. Rolling up of front or collapse of Austria, however, not to be feared. Turkey and Bulgaria to be relied on. Greece uncertain. Hopes of peace before winter, as result of Russian or French war-weariness, diminished by this development Apparently, if no great catastrophe occurs in East, Wilson's mediation possible and successful if we guarantee required restoration of Belgium. Otherwise, unrestricted submarine warfare would have to be seriously considered. Request you give purely personal opinion without inquiry in any quarter.

"BETHMANN-HOLLWEG."

To this inquiry I replied as follows:

TELEGRAM IN CIPHER No. 101

"Rye, 8th September, 1916.
"In reply to Telegram No. 74.

"Your question answered in substance by my telegram No. 100. I take it then that your Excellency intends yourself to invite Wilson's mediation. In so far as the United States of America concerns itself with territorial questions—which hitherto I have always categorically opposed — restoration of Belgium should constitute America's principal interest, since public opinion is almost exclusively favorable to this.

"If Wilson is re-elected, I think there is good prospect of his mediation before the end of the year.

"From this point of view the attainment of peace through unrestricted submarine war seems hopeless, since the United States would inevitably be drawn into the war—no matter what may be the result of the election—and consequently the war would be prolonged."

I should like particularly to draw the reader's attention to this telegram, because it expresses definitely my opinion that the submarine campaign could not bring us peace.

Soon afterwards I was again instructed by the Chancellor to hasten Mr. Wilson's peace movement. His telegram is here reproduced:

TELEGRAM IN CIPHER

"Berlin, 26th September, 1916.

"For Your Excellency's personal information.

"The enemy's intention of breaking through our fronts has not, so far, succeeded, and will not succeed, any more than his Salonika and Dobrudja offensives. On the other hand, the operations of the Central Powers against Rumania are making encouraging progress. Whether we shall succeed this year in gaining a victory there that will bring the war to an end is still doubtful; therefore, for the present we must be prepared for a further prolonging of the war. Meanwhile, the Imperial navy is confident that by the unrestricted employment of large numbers of submarines they could in view of England's economic position, meet with a success which would in a few months make our principal enemy, England, more disposed to entertain thoughts of peace. It is therefore essential that G.H.Q. should include a submarine campaign among their other measures to relieve the situation on the Somme Front, by impeding the transport of munitions, and so making clear to the Entente the futility of their efforts in this area.

"The whole situation would change if President Wilson, following out the plans he has already indicated, were to make an offer of mediation to the Powers. This would, of course, not have to include any definite proposals of a territorial nature, as these questions should form part of the agenda of the peace negotiations. Such a move, however, would have to be made soon, as otherwise we could not continue to stand calmly aside and watch England, realizing as she does the many difficulties to be reckoned with, exert with impunity increasingly strong pressure on the neutrals, with a view to improving her military and economic position at our expense, and we should have to claim the renewed liberty of action for which we stipulated in the Note of the 4th of May of this year. Should Mr. Wilson insist on waiting until immediately before or after the election, he would lose the opportunity for such a step. Also the negotiations should not at first aim at the conclusion of an armistice, but should be carried on solely by the combatant parties, and within a short period directly bring about the preliminary peace. A further prolongation would be unfavorable to Germany's military situation, and would result in further preparations being made by the Powers for the continuance of the war into next year, so that there would be no further prospect of peace within a reasonable time.

"Your Excellency should discuss the position cautiously with Colonel House, and find out the intentions of Mr. Wilson. A peace movement on the part of the President which bore the outward appearance of spontaneity would be seriously considered by us, and this would also mean success for Mr. Wilson's election campaign.

"Gerard has applied for leave, as the result of a private letter from Colonel House, but he has received no reply from the State Department.

"BETHMANN-HOLLWEG."

The explanation of the final sentence of the above telegram is as follows. I have already mentioned that Mr. Gerard was not popular in Berlin, owing to his very highly-strung temperament, his impetuosity and his want of tact. His recall was eagerly desired. Consequently, I had received instructions to arrange, if possible, for the replacement of Mr. Gerard, and in any case that the Ambassador should be recalled for a time to Washington, so that his nerves might have a chance to rest. As always, in strictly confidential matters, I referred this to Colonel House, who told me that in view of the existing political situation there could be no question of a recall of Gerard. He would, however, arrange for the Ambassador to be summoned at once to Washington for fresh instructions. If once Mr. Gerard learned that the President now had the definite intention of mediating with a view of peace, Colonel House thought he would be received in a more friendly manner in Berlin.

I answered the Chancellor's last telegram as follows:

TELEGRAM IN CIPHER

"Washington, 5th October, 1916.

"No. 121.

"Telegram No. 89 discussed according to instructions.

"No change here in the situation reported in telegrams Nos. 100 and 101.

"In view of possibility of surprises in war and election, Wilson, for reasons already stated, refuses to attempt mediation until re-elected. Result of election, which is being fought exclusively on foreign politics, uncertain. President showing surprising firmness. If unrestricted submarine campaign unavoidable, advise emphatically, postpone at least until after election. Now, immediate rupture with United States would be certain; after election Wilson's mediation probable on the one hand; on the other hand at least slight possibility of finding *modus vivendi* by negotiation with United States."

The instructions from Berlin gave me occasion for repeated conversations with Colonel House. The Imperial Government were now ready to accept Mr. Wilson's League of Nations programme, which provided for general disarmament, freedom of the seas, and compulsory arbitration. My reports to Berlin on this question had the result that on 9th November the Chancellor in a speech publicly espoused this programme, and that I, at my own suggestion, received permission to communicate officially the Chancellor's speech to the American Peace League, which published my communication.

On the other hand, the Imperial Government desired that the territorial questions should be regulated by direct negotiations between the combatant Powers. Mr. Wilson, as Colonel House told me, was in agreement with this. Mr. Wilson had already expressed himself to this effect in the above mentioned speech of the 27th May, and in general adopted the point of view that the United States had no interest in the details of territorial adjustment; but that it was of equally fundamental importance for America as for Europe that in future wars should be avoided. The President was only willing to intervene in so far as he was certain of having American public opinion behind him. In my conversations with Colonel House we never spoke of the evacuation of any German territory. We always confined ourselves exclusively to a real peace by negotiation on the basis of the *status quo ante*. With such a peace Germany's position in the world would have remained unimpaired. The freedom of the seas, a principal point in the Wilson programme, could not but be welcome to us. The President and Colonel House have been the sponsors of this idea in America. Both were indefatigable in their efforts to materialize this idea in such a way that war on commerce should be abolished and that all commerce, even in war-time, should be declared free. As a necessary result of this development of the laws of naval warfare Mr. Wilson hoped to bring about general naval disarmament, since navies would lose their *raison d'être* if they could only be used against each other and no longer against commerce and for purposes of blockade. It is a regrettable fact that at the Hague Conference we accepted the English standpoint on the question of war on commerce, and not the American.

In October I was again instructed from Berlin to speed up Mr. Wilson's peace movement. With regard to this new urgency Herr von Jagow, on the 14th April, 1919, granted an interview to the Berlin representative of the *New York Sun,* the substance of which was as follows:

"In the autumn of 1916 the Emperor, Count Bernstorff and I opposed the resumption of unrestricted submarine warfare, which was urged with increasing vigor by our military and naval departments, as being the only means of bringing the war to an early conclusion. Week after week we watched for the hoped-for peace move of President Wilson, which, however, did not come. At last, in October, the Emperor, upon whom increasing pressure was being brought to bear to give his consent to the unrestricted submarine campaign, sent a memorandum to the American Government, reminding them of certain mediation promises which had been made at the time of the *Sussex* crisis.

"When this memorandum, addressed to Mr. Gerard, reached Berlin Mr. Gerard had already left for America. I, therefore, cabled the text to Washington and instructed Count Bernstorff to hand the memorandum to Mr. Gerard on his arrival in New York. Count Bernstorff, who had been made fully aware that the Emperor wished to avert the submarine campaign and a rupture with the United States, was also informed by me that the memorandum had been written by the Emperor in person. For reasons which there is no need for me to mention here, Count Bernstorff handed the memorandum, not to Mr. Gerard, but to Colonel House, who certainly communicated it to the President."

The telegram in which the Emperor's memorandum was communicated to me read as follows:

TELEGRAM IN CIPHER

"Berlin, 9th October, 1916.

"His Majesty the Emperor desires that the following memorandum should be handed to Ambassador Gerard on the latter's arrival.

"Your Excellency should do this in strict confidence and say that the memoir is not intended to convey a threat of submarine warfare. I should only like you to remind the Ambassador before his interview with the President of the expectations we based in the spring on Wilson and to call his attention to the increasing ruthlessness with which the enemy is carrying on the war. I take it for granted that Gerard will treat my memoir as strictly confidential and will not publish it.

"Should Your Excellency, however, regard the delivery of the memorandum as indiscreet, I request that it may be deferred.

"For Your Excellency's information (strictly confidential):

"1. The memorandum is written personally by His Majesty.

"2. Unrestricted submarine warfare is for the present deferred.

"Memorandum

"Your Excellency hinted to His Majesty in your last conversation at Charleville in April that President Wilson possibly would try towards the end of summer to offer his good services to the belligerents for the promotion of peace. The German Government has no information as to whether the President adheres to this idea, and as to the eventual date at which his step would take place. Meanwhile the constellation of war has taken such a form, that the German Government foresees the time at which it will be forced to regain the freedom of action that it has reserved to itself in the Note of May 4th last, and thus the President's steps may be jeopardized."

Mr. Gerard arrived in New York a few days after I had received the Emperor's memorandum. He was accompanied by the American journalist, Herbert Swope, a correspondent of *The World,* who had spent a considerable time in Berlin. This gentleman professed to be Mr. Gerard's confidant, and even from the ship sent wireless messages to his paper in which he reported that the unrestricted submarine campaign was imminent. The Ambassador also, after landing in New York, expressed himself, as I at once learned, to the same effect, and Mr. Swope continued his open Press-campaign in this direction.

Under these circumstances I considered it inopportune to give Mr. Gerard the Emperor's memorandum, as I assumed that he would read into it merely a confirmation of his view, and would discuss it in that light. If, however, the idea spread abroad that we were about to begin the unrestricted submarine campaign all prospect of success for peace mediation was lost. It was indeed clear that the Entente would not accept American mediation if they could hope for the submarine campaign and consequent declaration of war by the United States. It must continually be repeated that mediation could only succeed if the Entente had already abandoned all hope of American assistance. On these considerations I handed the memorandum to Colonel House, of whose discretion I had two years' experience. In this way it came into the hands of the equally unusually discreet President, without anyone else learning anything about it. The memorandum at once produced a great effect, as now the American authorities had no further doubt that the Imperial Government would accept the intended mediation. This could, however, not be speeded up because Mr. Wilson did not want to undertake a great political movement so shortly before the election.

At this time I sent the following report to the Chancellor:

REPORT IN CIPHER

"Washington, 17th October, 1916.

"For a week there has again been some excitement here about foreign policy. This is due to a variety of causes. At first the rumor was that Ambassador Gerard was bringing with him a peace proposal from the German Government. In spite of all denials this rumor was believed for a time, because it was started by one of the first bankers of New York. Unfortunately Mr. Gerard heard of this canard while he was still on the ship, and as he was travelling with Herbert Swope a denial, sent by wireless, appeared in *The World,* which was worse than the rumor itself. In this Swope reported that Mr. Gerard was coming over to announce the approaching beginning of ruthless submarine war. Just at this moment the U53 appeared at Newport, and two days later I had an audience of the President, which had been arranged a long time before, that I might hand to Mr. Wilson the reply of His Majesty the Emperor and King on the question of Polish relief.

"Colonel House, with whom, as is known, I am in constant communication, expected that on his landing Mr. Gerard would let fall some intentional or unintentional diplomatic *lapsus linguæ,* and therefore went in the early morning to the quarantine station in order to protect Gerard from the reporters. Mr. Gerard received a very hearty reception, which, however, had certainly been engineered for election purposes, because it is to the interest of the Democratic Administration to extol their ambassador and their foreign policy. Immediately after the reception Gerard breakfasted with House, and there everything was denied that had been actually said or implied.

"As I have known Mr. and Mrs. Gerard for many years I had a longish conversation with them on the day after their arrival. The quintessence of the ambassador's remarks was that he was completely neutral, but that Berlin expected more than that.

"Now everything has calmed down again here, and nothing is talked about except the election, which will be decided in three weeks' time. As I have several times had the honor to report, the result is most uncertain. While four months ago a Republican victory seemed certain, to-day Wilson's success is very possible. This is explained by the fact that Mr. Hughes has made no permanent impression as a speaker, whereas Roosevelt blew the war trumpet in his usual bombastic fashion. If Hughes should be defeated he can thank Roosevelt. The average American is, and remains a pacifist, '*Er segnet Friede und Friedenszeiten,*' and can only be drawn into war by passionate popular excitement.''

With the facts contained in the above report the following telegram is also concerned, which I despatched after the visit to the President mentioned above:

TELEGRAM IN CIPHER

''Washington, 11th October, 1916.

''Wilson gave particular force to his remarks by pointing out that the leaders of the opposition, Roosevelt, Lodge and Co., desired war with Germany, which he was quite unable to understand. His only desire was to remain neutral, and to help to bring the war to an end, as a decision by force of arms seemed to him out of the question. He thought that neither of the belligerent parties would be able to gain a decisive victory. Therefore it was better to make peace to-day than to-morrow. But all prospect of ending the war would vanish if the United States were also drawn in.

''As Wilson always spoke as though he was holding himself in readiness, in case his services as mediator were required, I told him that in my opinion there was no prospect of any advances being made by the belligerent Powers.

''It was obvious that Wilson would have preferred to be directly encouraged to make peace before the election because in that case he would have been sure of being re-elected. If, however, he were re-elected without this, he would have to make up his mind to take the initiative himself. Result of the poll still very doubtful. Wilson surprisingly strong, as Hughes has little success as a speaker and Roosevelt does more harm than good."

To this I received the following reply from the Chancellor:

CIPHER TELEGRAM

"Berlin, 14th October, 1916.

"Demand for unrestricted submarine campaign increasing here with prolongation of war and improbability of decisive military blow, without, however, shaking the Government's attitude.

"Direct request for Wilson's mediation still impossible, in view of favor hitherto shown to Entente, and after last speeches of Asquith and Lloyd George. Spontaneous appeal for peace, towards which I again ask you to encourage him, would be gladly accepted by us. You should point out Wilson's power, and consequently his duty, to put a stop to slaughter. If he cannot make up his mind to act alone he should get into communication with Pope, King of Spain and European neutrals. Such joint action, since it cannot be rejected by Entente, would insure him re-election and historical fame.

"BETHMANN-HOLLWEG."

The incident of the Emperor's memorandum closed with the following telegram sent by me:

CIPHER TELEGRAM

"Washington, 20th October, 1916.

"I thought it better to give memorandum to Gerard for House, as in this way greater discretion is assured. Latter was incautious in his utterances to Press here. House will speak with Gerard. Both gentlemen see Wilson shortly, and are accordingly in constant touch.

"It is still not to be expected that Wilson will make peace advances before the election. Nor that he will get into communication with Pope or King of Spain as hitherto every suggestion of joint action has met with immovable opposition, chiefly based on tradition. Meanwhile prospect of Wilson's re-election becomes obviously greater every day. Should this occur I believe that Wilson will very soon attempt mediation and with success, chiefly because the feeling against England has greatly increased, which England is seeking to hide. If peace is not concluded serious Anglo-American differences of opinion are to be expected. Until now every fresh dispute with Germany with regard to the submarine question has always been exploited by our enemies here to bridge the differences with England. Already the agitation in the German Press for unrestricted submarine warfare is persistently used for this purpose.''

After a hard struggle Mr. Wilson was re-elected President. The pacifist tendency in the United States had won, for the battle was fought under the watchword that Mr. Wilson had preserved peace for the United States. ''He kept us out of the war'' had been the battle-cry of the Democrats. The few electioneering speeches made by the President breathed the spirit of neutrality and love of peace. It is particularly to be noticed that at that time, Mr. Wilson, in an address, dealt in a thoroughly objective way with the question of guilt for the origin of the war, which was later to be the determining factor in his attitude towards us. The way was now cleared for the opening of the peace movement. Public feeling had also become more favorable to us, inasmuch as the American war industry no longer attached so much importance to the prolongation of the war after the victorious Democratic party had drawn up an extensive armament programme and so indicated to the industry the prospect of great State contracts.

On the subject of my own attitude with regard to the election, innumerable legends have been spread through Germany. The few German-Americans who shared the views of the so-called "German-American Chamber of Commerce" have reproached me with having brought about Mr. Wilson's election by influencing the German-Americans. Anti-German-American newspapers maintained, on the other hand, that I had used every lever to bring about the election of the Republican candidate, Mr. Hughes, so as to punish Mr. Wilson for his attitude towards the submarine campaign. My position was an extraordinarily difficult one, as I could neither take part in the election nor give up the relations which naturally and in the course of my duty bound me to the German-Americans and pacifists. In general I may say that the vast majority of German-Americans had absolute confidence in me throughout. A splendid testimony of this was given at the great German bazaar which was held in New York in aid of the Red Cross. This undertaking made the astounding net profit of 800,000 dollars. At the opening nearly 30,000 people were present, who gave me an indescribably enthusiastic ovation simply because they believed that I had prevented war between Germany and the United States.

I never for a moment denied that I personally should be glad to see Mr. Wilson re-elected, as I was convinced that he had the determination and the power to bring about peace. It was at that time impossible for me to foresee that our Government would change its attitude to this question. All American pacifists belonged to the Democratic camp, all militarists belonged to the Republican party.

A change in our favor was, therefore, not to be expected from the election of Mr. Hughes. Apart from the usual relations with the pacifists and German-Americans already mentioned, which were in no way altered during the election, I held myself aloof as my position demanded. If it had been possible to accuse me of taking sides, the agents of the Entente would not have missed the opportunity of bringing me to book, as this they regarded as their object in life. I continually received letters from *agents provocateurs*, asking for my opinion on the elections. Of course I never replied to these. Neither were the false statements of anti-German newspapers any more successful which announced that on the day of the election I had openly shown my support of Mr. Hughes.

New York at night after the polling is one of the sights of America. All streets, squares, theatres and restaurants are filled to overflowing. The election results are displayed everywhere by electric light and cinematograph. Particularly when the result is very uncertain, as in 1916, the crowd are tremendously excited. At 11 p.m. the election of Mr. Hughes seemed certain, as the Eastern States had voted for him almost to a man, and it was said that a Democratic candidate can only gain the victory if he wins over New York State. Next day the picture changed, after the results had come gradually from the West, where the Democratic party was everywhere triumphant. The majority, however, was so slight that it was several days before Mr. Wilson's election was secure.

The malcontents among the German-Americans already mentioned maintain that if Mr. Hughes had been elected, Congress would have used the four months between the election and the 4th March, during which Mr. Wilson was powerless and Mr. Hughes had not yet got the reins into his hands, to rush through the warning of American citizens against travelling on British passenger-ships. In that case, Mr. Hughes, on assuming office, would have found himself faced with a situation which would have prevented him from entering the war, in view of the national inclination towards peace. Therefore, the German-Americans ought to have supported Hughes. This had been clear to the Germans in the East. They maintained that Wilson's re-election was due to the German votes in the Western States which had obeyed a more or less clear order from the German Embassy.

This line of argument is yet another proof that the Germans in question had no idea of the situation in America. They kept exclusively to themselves in the *Deutscher Verein,* and scarcely ever saw a real, true-bred American. To begin with, it is difficult to see why the Germans in the West should obey the alleged order from me if the Germans in the East did not do so. But the important thing is that Wilson had firmly made up his mind, in case Mr. Hughes was elected, to appoint him Secretary of State immediately and, after Hughes had informed himself on the political position in this office, to hand over the presidency and himself retire. Mr. Wilson considered it impossible to leave the country without firm leadership at such a dangerous moment.

Immediately after the official announcement of his re-election, Mr. Wilson wrote a Peace-Note, but unfortunately kept it in his desk, because, unhappily, just at that time a new anti-German wave swept over the country on account of the Belgian deportations. Mr. Wilson was at that time in the habit of typing the drafts of his Notes and speeches himself, and only submitting them to his advisers on points of law or other technicalities. Whether he still works in this way I do not know. If the unhappy measure of the Belgian deportations had not been adopted, and particularly just as we had informed the President that we did not want to annex Belgium, the history of the world would probably have taken a different course. The American mediation would have anticipated our peace offer and, therefore, would probably have succeeded, because we could not then have reopened the unrestricted submarine campaign without letting the mediation run its course.

In November several submarine incidents occurred in which there was a doubt as to whether the rules of cruiser warfare had been followed. The ships *Marina* and *Arabia* came under particular consideration. I will not go into these cases as they had no political importance. President Wilson caused the investigations to be carried on in a dilatory fashion because he did not want to see his peace move disturbed by controversies.

Of greater importance was the wish that was again cropping up in Berlin to open the so-called "intensified submarine campaign." I learned this in the following from Secretary of State von Jagow:

CIPHER TELEGRAM No. 112.

"Berlin, 8th November, 1916.

"Navy wishes at least torpedo armed enemy cargo-vessels without warning. Does Your Excellency consider this dangerous, apart from probable mistakes, particularly in view of fact that now many Americans are lured to travel on such steamers?

"VON JAGOW."

As the "intensified submarine campaign" would have destroyed all prospect of American intervention, I advised strongly against it in the two following telegrams:

(1) CIPHER TELEGRAM No. 152

"Washington, 17th November, 1916.

"It is urgently desirable not to reopen disputes about armed merchantmen, especially in view of Wilson's peace plan."

(2) Cipher Telegram

"Washington, 20th November, 1916.

"In reply to telegram No. 112 which was delayed.

"Pursuant to Telegram No. 152.

"Urge no change in submarine war, until decided whether Wilson will open mediation. I consider this imminent."

At the same time I received the first news of the intended peace offer of the German Government. To begin with, the following telegram arrived from Secretary of State von Jagow:

Cipher Telegram

"Berlin, 16th November, 1916.

"Desirable to know whether President willing to take steps towards mediation, and if so, which and when? Question important for decision of possible steps in same direction elsewhere.

"How does Mexican question stand?

"Von Jagow."

Then followed a further telegram which read as follows:

Cipher Telegram

"Berlin, 22nd November, 1916.

"Strictly confidential.

"For Your Excellency's strictly personal information. So far as favorable military position permits we intend, in conjunction with our Allies, immediately to announce our readiness to enter into peace negotiations.

"Von Jagow."

To the first of these two telegrams I sent the following reply:

CIPHER TELEGRAM
"Washington, 21st November, 1916.

"Wilson spontaneously commissioned House to tell me in strict confidence that he is anxious to take steps towards mediation as soon as possible, probably between now and the New Year. He makes it a condition, however, that until then, mediation should be spoken and written of as little as possible, and further, that we should conduct the submarine war strictly according to our promises and not allow any fresh controversies to arise.

"Wilson's reasons for the above conditions are as follows: He believes that he can only resort to mediation provided that public opinion over here remains as favorable to us as it has been during the last few months. On this account he deplores the so-called Belgian deportations. Any new submarine controversy would again affect public feeling adversely for us, whereas if this question can be eliminated the tension with regard to England will increase. The British reply on the subject of the black lists and the English Press utterances on Wilson's election have created a bad impression in Government circles over here. The submarine question, however, will always divert this resentment against us again.

"Wilson still hesitates to intervene because the State Department expects a refusal on the part of our enemies, while House urges it strongly and is very hopeful. I have, according to instructions, encouraged him as much as possible, by telling him, that in my opinion, our enemies would be quite unable to refuse to enter into negotiations, and that is all that Wilson has in view. House seemed very much impressed when I reminded him how, throughout the whole war, the English Government had tried by lying and diplomatic trickery to bring public opinion on to their side. This house of cards, built on lies and deception, would immediately collapse if our enemies were now to refuse negotiations and thus would have to admit openly their desire for conquest. I am rather afraid that England may make a pretense of entering into negotiations and then try to put us in the wrong.

"I chose this line of argument because Wilson fears above all things the humiliation of a refusal. If it does come to negotiations, even unsuccessful, Wilson will have scored a great success. Whether the negotiations will lead to a definite result I cannot judge from here. In any case, if it should come to negotiations, strong pressure will be exerted by the Government over here in the direction of peace.

"The Mexican question is still in a state of stagnation as a result of diplomatic negotiations. This affair interests practically no one any more and proved to have no influence on the election.

"If Your Excellency still desires Wilson to intervene it is necessary, in view of the above, to get rid as soon as possible of the *Marina* and *Arabia* incidents without further controversy and not to allow any fresh controversies to arise. I think that, with the help of House, I can bury these two incidents without attracting much attention, as this is the wish of Wilson himself. As House said, the President takes a tragic view of these incidents, because, after the *Sussex* Note, he could not possibly write another Note, and therefore, there is nothing left but to break off diplomatic negotiations, should it be impossible to dispose of the matter privately and confidentially with me.

"Next week Gerard will be in Washington for a day or two: he will lunch with me and dine with Lansing. House keeps him in strict control. In case Gerard's return to Berlin is not desired, please send me instructions. Otherwise he should be there again at the end of the year."

To this telegram, which announced very definitely the American mediation, I received from the Foreign Office the following reply:

CIPHER TELEGRAM No. 121

"Berlin, 26th November, 1916.

"Replacement, or at least further retention, of Gerard in America desired in Berlin, provided that it is possible without wounding his vanity and sensitiveness to our disadvantage, that it is certain that this hint from our side will not become known in America and that a suitable successor is available.

"We should prefer Wilson's peace move to the step on our part mentioned in our telegram No. 116 of the 22nd November. For this reason it is eminently desirable that Wilson should make up his mind for immediate action if possible at the opening of congress or immediately afterwards. If it is put off until the New Year or later, the lull in military operations during the winter campaign would moderate the desire of public opinion for peace, and on the other hand would make preparations for the spring offensive necessary which would probably strengthen the military opposition of a peace movement. Please place this point of view cautiously and without *empressement* before House as your personal opinion and keep me closely instructed by telegram as to the position.

"ZIMMERMANN."

To this telegram I sent the two following replies:

CIPHER TELEGRAM No. 164

REPLY TO TELEGRAM No. 121

"Washington, 1st December, 1916.

"To-morrow I shall see House in New York and will try to arrange that Gerard, who is to sail on 5th December, is kept back.

"Lansing expressed himself very strongly to me on the subject of the American protest with regard to the Belgian deportations. These have endangered the whole Belgian relief movement; in addition, feeling here has been poisoned against us, and that just at a moment when it looked as though peace negotiations might be begun. Lansing expressed the view that, if the Imperial Government could find a way of yielding to the protests of the neutrals, this would make a strong impression in our favor and that it would probably be possible immediately afterwards to propose the opening of peace negotiations. Hitherto, unfortunately, something has always intervened.

"The Federal Reserve Board's warning to the banks against unsecured promissory notes of foreign States is the first sign that the Government here wishes to put pressure on our enemies.

CIPHER TELEGRAM

"Washington, 4th December, 1916.

"Pursuant to Telegram No. 164 of the 1st inst.

"House told me in strict confidence question of Mr. Gerard's return has been thoroughly discussed by him with Mr. Wilson and Mr. Lansing. Mr. Gerard's unpopularity in Berlin and his unfriendly manner were well known here. However, no satisfactory successor was available, and Mr Gerard is at least straightforward and does exactly what he is told. He has received very detailed instructions here, and is even quite enthusiastic over the idea of assisting in bringing about peace. In addition, Mr. Gerard was so pleased at the appointment of the Secretary of State that he is sure to adopt a more friendly attitude in future.

"As a matter of fact, Mr. Gerard has everywhere described the changes in the personnel at the Foreign Office as extraordinarily favorable for German-American relations, and laid particular stress on his personal friendship with the Secretary of State.

"Everything is prepared for a peace move, but with Mr. Wilson still hesitating, it is still doubtful when he will take action. All the authorities here have now been won over to favor such a step. This may then come at any time, especially if it is possible for us to adopt a conciliatory attitude on the Belgian question. Mr. Wilson believes that he is so hated in England that he won't be listened to. This train of thought largely explains his eagerness in the Belgian question. In any case, so much is certain, that House is continually urging Mr. Wilson to take action; moreover, peace propaganda here is steadily increasing, notwithstanding that it is for the moment very seriously hampered by the Belgian question. If Mr. Wilson—as is to be expected—finds a strong feeling for peace in Congress, he should at last make up his mind."

After a stay of about two months in America, Mr. Gerard, furnished with fresh instructions, left for Berlin on the 5th December. When later the Ambassador, at the much discussed Adlon dinner, declared that the relations between the United States and Germany had never been so good as at that moment since the beginning of the war, this speech was the keynote of his instructions. If on the other hand Herr Helfferich said that the exuberance of the Ambassador astonished him, this is explained by the fact that Berlin never believed in Mr. Wilson's intention to bring about peace. Why such incredulity should persist notwithstanding that Colonel House had twice travelled to Berlin for this very purpose, and that the President's peace policy had been the burden of all my reports, I shall never be able to understand, while, on the other hand, I can quite understand that Mr. Wilson's passivity with regard to the English breaches of international law had engendered strong distrust of him in Germany.

For the rest, Mr. Gerard seemed to be imperfectly informed about the situation in Berlin. He was certainly right in his prediction of the unrestricted submarine campaign, but in this case the wish was father to the thought. It accorded with Mr. Gerard's anti-German feeling, to which he gave expression later in his gossipy literature and film production, that he should welcome the submarine campaign, and with it the rupture with the United States, as well as our defeat. But after all, the Ambassador proved at the Adlon dinner that he could "sing another tune."

When Mr. Gerard lunched with me in Washington, I had just learned by cable from Berlin that Herr von Jagow had resigned and had been replaced by Herr Zimmermann. On hearing this news, the Ambassador said that now there would be no rupture between Germany and the United States, for Herr Zimmermann was his personal friend and was opposed to war, while Herr von Jagow, as an aristocrat, did not love the Americans, and looked down on bourgeois Gerard. A grosser misreading of the actual situation in Berlin can scarcely be conceived, as the unrestricted submarine campaign was only made possible by the resignation of Herr von Jagow, who was the chief opponent in Berlin of the submarine campaign, and the pillar on which the idea of American intervention rested. As long as Herr von Jagow remained Secretary of State, a breach with the United States was regarded as impossible. One of his last official acts was to write a private letter to me on the 20th November, 1916, concluding with the following sentence:

"As you have seen from your instructions, we are thoroughly in sympathy with the peace tendencies of President Wilson. His activity in this direction is to be strongly encouraged. Naturally his mediation tendencies must not extend to concrete proposals (because these would be unfavorable to us.)"

We now come to the moment in this account when the peace offer of the Imperial Government got involved with Mr. Wilson's plans for mediation. It is not my intention to go closely into the events that occurred in Berlin or the considerations that took effect there, as I only know them through their reaction on the instructions sent to me. I will only mention briefly, that, according to the statement of Herr von Bethmann-Hollweg before the Commission of the National Assembly, the peace offer of the Imperial Government was made with a view to influencing the pacifist minorities in the Entente countries, and working, through the people, on the Governments. Beyond this there was no intention of cutting out Mr. Wilson's peace move, but the Imperial Government wanted to have "two irons in the fire." Finally, all the utterances of the Imperial Government, which do not seem to tally with these two principles of their policy, are to be regarded as based on purely tactical motives. Accordingly, the decisive turn in our policy did not occur until the 9th January, 1917, when the decision to resort to the unrestricted submarine war was taken. Until then the policy followed was that of "two irons in the fire."

This is the way in which I read the situation in Washington at the time. If I had been convinced that the resignation of Herr von Jagow and the German peace offer meant a definite departure from the policy which we had hitherto followed with regard to Mr. Wilson's peace step, I should have immediately sent in my resignation, as I was completely identified with this policy. However, I shall return to this side of the question later.

The following telegram from the Foreign Office gave me the official information of our peace offer:

CIPHER TELEGRAM No. 128

"Berlin, 9th December, 1916.

"Confidential, for your personal information.

"We have decided to make use of the favorable position created by the fall of Bukarest in order, according to telegram number 116 of the 21st November, to make a peace offer in conjunction with our Allies, probably on Thursday, the 12th December. We do not at the present moment run any risk of damaging our prestige or showing signs of weakness. Should the enemy reject the offer the odium of continuing the war will fall upon them. For reasons stated in telegram number 121 we could not wait any longer for President Wilson to make up his mind to take action.

"The American Embassy here will at the given moment receive a Note in which the American Government will be requested to communicate our peace offer to those of our enemies with whom they represent our interests. Our other enemies will be informed through the medium of Switzerland and Spain respectively. American reprsentative in conversation with Chancellor on 5th

December expressed himself, in confidence, on the President's mission, among other things, as follows: 'What the President now most earnestly desires is practical co-operation on the part of German authorities in bringing about a favorable opportunity for soon and affirmative action by the President looking to an early restoration of peace.' Chancellor replied to American representative, he was 'extremely gratified to see from the President's message that in the given moment he could count upon the sincere and practical co-operation of the President in the restoration of peace, as much as the President could count upon the practical co-operation of German authorities.' We think we may assume that our action meets the wishes of the President.

"Please interpret it in any case in this sense to the President and House.

"VON STUMM."

To this telegram I replied as follows:

CIPHER TELEGRAM

"Washington, 13th December, 1916.

"In reply to Telegram No. 128.

"Have carried out instructions with House, who is at present staying at the White House. I have not yet received answer from Wilson, but it is generally believed here that he will strongly support peace proposals.

"Mr. Gerard, in a speech at a farewell dinner given to him in New York, declared that Germany had won, and could not be robbed of her victory. Although not published, this speech attracted attention, especially as Mr. Gerard emphasized the fact that he had reported to Mr. Wilson in this sense."

Before the Commission of the National Assembly I

was asked whether I had made an attempt to stand in the way of our peace offer, lest it should interfere with Mr. Wilson's action. I took no such steps, because I thought that I was faced with a firm resolve of the Imperial Government, and because I did not think that our peace offer would substantially compromise Mr. Wilson's action.

It was also stated before the commission that I might have helped my policy to prevail in Berlin if I had insisted on it more strongly. With regard to this, I must say at once, that I did not consider stronger influence on my side really called for, as my instructions had always categorically laid down that I was to encourage Mr. Wilson to take peace action. I had also been informed that the Imperial Government would prefer such action to a peace offer from our side, and that the correct moment for the latter would have to depend on the military situation. I was, therefore, until the arrival of the Berlin telegram, number 128, not clear as to which of the actions would come first, especially as, according to my instructions, I was to keep our peace offer secret and could not discuss it with Colonel House.

Under ordinary circumstances, I should have travelled to Berlin several times during the war to confer with the authorities. Unfortunately, however, that was impossible, as the English would never have allowed me to travel to and fro. If I had had the ways and means to enlighten German public opinion on the situation in America, it would certainly have done a lot of good. According to the evidence given before the Commission of the National Assembly, the chief reason for our rejection of mediation was distrust of Mr. Wilson. Nevertheless, I still believe that ignorance and undervaluation of America was a stronger influence. At least I cannot conceive that all the authorities concerned would have voted for unrestricted submarine war if they had been firmly convinced that the United States would come into the war with all her military and economic power. However that may be, I tried at least to do what I could and I made an attempt to send Herr Albert, who was completely in accord with me, to Berlin on the submarine *Deutschland*. The captain of the *Deutschland,* however, had scruples against carrying passengers, and Herr Albert's voyage had therefore to be given up. After my experience of the journeys of Herren Meyer Gerhardt and Dernburg, I certainly do not think that Herr Albert would have done very much in Berlin. Even I could hardly have hindered the opening of the unrestricted submarine campaign where Herr von Jagow, Herr von Kühlmann and others had failed, and after all, that was the main point.

Mr. Wilson's intention of bringing about peace had been reported to me so definitely and so often that I took it for granted that the President would carry through his plan in spite of our peace offer. As I had received no instructions to the contrary, I held to my previous interpretation of the situation, and assumed that, although it was true that we had ourselves made a peace offer because Wilson's action was so long in coming, we should nevertheless still be glad to avail ourselves of the President's help. In my opinion, this was the only interpretation that could be put on the Foreign Office telegram number 128, given above. The President himself, as Colonel House told me, was very disappointed when he received the news of our peace offer. Colonel House told me that he would naturally have liked to take the first step himself. Apart from this, he had always warned us against mentioning peace, because this would be interpreted by the Entente as weakness. He therefore regarded our peace offer as an obstacle to action on his part, as it was bound to diminish the enemy's readiness to enter into negotiations. On the other hand, the step of the Imperial Government exerted a favorable influence on American public opinion, and this influence would have been even more favorable if the offer had been made less in the tone of a victor. The attitude of American public opinion, and the fear lest peace negotiations might be opened without his co-operation, must have been the chief reasons that influenced Mr. Wilson publicly to support our peace offer. In connection with this I sent the following information to Berlin:

Cipher Telegram

"Washington, 16th December, 1916.

"Lansing tells me the following statement, which I could not send by wireless to-day, comes from Wilson personally.

"President Wilson has decided that the Notes of the Central Powers, proposing a discussion of peace to the Entente Allies, will be sent forward by the American Government acting as intermediary without any accompanying offer of his own. He has not determined whether any action on behalf of peace will be taken later by the United States on its own account, but is holding himself in readiness to serve in any possible way towards bringing the warring nations together."

"From Lansing's remarks I gather that he is convinced that our enemies will agree to a conference and that then the American Government will have an opportunity to speak in favor of peace. As the Press here is also in general of the opinion that our enemies cannot refuse a conference without turning public opinion against themselves, I have grounds for assuming that the American

Embassy in London, in spite of the official statement mentioned above, will assert this view.

As I expected, the President did not allow himself to be turned from his purpose, and on the 18th December dispatched the Note which had long been ready, with certain alterations, to the belligerent Powers. He certainly would not have taken this step if he had not reckoned on certain success. Mr. Wilson's Note could not help but bear out our peace plans, and was therefore regarded throughout America as "pro-German." For this very reason it caused a sensation. On the New York Exchange it was followed by a slump in war industry values. A few anti-German newspapers, which began to suspect that I was the only diplomatist in Washington who knew anything of the President's intentions, declared that I had made millions by speculating on this probability. I had already been accused of every other imaginable crime by the Jingo and Entente Press. Mr. Wilson's son-in-law, Secretary of the Treasury McAdoo, was also suspected of having abused his political information to speculate on the Exchange. Soon afterwards, when I was dining with the President, he asked me in jest what I had to say to the accusation of the American Press that I had made millions in this way. I replied that I had gradually got used to such attacks, and they only amused me. Mr. Wilson replied: "That is right. My son-in-law takes the matter much too seriously. I tell him 'If you get so angry, people will think the story is true.'"

The American Press was thrown into the greatest excitement by the President's Note and stormed the State Department. Mr. Lansing was surrounded by questioners and remarked that the United States had the greatest interest in bringing the war to an end, because otherwise she would be drawn in herself. As of late, as has already been mentioned, several doubtful submarine incidents had occurred, the Press took this remark to mean that the United States would enter the war against us if the intervention move came to nothing. Mr. Wilson immediately, realized that such an interpretation of Mr. Lansing's words would seriously jeopardize his peace move. If the Entente could hope for American participation in the war, there would be no prospect of their consenting to a "peace without victory." In that case the direction of their policy was defined beforehand. They only required to reject the offer of mediation to reach the goal of their long-cherished hopes. The President therefore at once requested Mr. Lansing to contradict the statements of the Press. This was done, with the observation that there was no probability of the United States entering the war. The harm could not, however, be completely wiped out, as denials are always regarded with doubt.

The vital parts of Mr. Wilson's Note read as follows:

"The President suggests that an early occasion be sought to call out from all the nations now at war such an avowal of their respective views as to the terms upon which the war might be concluded and the arrangements which would be deemed satisfactory as a guaranty against its renewal or the kindling of any similar conflict in the future, as would make it possible frankly to compare them. He is indifferent as to the means taken to accomplish this. He would be happy himself to serve, or even to take the initiative in its accomplishment, in any way that might prove acceptable, but he has no desire to determine the method or the instrumentality. One way will be as acceptable to him as another if only the great object he has in mind be attained.

"In the measures taken to secure the future peace of the world the people and the Government of the United

States are as vitally and as directly interested as the Governments now at war.

"The President does not feel that it is right and his duty to point out their intimate interest in its conclusion, lest it should presently be too late to accomplish the greater things which lie beyond its conclusion, lest the situation of neutral nations, now exceedingly hard to endure, be rendered altogether intolerable, and lest, more than all, an inquiry be done civilization itself which can never be atoned for, or repaired.

"Yet the concrete objects for which it is being waged have never been definitely stated.

"The leaders of the several belligerents have, as has been said, stated those objects in general terms. But, stated in general terms, they seem the same on both sides. Never yet have the authoritative spokesmen of either side avowed the precise objects which would, if attained, satisfy them and their people that the war had been fought out. The world has been left to conjecture what definite results, what actual exchange of guaranties, what political or territorial changes or readjustments, what stage of military success even, would bring the war to an end.

"It may be that peace is nearer than we know; that the terms which the belligerents on the one side and on the other would deem it necessary to insist upon are not so irreconcilable as some have feared; that an interchange of views would clear the way at least for conference and make the permanent concord of the nations a hope of the immediate future, a concert of nations immediately practicable.

"The President is not proposing peace; he is not even offering mediation. He is merely proposing that soundings be taken in order that we may learn, the neutral with the belligerent, how near the haven of peace may be for which all mankind longs with an intense and increasing longing. He believes that the spirit in which he speaks and the objects which he seeks will be understood by all concerned, and he confidently hopes for a response which will bring a new light into the affairs of the world.''

As this Note in its positive proposals was considered rather tentative and obscure—with the intention, of course, of making a direct negative answer impossible—I asked Mr. Lansing what procedure the President would like. With regard to this conversation I reported to Berlin in the following telegram:

CIPHER TELEGRAM No. 188

''Washington, 21st December, 1916.

''Lansing informed me a few days ago of Wilson's Peace Note, and said that the American Government were becoming more and more involved in an intolerable position as a result of repeated infringements of their rights. Therefore they hoped for frank statements from the belligerent Powers on their peace conditions. I gave it as my personal opinion that this would be difficult except through a conference because of the press, etc. Lansing replied that the statements could be confidential, and might gradually lead to a conference. This seems to bear out the view, widely held here, that Wilson would like to act as a 'clearing house' for the further steps towards peace. He has American public opinion behind him with the exception of our inveterate enemies, who regard Wilson's Note as pro-German.''

My conversation with Mr. Lansing, and the wording of the American Note, made it perfectly clear that the President, in the first place, only wished to be informed of the peace conditions of both sides. This was just what the

Berlin Government did not want, because it would have aroused a bitter struggle between the different shades of public opinion as to the "war aims." My telegram therefore received the following negative reply:

CIPHER TELEGRAM No. 142

"Berlin, 26th December, 1916.

"In reply to Telegram No. 188.

"I would reply to the American Peace Note that a direct interchange of ideas seems to us most likely to attain the desired result. We should, therefore, propose immediate conference of delegates of belligerent States in neutral place. We share President's view that work of preventing future wars could only begin after conclusion of present war.

"For your exclusive personal information: as place for possible conference of delegates only neutral Europe can be considered Apart from the difficulty of getting to and from America, the Portsmouth experiences teach that American indiscretion and interference make appropriate negotiations impossible. Interference by President, even in form of 'clearing house,' would be detrimental to our interests and is, therefore, to be prevented. The basis for future conclusion of peace we must decide in direct conference with our enemies if we are not to run the risk of being robbed of our gains by neutral pressure. We, therefore, reject the idea of a conference. On the other hand, there is no objection, after conclusion of peace, to sending delegates to an international congress to confer on problem of safeguarding future world peace.

"ZIMMERMANN."

From this telegram it might be assumed that the Imperial Government wished to limit Mr. Wilson's activity to bringing the belligerent parties to the conference table. We might also very well have gone on working with the President if the unrestricted submarine campaign had not intervened. It was, however, understandable that the Imperial Government, on grounds of domestic politics, should not want to name our peace terms at once. Accordingly the answer to the Wilson Note, which reached Berlin with extraordinary promptness on the 26th December, amounted to a friendly negative.

The German Note ran as follows:

"The Imperial Government have received and considered the President's magnanimous suggestion, that the foundation should be laid on which to build a lasting peace, in the friendly spirit which permeates the President's communication. The President points to the goal which is dear to his heart, and leaves the choice of the way open. To the Imperial Government a direct interchange of ideas would seem the most appropriate way of attaining the desired result. They, therefore, have the honor to suggest, in the sense of their statement of the 12th inst., in which they offered the hand to peace negotiations, an immediate conference of delegates of the belligerent States in a neutral place.

"The Imperial Government are also of the opinion that the great work of preventing future wars cannot be begun until after the conclusion of the present struggle of the nations. When this time has come they will gladly be ready to co-operate with the United States of America in this noble work."

The reasons of domestic politics which prevented the Imperial Government from naming our peace conditions were not understood in America. When Secretary of

State Lansing discussed with me the German Note of 26th December he said that he did not understand why we refused to name our conditions. If both the belligerent parties communicated their conditions a compromise would eventually be reached. To my objection that our demands were so moderate that they would be interpreted as weakness he replied that we ought to ask for more, indeed, ask for anything at all so long as we said something that would provide a starting-point from which negotiations could be opened and settled.

This conversation had no immediate practical results, as Colonel House asked me on the same day to call on him in New York With regard to the result of our conversation I telegraphed to Berlin as follows:

CIPHER TELEGRAM No. 192

"Washington, 29th December, 1916.

"House told me it is Wilson's opinion that a conference will not come about without previous confidential negotiations, for our enemies, as things are at present, would refuse the invitation or make their consent dependent on conditions. These words of Colonel House were accompanied by an invitation to strictly confidential negotiations, of which only he and Mr. Wilson should know. Under these circumstances complete discretion was assured, as Wilson and House, unlike most Americans, are both fairly clever at keeping secrets.

"I beg for early instructions as to whether I should reject such negotiations, or whether your Excellency wishes to authorize me to accept and will furnish me with instructions accordingly. As I have always reported, Wilson lays comparatively little importance on the territorial side of the peace conditions. I am still of the opinion that the chief emphasis should be laid on what are here called the guarantees for the future. If we could give Wilson these as fully as possible he thinks he could bring about a conference, for with that the chief argument of our enemies would be disposed of. The latter maintain that we would like to make peace now in order to begin the war when a more favorable opportunity occurs, while our enemies are obliged to hold together the coalition that has been formed against us in order to attain a lasting peace. Wilson's ideas about such guarantees are known to Your Excellency. They consist, in the first place, of disarmament by land and sea (freedom of the seas), provisions for arbitration and a peace league. I think, from Your Excellency's speech in the Reichstag, that the Imperial Government would give such guarantees on condition that peace was restored.

"With House I adopted chiefly a listening attitude in order not to compromise Your Excellency in any way. However, I agree with Colonel House's view that a peace conference cannot be brought about without the help of the United States. Our enemies will try to put us in the wrong by saying that we did, indeed, propose a conference but would not breathe a word about our conditions or guarantees. I can, of course, only judge from the American standpoint. We have, by our peace offer, brought about a great change in public opinion over here. This advantage we shall lose entirely if the idea spread by our enemies that we have only made a deliberately theatrical peace gesture for the benefit of German public opinion is confirmed. What steps Wilson will take should Your Excellency empower me to enter upon such negotiations is not yet certain and depends entirely on Your Excellency's instructions. House had an idea of travelling to England in person. The more detailed the information Your Excellency can give me as to our conditions and readiness to give guarantees the better from my point of view. However, I do not know whether Your

Excellency may not perhaps prefer to let the negotiations break down rather than accept American help. In my opinion it is not necessary that the United States should take part in all the negotiations. All that is necessary would be for us to pledge ourselves to the guarantees, which would be settled in detail at a general conference, after a conference of the belligerents had concluded a preliminary peace.

"I submit to Your Excellency the above proposal because I am convinced that our enemies will not consent to negotiations unless strong pressure is brought to bear. This, however, will, in my opinion, occur if Your Excellency thinks it possible to accept American intervention. With the exception of the Belgian question the American Government ought to bring us more advantage than disadvantage, as the Americans have only just come to realize what England's mastery of the seas means."

This telegram I consider the most important of the entire negotiations, inasmuch as it reached Berlin on the 3rd January, therefore six days before the decision in favor of unrestricted submarine war. When I re-read my telegrams to-day, I still—even after the evidence given before the Commission of the National Assembly— have the same impression as at that time, that Mr. Wilson agreed with our wishes and regarded it as his principal task to bring about a conference of the belligerent parties. I cannot, therefore, understand how it was possible to regard this American offer as anything but an offer of peace mediation, and how the Foreign Office could declare to G. H. Q. that there had never been any question of peace mediation by Mr. Wilson. On the other hand, I quite understand that Bethmann-Hollweg, as he stated before the Commission of the National Assembly, was very sceptical with regard to the President's policy.

Nevertheless, an offer of mediation was made which had to be accepted or refused. In the first case it was necessary to bring forward the submarine war as little as possible; in the other we should have to create a clear diplomatic situation in Washington, if we were to avoid the reproach of having negotiated with Wilson on the subject of peace while at the same time planning the submarine campaign, which was bound to bring about a rupture with the United States.

When I spoke with Colonel House at that time I assumed that the principal aim of the German Note of the 26th December was to lay particular emphasis on our old point of view, already known to Mr. Wilson, according to which the regulation of territory was to be dealt with by the belligerent Powers, and the League of Nations question in a world conference under the American presidency. At the time Colonel House himself always spoke of two conferences which the President hoped to bring together at the Hague. The one was to consist only of the belligerent Powers and settle the territorial questions, the other was to be a world conference to found the League of Nations. Mr. Wilson did not wish to invite the conference to Washington because of the great distance from Europe and the peculiar position of the American Press.

As I have already mentioned, their opening of the "intensified submarine campaign" had been planned weeks before. This question had now become acute, and I received the two following Foreign Office telegrams on this subject:

CIPHER TELEGRAM No. 145

"Berlin, 4th January, 1917.

"Question of armed merchantmen in opinion of navy and G. H. Q. cannot be further postponed.

"Request you discuss with Lansing following memorandum which is closely connected with American memorandum of 25th March and leave with him as *aide-memoire*. Our action against armed merchantmen, which will follow the lines of the memorandum, does not, of course, imply any withdrawal of our assurance in the Note of 4th May, 1916, as to sinking of merchantmen.

"ZIMMERMANN."

CIPHER TELEGRAM No. 148

"Berlin, 5th January, 1917.
"Pursuant to Telegram No. 145 of 4th January.

"Please telegraph to me immediately Your Excellency's personal opinion as to impression and consequent action with regard to Telegram No. 145. This must, not, however, be discussed with Lansing, as, for your own strictly personal information, action against armed ships will begin immediately.

"VON STUMM."

As the question of the "intensified submarine war," in consequence of the further course of events, became of no importance, there is no need for me to go into detail, and I will confine myself to giving my two answers as follows:

(1) CODED WIRELESS TELEGRAM

"Washington, 9th January, 1917.
"Telegrams Nos. 145 and 148 received to-day.
"Request most urgently to postpone further steps till you have received my answer."

(2) Cipher Telegram

"Washington, 10th January, 1917.
"In reply to Telegram 1488.

"Memorandum Lansing received. In my opinion steps in sense of this memorandum will cause collapse of Wilson's peace mediation, and bring about instead a rupture with America, unless action is postponed at least until agreement is reached with American Government. It may perhaps be possible to arrange that Americans should be warned against serving on ships armed for attack. In any case, however, time must be allowed the Government here to bring this about. As everything is decided by Wilson, discussion with Lansing is mere formality. He never gives an answer until he has received instructions from Wilson. In present case latter must read memorandum first.

"How much importance Your Excellency attaches to Wilson's peace mediation I cannot judge from here. Apart from that it is my duty to state clearly that I consider rupture with the United States inevitable if immediate action be taken on the lines of the memorandum."

At the time of sending the telegram I received, in the following telegram, the reply of the Foreign Office to Mr. Wilson's last proposals, which had been communicated to me through Colonel House:

Cipher Telegram No. 149

"Berlin, 7th January, 1917.
"In reply to Telegram No. 192 of 29th December.
"For your personal information.

"American intervention for definite peace negotiations is entirely undesirable to us owing to public opinion here. Also at the present moment we must avoid anything that might deepen the impression among our enemies that our peace offer is in any way the result of our finding ourselves in a desperate position. That is not the case. We are convinced that economically and from a military point of view, we can bring the war to victorious conclusion. The question of stating our conditions, therefore, Your Excellency will handle dilatorily. On the other hand, I authorize you to state now our readiness to co-operate in that part of the programme in which the President is particularly interesting himself, and which seems to be identical with the so-called 'Second Convention' outlined by Colonel House here. In this we include arbitration machinery, peace league, and examination of the question of disarmament and of the freedom of the seas. We are, therefore, in principle, prepared for those guarantees which could be settled in detail in a general conference after a conference of the belligerents has brought about a preliminary peace. To prove our *bona fides* in this direction, we are also ready in principle to open immediate negotiations with the United States.

"Your Excellency will be so good as to inform the President of this, and request him to work out the programme for the conference to secure world peace, and to communicate it to us as soon as possible.

"Please also emphasize to Colonel House and President Wilson that our actual peace conditions are very moderate, and, in contrast to those of the Entente, are kept within thoroughly reasonable limits; this is also particularly the case with regard to Belgium, which we do not wish to annex. Moreover, we desire regulation of commercial and traffic communications after the war without any idea of a boycott, a demand which we think will be understood at once by all sane people. On the other hand, the question of Alsace and Lorraine we cannot consent to discuss.

"I should like to know how Your Excellency thinks that pressure could be brought to bear by President Wilson to incline the Entente to peace negotiations. In the light of our experience during the two years of war, it seems to us that a prohibition of the export of war material and foodstuffs, which would be the step most likely to bring the Entente into line and would also be the best for us, is unfortunately little likely to be realized. Only an effective pressure in this direction could relieve us on our side of the urgent necessity of resorting again to unrestricted submarine warfare. Should Your Excellency have proposals to make as to how the unrestricted submarine warfare can be conducted without causing a rupture with America, I request you to report immediately by telegram.

"ZIMMERMANN."

I understood from this telegram that I was to continue the negotiations with Colonel House. The refusal contained in this telegram was only concerned with a demand which had never been made by the United States. Moreover, I have never personally had much faith in the appeal to public opinion which would have nothing to do with Mr. Wilson. If the Imperial Government had a few weeks before desired such intervention, they must have believed that German public opinion would agree to it. In my opinion, too, an agitation in favor of American intervention would have set in in Germany quite on its own account if the German people had known that such action by President Wilson offered good prospects of leading to a peace by understanding. Later, when I returned from America to Germany, I was struck by the small number of my countrymen who privately favored the submarine war. I therefore still think that German public opinion could easily have been persuaded to accept Mr. Wilson's mediation, if the terrorism of the supporters of submarine war had been dealt with in time. Herr von Bethmann-Hollweg has spoken before the Commission of the National Assembly of the hypnotic effect exerted on German public opinion by the submarine war.

Though the Foreign Office telegram of the 7th January mentions the ways in which President Wilson could bring pressure to bear on the Entente, it had already struck me at that time that the first step taken by the United States to force the conclusion of peace had not made the impression in Germany that its importance warranted.

The various "War Memories" that have now been published in Germany do not touch on this point. As has already been mentioned, the "Federal Reserve Board," which corresponds to our Reichsbank, had issued a warning against the raising of loans for belligerent States. In this way the American source of funds was practically cut off. Already foreign securities were in general unwillingly handled. If the loans had been completely forbidden, such results would not have transpired, as the American avails himself of bank credit to a far greater extent than is usual in other countries. It is well known that the Government of the United States, after they had entered the war, themselves raised "Liberty loans," and advanced money to their Allies because this procedure accorded much more closely with American inclinations than the raising of foreign loans.

As is well known, after the German peace action had failed, the definite decision to declare unrestricted submarine war was taken in Pless on the 9th January. In this way, as the Chancellor said, the Rubicon was crossed. War with the United States seemed inevitable, unless it were found possible at the eleventh hour to annul the decision of the German Government. Herr von Beth-mann-Hollweg has declared before the Commission of the National Assembly that he had not sufficient faith in Mr. Wilson's peace intervention to advise the Emperor to oppose the demand of G. H. Q. for the declaration of un-restricted submarine war.

At the end of this chapter I give a report which I drew up on the attitude of American public opinion towards intervention.

I should like once more to emphasize that in judging and estimating American politics I have always given more weight to public opinion than to the views or inten-tions of any individual statesman.

"Washington, 11th December, 1916.

"During the last phases of the presidential elections the American Press used to be so much occupied with questions of domestic policy that there was little space left for the discussion of foreign events. In contrast with this, in this year's campaign the Press politics on ques-tions of foreign policy played a very important part, but the discussion was naturally so much under the influence of the aims and considerations of party politics that a report on the attitude of the Press towards the European belligerents at that time could not have given a true pic-ture. This was quite particularly the case with regard to Germany. On one hand the Republican organs, out of regard for the votes of the German-Americans, found it necessary considerably to moderate their speech, while on the other the Democratic Press branded the Republi-can candidate as a 'Kaiserite,' owing to his German-American following, and at the same time threw more mud than ever over Germany and everything German; until in the last weeks of the election campaign the dawn-ing hope of bringing over great masses of *Bindestrichler* into the Democratic camp brought about a sudden moderation in the tone of this organ.

"Only now, after the absurdities of the presidential election are over, is it again possible to arrive at an approximately clear judgment as to the attitude of the Press towards Germany and the other belligerent nations.

"This judgment may be briefly stated as follows:

"The American Press in general takes sides less passionately with either party than was formerly the case, and is heartily tired of the war. This does not in any way imply that our enemies have not still the support of a number of very influential partisans, who are all the time fighting loyally for the 'Cause of the Allies,' let slip no opportunity to malign Germany and, in the event of a threatened crisis, form an element of danger for us which should not be underestimated. It may even be admitted that the tone which the organs of this tendency, particularly strongly represented in New York, Boston and Philadelphia, adopt against Germany has become, if possible, more bitter during the last few months. But it is questionable whether the great mass of the influential papers, particularly in the remoter districts of the Atlantic coast, have become more impartial. They don't like us and don't trust us, but have also gradually got to know but not to esteem England.

"The present attitude of America towards the cause of the Entente Powers, with which that of the greater part of the independent Press coincide, was defined as follows by the *New York Tribune,* one of the most inveterate champions of our enemies at the present time: 'Despite a very widespread sympathy for France and a well-defined affection for Great Britain in a limited circle of Americans, there has been no acceptance of the Allied points of view as to the war, and there is not now the smallest chance that this will be the case. . . . The thing that the British have failed to get before the American people is the belief that the war was one in which the question of humanity and of civilization was uppermost for the British. The Germans have succeeded in making Americans in very great numbers believe that it is purely and simply a war of trade and commerce between the British and the Germans, and the various economic conference proposals have served to emphasize this idea.'

"The violation of Greece, the ruthless procedure against Ireland since the Easter rebellion—on which a well-directed Press service of American-Irish, in spite of the strict English censorship, keeps public opinion constantly informed—the selfish sacrifice of Serbia, Montenegro and Rumania, as well as the illegal economic measures against Holland and Scandinavia, have seriously shaken England's reputation here as the protectress of the small nations.

"Certain remarks of the English Press of altogether too free a nature on the American Government, their disparaging cartoons of the President and the patronizing air adopted by many English war journals and often in the English daily Press towards America—as, for example, in a recent number of the *Morning Post,* alleged former German hankerings for colonies in South America, from the realization of which the Union is said to have been protected by England—are arousing increasing dissatisfaction here. The persistent and systematic attempts of the British Press Bureau to sow dissension between America and Germany on the question of the submarine war are resented. The sharp British replies to American representations on the question of the 'black list' and the 'post-blockade,' and, England's latest pinprick, the refusal of the request for a free passage for the Austrian Ambassador, condemned even by such a pro-British paper as the Philadelphian *Public Ledger* as a 'British affront,' have created a very bad impression. 'It is unmistakable,' says the pro-Entente *Evening Sun,* 'that American opinion has been irritated and sympathy estranged by many acts which have damaged our interests and wounded our national self-respect.'

"Above all, however, the serious shortcomings of the enemy General Staffs, which are criticised here with unprofessional exaggeration, and their ineffectiveness—'a lamentable succession of false moves,' as they are called by the respected *Springfield Republican*—have produced a general disillusionment as to the efficiency of our enemies, which has damped even the old enthusiasm over the heroic bearing of the French army and its commander-in-chief, who is very popular over here. 'We give thanks for Joffre,' was the heading of a typical leading article in the *New York Sun* on Thanksgiving Day. The recent warning of the American banks by the Federal Board against accepting through the post large quantities of unsecured foreign treasury notes—a warning which could only refer to the issue by the Morgan bank of English and French short-dated securities—has also shattered the belief in the inexhaustible economic resources of France and England. With a quite exceptional expenditure of effort the newspapers under British or French influence, of which the most important are the *New York Times, New York Herald* and *Evening Telegram;* the Philadelphian *Public Ledger,* the *Chicago Herald,* and the *Providence Journal,* in addition to a number of other sworn partisans of the Entente Powers, among which may be mentioned particularly the *New York Tribune,* New York *Sun* and *Evening Sun; New York Evening Post, Journal of Commerce, New York Globe;* Brooklyn *Daily Eagle,* Boston *Evening Transcript* and Philadelphian *Inquirer,* have lately been trying to raise our enemies in the esteem of public opinion here. This is shown particularly in the headlines and the arrangement of the war news in these papers. All news that is detrimental to the German cause, even when it comes from an unreliable source, is printed in heavy type in the most striking position. Every gain of ground by the Allies, however, slight, is hailed as a great victory, and even the communications of private agencies which are in contradiction to the official reports of the enemy, and obviously inventions, appear as accomplished facts in the headlines of the papers. Their leading articles pour out hatred and malice against Germany. Their letter boxes are filled with contributions which are full of venom and gall against Germany and her allies, and their feuilletons or Sunday supplements contain about the strongest attacks that have ever been brought against us even in the American Press. But it looks as though their tactics no longer have the same success as of old. Their utterances, apart from such as deal with the Belgian or *Lusitania* themes, no longer make any impression.

"On the other side the consistently friendly attitude of the ten papers of the Hearst syndicate, which come daily into the hands of more than three million readers in all parts of the country, has of late become even much more friendly as a result of the English boycott of the International News Service and the exclusion of all the Hearst publications from circulation in Canada. Mr. Hearst has replied to the inconceivably shortsighted policy of the British authorities towards his news service in a series of forcible, full-page leading articles against the British censorship which must have seriously shaken the confidence, apart from this already weakened long ago, of the American Press in all news coming from England. Not only did the articles in question contain a crushing criticism of the English system of suppressing and distorting the truth, but they also proved that for years America had been misled systematically from London in its judgment of foreign nations—e.g., the 'degenerate' French. Apart from this the Hearst newspapers repeatedly explained in detail how in the autumn of 1916 the position of the Central Powers was excellent, while that of England and her allies was completely hopeless. It should be emphasized that the Hearst newspapers are, nevertheless, not to be regarded as blindly pro-German, for they publish a good deal that can hardly be desirable for us—e.g., occasional articles on the 'German Peril,' for which new food was provided by the exploits of the *Deutschland,* and more especially U53, and was exploited here to support the idea of increasing the army and navy. The papers named are based on a sound American policy, but with their sharp, anti-English tendency do us much more good than papers with admitted pro-German bias. The chief value of the pro-German attitude of the organs of the Hearst syndicate lies in the fact that their influence is not limited to any particular town or district, but extends over the whole Union. An English critic, S. K. Ratcliffe, recently wrote about American newspapers in the *Manchester Guardian.* . . . 'Northern papers are of no account in the South; the most influential New York journals do not exist for the people of the Pacific coast, and carry little weight in the Middle States. Hence, summaries of opinion—confined to a small number of papers published east of the Mississippi—are imperfectly representative of the Republic.' This accurately observed geographical limitation of the influence of the leading American newspapers is substantially overcome by the Hearst organization, for the leading articles which appear in the *New York American* to-day will appear to-morrow in the allied papers of Boston, Chicago

and Atlanta, and the day after in San Francisco and
Los Angeles.

"Another factor that has improved the attitude of the
American Press towards Germany is the recent important development of the wireless news service. By this
I do not mean so much the extension of the trans-Atlantic
service, in the communications of which a considerable
part of the Press here seems unfortunately to take little
interest, but the radiographic transmission of the full
reports of American correspondents in Berlin and on the
German fronts to the American newspapers or news
agencies. Among the interesting reports that have been
received direct and unmutilated in this way those of
Messrs. William B. Hale, Karl von Wiegand, Cyril Brown
and Karl W. Ackerman have exerted a particularly favorable influence for us, especially at the critical moments of the break-through in southern Galicia and the
battles of the Somme, when, without the special news
service via Nauen, the American Press would have been
completely misled by the mass of reports that were flow-
ing in from London. Among American journalists who
worked in Germany, Herbert Swope should be particularly mentioned, who, after his return, published in *The
World* and other Pulitzer papers, a series of fourteen
articles on the situation and feeling in Germany which
attracted the attention of both the Press and the reading
public. In a most undesirable way Mr. Swope in his first
articles, which appeared immediately before the election
—it was simply an electioneering monœuvre—emphasized
the deep hatred of the German people for the United
States, and the alleged general wish of all German circles
to see Mr. Wilson defeated at the election as a punishment for his unneutral attitude. To compensate for this
he performed a very valuable service for us in his later
articles by giving a convincing account of the economic

situation in Germany at that time, which removed all doubt over here as to the ability of our enemies to starve Germany out, and revived public respect for Germany's efficiency and organizing-power.

"The great and respectful tribute which the American Press pays to German 'efficiency' at every opportunity—and during the last few months there have been many such opportunities—can, however, do little or nothing to alter the deep 'sentiment' against Germany. As soon as the above-mentioned themes of Belgium and the *Lusitania* are mentioned, there are few papers that do not indulge, either in aggressive or more moderate terms, in expressions of horror at German 'frightfulness' and 'ruthlessness.'

"This deep-rooted feeling of the whole Press has been once more revived in very regrettable fashion by the recent Belgian deportations. The indignation of the Press at this 'slavery' which is being imposed on Belgium is general, deep-rooted and genuine. Even newspapers which express themselves in pretty harsh terms on the subject of the English illegalities condemn these deportations in no measured terms. The interview given by Governor-General von Bissing to the journalist Cyril Brown on the subject of these deportations, published on the front page of the *New York Times*, has unfortunately not made the slightest impression here. General von Bissing's second statement on the same subject in which, among other things, he emphatically declared it his duty to see that as few Germans as possible should be kept out of the firing line to guard Belgium, was grist for the mill of the enemy Press. 'The cat is out of the bag,' writes the *New York Times*, which does not miss the opportunity of reminding its readers of General von Bissing's responsibility for the shooting of Edith Cavell. 'Not a word about economic necessity, Germany needs men at the front. Simple, almost crude in fact, and completely German.' The Philadelphian *Public Ledger* says: 'The original offence, the invasion of Belgian territory, regardless of treaty obligations, has almost been obliterated by the cruelty which is now depopulating the land, stripping it of all its resources, sending its people into exile and slavery, making a wilderness and calling it order. There has not been such a tragedy since the fierce barbarian tribes swept over Europe; none would have believed two years ago that it could be enacted.' Such expressions as 'Huns,' 'Attila,' 'Hohenzollern slave trade,' and others of a similar nature are the order of the day, and the excitement is further fanned by reports from London and Le Havre, which no one here can verify, and provocative interviews, among which special mention must be made of that of Herr Carton de Wiart with the *World* correspondent. The news that Mr. Lansing had forwarded to Berlin a protest against the Belgian deportations was received with great applause by the whole of the Press. The resulting official statement that this protest had been made not in the name of the United States but in the name of the Kingdom of Belgium, represented by the American Government, caused dissatisfaction and a demand that the United States Government should also protest to Berlin on its own account. Resolutions of protest were sent to the President and published in the Press, and indignation meetings on a large scale are announced to take place in Boston and New York which will offer the Press further opportunities for anti-German demonstrations.

"With regard to the question of submarine warfare the American Press are quite unanimous on one point, that a withdrawal of the assurances given by Germany after the *Sussex* incident, or even an intentional breach of these, is bound to bring about, as it were, automatically, a breaking-off of diplomatic relations with Germany; and it is also clear that such a rupture would only be the first step towards open war. The great majority of the leading American newspapers express at every opportunity the genuine hope that such a contingency will not arise. Only the chauvinistic, anti-German element in the Press holds that the *casus ruptionis* has actually arisen and devotes itself to publishing and commenting on, in the most sensational manner, the alleged crimes of the German submarines. The newspapers of this order are abundantly supplied with pertinent material, particularly news of alleged sinkings without warnings, of which they on their side—probably with the co-operation of the British authorities here—know how to increase the effect by means of exaggerated reports of out-of-date 'sacrifices to German frightfulness,' which are eagerly swallowed here. In spite of the masterly skill with which this working on public feeling against the handling of our submarine war is managed, it may be taken for granted that it does not get a hold. However deep and however genuine may be the horror with which the American people regard such incidents as the sinking of the *Lusitania*—a fact that must be continually emphasized—equally great is obviously their indifference towards the destruction of non-American neutral shipping, *so long as the rules of cruiser warfare continue to be observed*. People over here have gradually got accustomed to reading daily reports of the sinking of another half dozen British or other vessels. The daily papers print them quite as a matter of course, and only in a prominent position when the bag reaches an unusually high figure. In the editorial columns of many papers a certain malicious joy is even observable, that England, who boasts of having mastered the submarine, should now be so mercilessly and persistently bled.

"One phase of the submarine war has, indeed, thrown nearly the whole of the American Press into a state of excitement, namely, the piratic exploits of U53 off the coast of New England. The destruction wrought by this boat so close at hand, and the consequent paralysis for several days of all merchant shipping, was too much even for the moderate papers, and resulted in strong outbursts against our 'ruthlessness.' Apparently this circumstance has recently been exploited by our enemies as a new way of influencing public opinion against us. Mysterious British battleships off the Atlantic coast are supposed to send out wireless warnings against the alleged approach of German submarines, and these are published in the American Press partly under panic headlines, and arouse indignation. This shady procedure, in which the pro-English press naturally takes the lead, recently aroused Mr. Lansing to make a forceful speech against the unknown originators of these rumors. It may be particularly emphasized, speaking quite generally, that the great influence exerted by the State Department on the Washington correspondents of the leading newspapers during the last few months, during which there has been a constant threat of the submarine question coming to a head, has always been on the side of peace, with the result that in more than one case, and particularly in the cases of the sinking of the *Marina* and *Arabia,* any serious agitation on the part of the Press has been avoided. With regard to the general war situation, the conviction has for some time been gaining ground with the great majority of the leading American newspapers, that a decisive victory by either of the two belligerent groups of Powers is no longer to be expected. With the exception of a continually dwindling minority which even to-day still promise their readers the 'ultimate victory' of the Entente Powers, the verdict of the

American Press on the probable result of the war is 'a draw,' 'a stalemate.' Only a few newspapers, to which belong those of the Hearst Syndicate, confess to the belief in 'a stalemate, or a victory of the Teutonic Allies.' How those newspapers which are at the service of our enemies, and which still hold to the legend of a miscarried German war of aggression, really judge the situation is only seen occasionally from incidental statements like the following confession of the *New York Tribune,* which preaches against a peace on the basis of the present position; this paper says that the American people should see that if the Allies were to conclude peace now the result would be a tremendous victory for Germany. Such isolated, misleading views as this do not, however, succeed in affecting in any way the general impression that by far the greater part of the leading newspapers regard the war as indecisive, especially after the fruitless conclusion of our operations before Verdun, the collapse of the great offensives on the Somme and in southern Galicia, as well as in view of the fact, confirmed on many sides, that the British blockade has not attained its end, the starvation of Germany.

"Our recent feats of arms in Rumania have hardly affected this opinion. In view of the great hopes, placed by our enemies and the newspapers in their service, on Rumania's entry into the war, these successes are recognized on all sides readily or grudgingly and without any spark of sympathy for the defeated country, and in some cases are even hailed as brilliant military achievements of the first rank. The preponderating opinion of the Press, however, passes over the fact that the conquest of Rumania, although opening up to Germany important new resources, is scarcely likely to influence to any considerable degree the situation which has resulted from the war of positions in East and West, and the still unbroken British mastery of the seas.

"The view that the war has reached a stalemate which, since President Wilson's speech at Charlotte in May of this year, had been maintained by several papers, but which has recently become general, apart from the definitely pro-Ally organs, is closely connected with the discussion of the question of peace restoration which for the American Press is in many cases synonymous with the question of intervention by the United States or all the neutral nations.

"There was a time when a very important part of the American Press seemed to stand on the level of the catch-phrase which was going the round at that time: 'Wall Street now fears nothing except the outbreak of peace.' These times, however, are long since past. The desire for a speedy end of the hostilities in Europe is to-day genuine, and shared by almost the whole Press. From the enemy camp we get the following testimony in the *New York Tribune,* which would like to convert its readers to less humane views: 'For millions of Americans this war is a tragedy, a crime, the offspring of collective madness,' and in its view the greatest service that America can render to the world—an allusion to the catch-phrase coined by Henry Ford for his ill-starred peace mission is—'to fetch the lads out of the trenches.' The discussion of the premises for the conclusion of peace, therefore, has for some time occupied an important place in the daily papers, and also to some extent in the reviews. Reports on the meetings of the many American peace societies are given with the greatest fulness, and anything in the overseas news connected with the question of a restoration of peace is printed in a prominent position and duly discussed in the leading articles.

"It would lead me too far to give even an approximately complete picture of this discussion with which the whole Press is occupied. But one point demands closer examination: the attitude of the leading papers to the German readiness for peace, publicly expressed by Your Excellency on three different occasions in the last few weeks.

"Your Excellency's great speech before the Budget Committee of the Reichstag unfortunately reached here at a time when the whole interest of the Press and public was directed to the at first uncertain result of the presidential election. Though generally printed, in the evening papers for the most part only in extracts, it was practically passed over in the editorial columns. An attempt to start a belated Press discussion of the speech by circulating it in the form of specially printed brochures, or at least to induce those papers which had only given extracts to publish the whole text, unfortunately failed; only the *Current History,* a special war magazine of the *New York Times,* felt itself called upon to reprint the speech *in extenso* in its December number. On the other hand, the passage of the speech which stated our readiness after this war to take a part in international organizations for insuring peace was widely circulated here, and attracted corresponding attention. As I, according to instructions, communicated this passage to the 'League to Enforce Peace' as the official German message for their banquet held here on the 24th inst., it was circulated throughout the country in the detailed Press reports on this association, which is greatly respected here, and commented on by many newspapers with all the more sympathy since Germany's sceptical reserve hitherto towards the question of a peaceful settlement of international differences has always worked strongly against us here.

"The interview granted by Your Excellency to the

American journalist Hale has been printed particularly fully by the ten Hearst newspapers, and further by all the other subscribers to the International News Service. In the *New York American* on Thanksgiving Day it occupied, together with a portrait of Your Excellency, the whole front page. At special request from many quarters the paper repeated the report three days later.

"Germany's readiness to enter into peace negotiations, expressed once more by Your Excellency at this interview, as well as Your Excellency's statement in the Reichstag on the 29th inst., that Germany is ready for any peace that will guarantee her existence and future, have during the last few days been fairly thoroughly discussed in the New York papers, which particularly dwell on the words 'a peace guaranteeing our existence and future,' and agree unanimously as to the urgent desirability of a further and more exact formulation of the German peace conditions.

"The *New York Times* says: 'All depends on what guarantees of the existence and the future of Germany are expected.' The paper goes on to ask how Germany could imagine her future assured from a territorial point of view, but points out in conclusion that these are only external details, and concludes, returning to its favorite theme, as follows: 'Deeper than all, fundamental in any discussion of peace, is the question of the German political ideals, of German *Machtpolitik* and *Weltpolitik*, of Prussian militarism.' . . . 'The fear, the practical certainty, that Von Bethmann-Hollweg's guarantees would be not merely guarantees of the existence and future of Germany, but of new and not distant wars with her, stands in the way of any serious discussion of his remarks.'

"The *Evening Sun* remarks sarcastically that obviously no such guarantees as *Deutschland über Alles* should be given to any country. Its verdict, too, is that: 'The peace that Germany craves still is a peace that will enable her to begin the next war in five or ten years, with a certainty of immediate victory and complete conquest of the over-lordship of Europe, if not America.' The *Brooklyn Daily Eagle* writes: 'If an inconclusive peace, a peace based upon the theory that the war is a draw, a peace fertile in the liabilities to future trouble, is not in the mind of the German Chancellor, what is in his mind? He should speak out. He will never have a better opportunity to be specific. The whole neutral world is listening, ready to give careful and intelligent consideration to his words.'

"More important than these and other utterances of the papers which follow in our enemies' wake is the trenchant leading article of the *World*, which on foreign questions generally expresses the point of view of the Administration. This paper says: 'If Germany is ready to end the war, the first thing for the Imperial Govern-ment to do is to make definite proposals for peace. Those proposals need not be made officially to the Allies, to the United States, or any other intermediary. They could be made to the world at large. The Chancellor could describe to the Reichstag the conditions under which Ger-many would regard her Existence and Future assured.' 'Germany began the war. It is proper that Germany should take the first steps towards ending the war, but something more than vague generalizations is necessary. At present there is nothing to talk about. There are no terms, not even extravagant and ridiculous terms, that can be discussed as a possible basis of settlement. Thus far there has been no evidence of good faith in the repeated German professions of a desire for peace. In consequence nobody takes them seriously until there is at least a tentative proposal of terms. When that is made, the responsible Ministers of other belligerent Governments will be forced to meet the issue. Public opinion in Great Britain and France, no less than in Germany and Austria-Hungary, will have a chance to make itself heard. When peace comes it cannot be merely the peace of diplomats and of Governments. It must be a peace in which popular sentiment has the final word, and popular sentiment has no means of expression until there is something tangible to discuss.'

"The general impression left by the utterances of the American Press on the subject of peace is that on the one hand—apart from a small number of influential papers—it is anxious for peace, from which anxiety it is obvious that it intends to pass over the extravagant war aims so often heard from the Entente statesmen; but that on the other hand it cannot as yet find any practicable way of bringing about an early conclusion of peace, and also that it cannot see any advance in this direction in the last statements of Your Excellency, which only a few papers have discussed to any extent.

"The change in the direction of the Foreign Office has been discussed at comparative length in the leading articles of the important newspapers, which, as a rule, deal with European Ministerial changes only in their news columns—less with regard to the personality of the retiring Minister, who was not very well known here, than that of the new Secretary of State. The only paper which devoted a few friendly words to Herr von Jagow was the *New York Times,* which described him, in connection with his conferences with Baron Beyens and Sir Edward Goschen at the outbreak of war, as a 'Gentleman in War and Peace,' and also recognized his sympathetic attitude during the negotiations on the submarine war controversy. Herr Zimmermann's appointment as Secretary of State, on the other hand, was greeted by many papers, and indeed by the Press in general—only a few papers were made somewhat uneasy by the news received lately by telegram, of his attitude towards the question of armed merchantmen—with great applause. The tone of these comments must have been set by the flattering and sympathetic utterances of Ambassador Gerard and the journalist Swope, on the subject of the new Secretary of State, and a longer article by Gilbert Hirsch published by the *New York Evening Post* and other papers under the heading 'Our Friend Zimmermann.' The note struck by this article and by the German Press comments transmitted and printed everywhere over here, that Herr Zimmermann is a particularly warm friend of the United States, was joyfully echoed by the whole American Press. Also the fact was everywhere emphasized that in Herr Zimmermann the important post of chief of the Foreign Office, hitherto reserved for 'Prussian Junkerdom,' had been given to a member, not of the diplomatic, but of the humbler consular service, and indeed, to a bourgeois. Here and there speculation was indulged in as to whether this appointment might not be interpreted as the first step towards a 'Liberal régime,' in which a not unimportant section of the American Press still sees the future salvation of Germany and of the world.

"The announcement of autonomy for Poland is, to say the least of it, received with scepticism by the American Press, which is comparatively well informed on the Polish question. The words of the virtuoso Paderewski, who is working here in the interests of the Polish sufferers through the war: 'This means only more suffering for my people; it means that another army will be raised, and that there will be more killing and more devastating,' were reproduced by many newspapers and regarded as an authoritative statement of what might be expected from the German-Austrian proclamations. Many papers declared it to be simply a move to raise more recruits.

Others sarcastically pointed out that the proclamation left the most vital questions, such as the boundaries of the new State and its form of government, to be settled later. Only a few of the leading newspapers, among them the *New York Evening Post* and the Philadelphia *North American*, allowed the Allied Governments a certain modicum of recognition, for, as they pointed out, in no case could the heavy hand of Russia, which had so long oppressed the country, be forgotten. The Polish Press here was at first very reserved. Their point of view is represented by the following leading article of the weekly paper *Free Poland*, founded since the war and published by the Polish National Council of America: 'What the Poles desire is an independent Poland. The Powers have acknowledged Poland's right to live, but either with a limitation of independence or diminution of territory. The Russians would fain lop off eastern Galicia. And now the Germans grant Poland an autonomy, but without Posen, West Prussia, or Silesia, in return demanding a Polish army to take up their cause against Russia. Though this move on the part of Germany will at least draw the world's attention to the inalienable rights of Poland as a nation, and make of the Polish question an international one, yet it must not be forgotten that the Poles in Europe will vehemently protest against any curtailment of their national aims and aspirations.

"The impression, on the whole unfavorable, made by the Polish measures on the American Press was gradually in part balanced by the announcement that the Polish Jews had been recognized as an independent religious community. Since it was thought in many quarters that this might be taken to be the first step towards cultural and political emancipation of the Eastern Jews, it was discussed with great interest, in view of the strong influence exerted by the American Jewish community on an important section of the American Press, particularly that of New York.

"Finally, there remains to be examined the attitude of the Press towards one question, in itself of a purely domestic, economic interest, but which promises to become of the most wide-reaching importance for foreign politics, namely, that of an embargo on corn. The price of most articles of food has risen to such an abnormal height during the last few months that the *New York Sun* can say without too great exaggeration, that if the war had lasted two more years the cost of living in Berlin and Vienna would have risen to the level of that of New York. In particular the serious position of the wheat market and the fairly certain prospect of an acute rise in the price of wheat in the course of the winter or next spring prompt the Press to constant discussion, the burden of which is the question whether the Government of the United States should or should not prohibit the exportation of corn. The opponents of such a measure, among which are the *World, New York Times, New York Evening Post, Journal of Commerce,* the Boston *Evening Transcript,* the Philadelphia *Public Ledger,* the Saint Louis *Globe-Democrat,* the *Pittsburg Post,* the Saint Paul *Pioneer Press,* the Indianapolis *News* and many others, maintain that the supporters of the embargo, whose main object is to injure the Allies, represent the situation as much more threatening than it is in reality. The *World* tries to console its readers by explaining that the high price of food represents the American people's contribution to the cost of the greatest war of destruction in the history of the world; while the *New York Times* points out the danger of estranging the Allies through an embargo. The newspapers which are friendly to Germany, particularly the Hearst newspapers, and the Milwaukee

Free Press, energetically urge an embargo on all articles of food, by which, as they more or less openly allow it to appear, England would be forced to make peace. But in addition a number of the most bitter opponents of Germany, for example the Philadelphia *Inquirer,* favor an early embargo for purely material reasons. It is to be expected that this question will be one of the first to come up at the opening of the approaching session of Congress, when the Press polemics of the opponents of the embargo, with the *arrière pensée* of protecting England's interests and those of her Allies, should reach their climax."

CHAPTER XI

THE RUPTURE OF DIPLOMATIC RELATIONS

BEFORE I received official notice of the opening of the unrestricted U-boat campaign, I had a further interview with Mr. House, concerning the peace activities of the President, and the telegram describing it which I sent to the Foreign Office, Berlin, is reproduced below:

CIPHER TELEGRAM No. 212

"(Answer to Telegram No. 149 of the 7th January.)

"Washington, January 16th, 1917.

"Your Excellency's authority in regard to Mr. House duly availed of. He told me Wilson considered this pronouncement of Imperial Government supremely valuable. As regards further developments of Wilson's efforts for peace, I can say nothing definite. This much only is certain, that at present moment President has no other thought than that of bringing about peace, and will endeavor to achieve this end with the utmost energy and all means in his power. A further pronouncement of Wilson's is expected almost immediately; it will probably take form of a communication to Congress. Apparently it will consist of an appeal to the American people to help him to enforce peace; in any case both he and House praise the Hearst Press article, which is written from that point of view. Whether means adopted will be to place an embargo on all exports is difficult to say.

Maybe the threat of an embargo will be enough to force our enemies to a conference.

"From the above it is clear that we cannot afford to have any difficulties over the old U-boat question. As regards the question of armed merchant vessels, I hope to arrive at a *modus vivendi*. But we must be careful not to act hastily and carelessly, so as not to create conflict before President has taken further steps. Remarkable as this may sound to German ears, Wilson is regarded here very generally as pro-German. His Note was traced to our influence, and Gerard's speech strengthened this impression. This speech is in accordance with instructions which Mr. Gerard is receiving. Our present enemies have gone literally raving mad, and leave no stone unturned in order to put obstacles in Wilson's way. This explains the attacks against the President, as also the scurrilous attempt engineered by the Republicans to charge the Administration with Stock Exchange speculations. Without any justification, of course, my name also was mentioned in this regard. The German Embassy, as is well known, is held responsible for everything by our enemies in this country."

At the same time as the above telegram, I wrote the following report describing the prevailing political attitude in Washington:

CIPHER REPORT
"Washington, 14th January, 1917.

"Ever since the Presidential election the political situation here has not changed. Apart from the question of ending the world-war, the public mind has not been constantly or earnestly concerned with any matter.

"Congress has dealt with the customary Budget proposals, and the fruitless negotiations about the Mexican question drag slowly on.

"Meanwhile, the attitude towards ourselves, which after the *Sussex* incident took a decided turn for the good, has slowly improved. This change in the public temper can be observed on all sides. It is true that it is only very slightly noticeable, if at all, in the Press, and our most rabid opponents are driven, owing to the general improvement in German-Americans' relations, to ever more violent attacks against us. Since President Wilson dispatched his Peace Note, our enemies' fury knows no bounds. Without exaggeration, it can be said that this note voices the spirit of almost the whole American people.

"Only Wall Street and the anti-German ring, as also their friends in the press, are dissatisfied and are endeavoring to put obstacles in the President's way. In these circles, which are always under English influence, the belief has taken root, that Mr. Wilson has fallen under German spell. The well-known anti-German Republican, Senator Lodge, boldly expressed this view in the Senate; but he could not prevent the Senate from voting in favor of Mr. Wilson's Peace Note, by a huge majority.

"The public mind is engaged principally with the question why precisely the President dispatched his note immediately after the German offer of peace. It is well-known that this Note had been prepared for some time, and would have been sent off at Christmas, quite irrespective of our own proposals, although, in view of Mr. Wilson's inclination to temporize, and to treat all questions somewhat dilatorily, this is by no means certain. I believe that the President's principal motive was his pressing desire to play the rôle of mediator—a prospect which seemed to be imperilled if our enemies agreed to deal directly with us. This may possibly explain why that particular moment was chosen, for which our enemies regard Mr. Wilson so unfavorably. A cartoon published by that most anti-German paper, the *New York Herald,* depicts Mr. Wilson's dove of peace as a parrot, faithfully babbling out the German proposals.

"Apart from the choice of this particular moment for its expression, the President's desire to bring about peace is in any case very comprehensible, seeing that he was re-elected principally on the basis of this programme. Furthermore, the Americans are genuinely alarmed by the extension of Japanese power in the Far East, and finally, since our Rumanian victories, Mr. Wilson has ultimately come to the conclusion that our enemies are no longer able to defeat us. One is constantly hearing the opinion expressed, both by members of the Cabinet and other friends of the President, who enjoy his confidence, that neither of the belligerent parties will now be able to achieve a decisive victory, and that further bloodshed is therefore useless.

"As already stated above, the anti-German party is doing its utmost to put every possible obstacle in Mr. Wilson's way, while the Press does not cease from repeating that the Peace Note is to be regarded as a menace against Germany. It is thus hoped to stiffen our enemies' backs, by dazzling them with the expectation of America's entry into the war; much, too, is made of the argument—and this was particularly so in the Senate— that Mr. Wilson's intervention was imperilling the traditional policy of the United States, which rests primarily upon the Monroe Doctrine, and upon the principle of non-interference with European affairs. Finally, a scurrilous attempt has been made by the Republican party to attack Wilson in the flank, by getting a notorious Stock Exchange speculator publicly to proclaim that members of the Administration, who knew beforehand of Wilson's action, had taken advantage to speculate heavily upon it. As this man could, however, produce no proofs, he simply made himself ridiculous.

"I have already frequently called attention in my report to the fact that the prolonged war hysteria over here has created an atmosphere of gossip and tittle-tattle, which at other times would have been regarded as impossible. For instance, even quite responsible people believe that I have obtained for cash certain compromising letters of Wilson's in order to be able to get a hold over him by this means. Senator Lodge, in his own house, privately expressed the view that this was a credible rumor, and then turned it to account in the Senate. The President is so terribly put out by this and other similar machinations on the part of the Republicans, who refuse to grant him the fame of the peacemaker, that he recently kept away from a public festival, because Mr. Lodge was to be the principal speaker there.

"Owing to the incredible rumors which are bandied from mouth to mouth here, I regarded it as necessary to bring an action against one notorious swindler and blackmailer. I wanted to convince public opinion that the Embassy had nothing to fear. I intend doing the same thing in the case of all future attempts at blackmail, once we have got a clean slate in regard to all compromising questions. Our enemies will, however, persist in leaving no stone unturned in order to cast a slur upon the Embassy, for their principal object is to succeed in bringing about my recall, or the rupture of diplomatic relations with Germany. Once they have accomplished this, they are convinced that it will be an easy matter to draw the United States into the war.

"As is well known, President Wilson received a reply from the Entente, in response to his peace move, which contained conditions utterly unacceptable to us. Messrs. Wilson and House regarded these conditions as 'bluff,' and were as convinced, as they had previously been, that the Entente would accede to a peace by arrangement. People frequently alluded in those days to the fact that in the last Anglo-American War of 1812-1814, the English, very shortly before the peace settlement, had proposed unacceptable peace terms which they suddenly allowed to drop later. I also believed, and believe still, that the Entente were perfectly well acquainted with the political situation in Germany, and wished by proposing such conditions to strike panic amongst us and compel us to declare an unrestricted U-boat war. The Entente never diverged from its one object, which was to draw the United States into the war, and thus to bring about a decision. Moreover, the negative reply sent to our Government by the Entente had sufficed to achieve this object; for the final resolution to declare an unrestricted U-boat war was formed before the peace conditions framed by the Entente became known in Berlin.''

On the 19th of January I received official notice that the unrestricted U-boat campaign would begin on February 1st, and I was to give the American Government notice accordingly on the evening of the 31st January. After all that had happened, I could but regard this intimation as a declaration of war against the United States, and one which, in addition, put us in the wrong; because it put an end to the peace overtures made by Mr. Wilson, which had been started with our approval. I did my utmost to try to get the Berlin resolution cancelled, or at least to obtain a postponement of the date on which it was to come into force, and with this end in view I sent the following telegram to Berlin:

CIPHER TELEGRAM

"Washington, 19th January, 1917.

"War inevitable in view of the proposed action. Danger of rupture could be mitigated by the fixing of a definite interval of time, say one month, so that neutral vessels and passengers may be spared, as any preliminary and timely warning seems impossible if present programme is carried out. I shall have to give the password for unnavigable German steamers on February 1st, as effect of carrying out of my instructions here will be like declaration of war, and strict guard will be kept. In any case an incident like that of the *Lusitania* may be expected soon.

"If military reasons are not absolutely imperative, in view of my Telegram 212, postponement most urgently desirable. Wilson believes he can obtain peace on the basis of our proposed equal rights of all nations. House told me again yesterday, that Wilson proposed to take action very shortly, for in view of our declaration regarding future Peace League, etc., he regards prospects of a Peace Conference as favorable."

In my efforts to avoid a breach with the United States, the President helped me to the extent of making a communication to the Senate on January 22nd, which he personally read to them in solemn session. In this communication, Mr. Wilson exhaustively developed his programme of a "Peace without Conquest." As the President officially communicated this proposal to all the belligerent Powers on the same day, it was to be regarded as a fresh and most solemn step towards peace. As, on the other hand, it is also a document which expresses most plainly Mr. Wilson's desires and intentions before his entry into the war, I quote it verbatim below. Those who read it to-day cannot help feeling that certainly no more scathing criticism of the Versailles Peace has ever been written,—a peace which contained all the signs of having been imposed upon the vanquished, and against which the President's communication was a warning.

"On the eighteenth of December last I addressed an identical note to the governments of the nations now at war requesting them to state, more definitely than they had yet been stated by either group of belligerents, the terms upon which they would deem it possible to make peace. I spoke on behalf of humanity and of the rights of all neutral nations like our own, many of whose most vital interests the war puts in constant jeopardy. The Central Powers united in a reply which stated merely that they were ready to meet their antagonists in conference to discuss terms of peace. The Entente Powers have replied much more definitely and have stated, in general terms, indeed, but with sufficient definiteness to imply details, the arrangements, guarantees, and acts of reparation which they deem to be the indispensable conditions of a satisfactory settlement. We are that much nearer a definite discussion of the peace which shall end the present war. We are that much nearer the discussion of the international concert which must thereafter hold the world at peace. In every discussion of the peace that must end this war it is taken for granted that that peace must be followed by some definite concert of power which will make it virtually impossible that any such catastrophe should ever overwhelm us again. Every lover of mankind, every sane and thoughtful man must take that for granted.

"I have sought this opportunity to address you because I thought that I owed it to you, as the council associated with me in the final determination of our international obligations, to disclose to you without reserve the thought and purpose that have been taking form in my mind in regard to the duty of our Government in the days to come when it will be necessary to lay afresh and upon a new plan the foundations of peace among the nations.

"It is inconceivable that the people of the United States should play no part in that great enterprise. To take part in such a service will be the opportunity for which they have sought to prepare themselves by the very principles and purposes of their polity and the approved practices of their Government ever since the days when they set up a new nation in the high and honorable hope that it might in all that it was and did show mankind the way to liberty. They cannot in honor withhold the service to which they are now about to be challenged. They do not wish to withhold it. But they owe it to themselves and to the other nations of the world to state the conditions under which they will feel free to render it.

"That service is nothing less than this, to add their authority and their power to the authority and force of other nations to guarantee peace and justice throughout the world. Such a settlement cannot now be long postponed. It is right that before it comes this Government should frankly formulate the conditions upon which it would feel justified in asking our people to approve its formal and solemn adherence to a League for Peace. I am here to attempt to state those conditions.

"The present war must first be ended; but we owe it to candor and to a just regard for the opinion of mankind to say that, so far as our participation in guarantees of future peace is concerned, it makes a great deal of difference in what way and upon what terms it is ended. The treaties and agreements which bring it to an end must embody terms which will create a peace that is worth

guaranteeing and preserving, a peace that will win the
approval of mankind, not merely a peace that will serve
the several interests and immediate aims of the nations
engaged. We shall have no voice in determining what
those terms shall be, but we shall, I feel sure, have a
voice in determining whether they shall be made lasting
or not by the guarantees of a universal covenant; and
our judgment upon what is fundamental and essential as
a condition precedent to permanency should be spoken
now, not afterwards when it may be too late.

"No covenant of co-operative peace that does not include the peoples of the New World can suffice to keep the
future safe against war; and yet there is only one sort of
peace that the peoples of America could join in guaranteeing. The elements of that peace must be elements that
engage the confidence and satisfy the principles of the
American governments, elements consistent with their
political faith and with the practical convictions which
the peoples of America have once for all embraced and
undertake to defend.

"I do not mean to say that any American government
would throw any obstacle in the way of any terms of
peace the governments now at war might agree upon, or
seek to upset them when made, whatever they might be.
I only take it for granted that mere terms of peace between the belligerents will not satisfy even the belligerents themselves. Mere agreements may not make peace
secure. It will be absolutely necessary that a force be
created as a guarantor of the permanency of the settlement so much greater than the force of any nation now
engaged or any alliance hitherto formed or projected
that no nation, no probable combination of nations could
face or withstand it. If the peace presently to be made
is to endure, it must be a peace made secure by the organized major force of mankind.

"The terms of the immediate peace agreed upon will determine whether it is a peace for which such a guarantee can be secured. The question upon which the whole future peace and policy of the world depends is this: Is the present war a struggle for a just and secure peace, or only for a new balance of power? If it be only a struggle for a new balance of power, who will guarantee, who can guarantee, the stable equilibrium of the new arrangement? Only a tranquil Europe can be a stable Europe. There must be, not a balance of power, but a community of power; not organized rivalries, but an organized common peace.

"Fortunately we have received very explicit assurances on this point. The statesmen of both of the groups of nations now arrayed against one another have said, in terms that could not be misinterpreted, that it was no part of the purpose they had in mind to crush their antagonists. But the implications of these assurances may not be equally clear to all,—may not be the same on both sides of the water. I think it will be serviceable if I attempt to set forth what we understand them to be.

"They imply, first of all, that it must be a peace without victory. It is not pleasant to say this. I beg that I may be permitted to put my own interpretation upon it and that it may be understood that no other interpretation was in my thought. I am seeking only to face realities and to face them without soft concealments. Victory would mean peace forced upon the loser, a victor's terms imposed upon the vanquished. It would be accepted in humiliation, under duress, at an intolerable sacrifice, and would leave a sting, a resentment, a bitter memory upon which terms of peace would rest, not permanently, but only as upon quicksand. Only a peace between equals can last. Only a peace the very principle of which is equality and a common participation in a common benefit. The right state of mind, the right feeling between nations, is as necessary for a lasting peace as is the just settlement of vexed questions of territory or of racial and national allegiance.

"The equality of nations upon which peace must be founded if it is to last must be an equality of rights; the guarantees exchanged must neither recognize nor imply a difference between big nations and small, between those that are powerful and those that are weak. Right must be based upon the common strength, not upon the individual strength, of the nations upon whose concert peace will depend. Equality of territory or of resources there of course cannot be; nor any other sort of equality not gained in the ordinary peaceful and legitimate development of the peoples themselves. But no one asks or expects anything more than an equality of rights. Mankind is looking now for freedom of life, not for equipoises of power.

"And there is a deeper thing involved than even equality of right among organized nations. No peace can last, or ought to last, which does not recognize and accept the principle that governments derive all their just powers from the consent of the governed, and that no right anywhere exists to hand peoples about from sovereignty to sovereignty as if they were property. I take it for granted, for instance, if I may venture upon a single example, that statesmen everywhere are agreed that there should be a united, independent, and autonomous Poland, and that henceforth inviolable security of life, of worship, and of industrial and social development should be guaranteed to all peoples who have lived hitherto under the power of governments devoted to a faith and purpose hostile to their own.

"I speak of this, not because of any desire to exalt an abstract political principle which has always been held very dear by those who have sought to build up liberty in America, but for the same reason that I have spoken of the other conditions of peace which seem to me clearly indispensable,—because I wish frankly to uncover realities. Any peace which does not recognize and accept this principle will inevitably be upset. It will not rest upon the affections or the convictions of mankind. The ferment of spirit of whole populations will fight subtly and constantly against it, and all the world will sympathize. The world can be at peace only if its life is stable, and there can be no stability where the will is in rebellion, where there is not tranquillity of spirit and a sense of justice, of freedom, and of right.

"So far as practicable, moreover, every great people now struggling towards a full development of its resources and of its powers should be assured a direct outlet to the great highways of the sea. Where this cannot be done by the cession of territory, it can no doubt be done by the neutralization of direct rights of way under the general guarantee which will assure the peace itself. With a right comity of arrangement no nation need be shut away from a free access to the open paths of the world's commerce.

"And the paths of the sea must alike in law and in fact be free. The freedom of the seas is the *sine qua non* of peace, equality, and co-operation. No doubt a somewhat radical reconsideration of many of the rules of international practice hitherto thought to be established may be necessary in order to make the seas indeed free and common in practically all circumstances for the use of mankind, but the motive for such changes is convincing and compelling. There can be no trust or intimacy between the peoples of the world without them. The free, constant, unthreatened intercourse of nations is an essential part of the process of peace and of development. It need not be difficult either to define or to secure the freedom of the seas if the governments of the world sincerely desire to come to an agreement concerning it.

"It is a problem closely connected with the limitation of naval armaments and the co-operation of the navies of the world in keeping the seas at once free and safe. And the question of limiting naval armaments opens the wider and perhaps more difficult question of the limitation of armies and of all programmes of military preparation. Difficult and delicate as these questions are, they must be faced with the utmost candor and decided in a spirit of real accommodation if peace is to come with healing in its wings, and come to stay. Peace cannot be had without concession and sacrifice. There can be no sense of safety and equality among the nations if great preponderating armaments are henceforth to continue here and there to be built up and maintained. The statesmen of the world must plan for peace and nations must adjust and accommodate their policy to it as they have planned for war and made ready for pitiless contest and rivalry. The question of armaments, whether on land or sea, is the most immediately and intensely practical question connected with the future fortunes of nations and of mankind.

"I have spoken upon these great matters without reserve and with the utmost explicitness because it has seemed to me to be necessary if the world's yearning desire for peace was anywhere to find free voice and utterance. Perhaps I am the only person in high authority amongst all the peoples of the world who is at liberty to speak and hold nothing back. I am speaking as an individual, and yet I am speaking also, of course, as the responsible head of a great government, and I feel confident that I have said what the people of the United States would wish me to say. May I not add that I hope and believe that I am in effect speaking for liberals and friends of humanity in every nation and of every programme of liberty? I would fain believe that I am speaking for the silent mass of mankind everywhere who have as yet had no place or opportunity to speak their real hearts out concerning the death and ruin they see to have come already upon the persons and the homes they hold most dear.

"And in holding out the expectation that the people and Government of the United States will join the other civilized nations of the world in guaranteeing the permanence of peace upon such terms as I have named I speak with the greater boldness and confidence because it is clear to every man who can think that there is in this promise no breach in either our traditions or our policy as a nation, but a fulfilment, rather, of all that we have professed or striven for.

"I am proposing, as it were, that the nations should with one accord adopt the doctrine of President Monroe as the doctrine of the world: that no nation should seek to extend its polity over any other nation or people, but that every people should be left free to determine its own polity, its own way of development, unhindered, unthreatened, unafraid, the little along with the great and powerful.

"I am proposing that all nations henceforth avoid entangling alliances which would draw them into competitions of power, catch them in a net of intrigue and selfish rivalry, and disturb their own affairs with influences intruded from without. There is no entangling alliance in a concert of power. When all unite to act in the same sense and with the same purpose all act in the common interest and are free to live their own lives under a common protection.

"I am proposing government by the consent of the

governed; that freedom of the seas which in international conference after conference representatives of the United States have urged with the eloquence of those who are the convinced disciples of liberty; and that moderation of armaments which makes of armies and navies a power for order merely, not an instrument of aggression or of selfish violence.

"These are American principles, American policies. We could stand for no others. And they are also the principles and policies of forward looking men and women everywhere, of every modern nation, of every enlightened community. They are the principles of mankind and must prevail."

In Helfferich's account of these matters, the author charges this appeal of Mr. Wilson's with having favored the Entente side, because in it the conditions laid down are regarded as an acceptable basis for peace. When I returned to Germany the Imperial Chancellor advanced the same argument in my presence; I have heard it repeated again and again at home, and among other places, before the Examination Committee of the National Assembly. It seems to me that this view is rather a Berlin *fable convenue*. There is no word in the document which would justify one in drawing such a conclusion. The President stated simply that he had invited both belligerent parties to define the conditions under which they would make peace, and that the Entente had replied fully to the invitation, whereas the Central Powers had not submitted their terms. He then proceeded to say that in so far as the conditions insisted upon by one side had become known, we had advanced a step nearer to the discussion of peace. If we read the wording of the document without prejudice, and in connection with the views expressed by American statesmen, it becomes abundantly clear that the President regarded the terms laid down by our enemies as maximum conditions, and further, that he believed that we also would submit our maximum terms, and finally come to an agreement by adopting a middle course.

Herr Helfferich makes a similar charge against Wilson's Note of the 18th December, owing to the threats that it contained. But this charge strikes me as being just as gratuitous as the first. The threats were uttered in London quite as plainly as they were in Berlin. The charge of partiality would have been justified only if the threats had been contained simply in the version of the Note which was sent to Berlin.

Besides, in all Entente countries, it was maintained that both the Note of the 18th December and the appeal of the 22nd January revealed partiality for the Central Powers. The diplomats of the Entente in Washington were quite beside themselves with anger, and plainly revealed their displeasure to Mr. Wilson. I am not concerned now with criticizing the President's efforts for peace in retrospect. The fact that Mr. Wilson became our personal enemy after the 31st January, 1917, and that he consented to the Peace of Versailles, is no proof of the contention that, before the 31st January, 1917, he would have proved a similar failure as a peacemaker. The President's spiteful censure and treatment of us, both during the war and at Versailles, may be explained psychologically, by the fact that we rejected his efforts as a mediator, and declared the U-boat war.

Mr. Wilson's personal sensitiveness and egocentric nature played an essential part in all the negotiations. When the French and English Press derided the President, in November, 1916, after the first cables had announced the election of Mr. Hughes, Mr. Wilson was deeply mortified. A further improvement in his attitude towards us followed, when we showed that we were favorably disposed to his mediation for peace. The fact that Germany relied on him, stimulated his self-esteem to such an extent that he became, to a certain degree, interested in bringing about a peace that would be satisfactory to Germany. Nor should the interest he showed in this matter be underrated. I openly confess that it was also my ambition to assist in restoring peace, in order to save our country from the catastrophe that threatened to overtake it, and to spare the world any further suffering. To this day I am still convinced that, had the Germans skilfully conducted their share in these peace negotiations, we should have achieved all we wanted to achieve. The happy personal relations which, in that case, would have prevailed between Mr. Wilson and the German representatives at the Peace Conference, would, in view of the element of chance, which is so conspicuous at such congresses, have turned the scales in our favor to a surprising extent. On the other hand, I was, and am still, of the opinion that the peace which would have been settled at that time, would not have satisfied the public opinion of the moment in Germany. But I attached no importance whatever to this consideration. He who practises politics in the interests of his native country, must be ready at any moment to plunge like Curtius into the abyss, in order to save his nation. This, however, is what made Curtius immortal. Besides, in a few years, if not sooner, the German people would surely have realized that "Peace without Victory" constituted a victory for Germany.

After the 31st January, 1917, Mr. Wilson was incapable of an impartial attitude towards Germany. He saw red whenever he thought of the Imperial Government, and his repugnance against it knew no bounds. Even to-day the bitter feeling still rankles within him, that the German Government deprived him of the glory of being the premier political personage on the world's stage. It goes without saying, that at Versailles the Entente exploited with a vengeance both this attitude on the part of the President, and his peculiar idiosyncrasies. Intercepted wireless messages from Paris had made us aware of the fact that the original American interpretation of the fourteen points entirely agreed with our own; and thus we in Berlin were filled, not without reason, with certain hopes of America's help. But Mr. Wilson, who would have acted more wisely had he never gone to Versailles, sat there alone, facing three European statesmen, for whom he was no match. They played upon his weakest point, by suggesting to him the view that, in addition to the German Government, the German people, who were guilty, too, should also be punished, and that the obligation to punish the guilty took precedence of the fourteen points. Had Mr. Wilson, after January, 1917, really come to the definite conclusion that he held the proofs of Germany's war guilt and lust of world empire? Whereas, theretofore he had considered the question of war guilt impartially, he now agreed that the Germans would have been able to obtain a reasonable peace through his mediation, but had rejected it and chosen to declare the U-boat war instead, in order to achieve a complete victory. Consequently, the Germans had not been concerned all this time with bringing about a reasonable peace, but with gaining the empire of the world, a conclusion from which their war guilt was also to be inferred. It was as the result of these ideas that Mr. Wilson preached the crusade against militaristic and autocratic Germany, who wanted to achieve the mastery of the world. Only by means of the belief in a crusade could the peace-loving American people be prevailed upon to wage war.

Regarding the effect upon the Senate of the President's appeal, I sent the following telegram to the Foreign Office:

CIPHER TELEGRAM

"Washington, January 23rd, 1917.

"Wilson's appeal has met with general approval in Senate, and is regarded as a further energetic step in peace movement. Only our wildest opponents have again attacked President as a pro-German. Almost throughout views expressed about appeal contain the wish that Central Powers will also state their peace terms now. House also begged me urgently that this might be done, either publicly or secretly. Then Wilson would immediately propose Peace Conference; President also seems inclined to conclude the Bryan Treaty with us. Time is now, alas, too short, otherwise treaty might perhaps have helped us to avert war.

"As result of proposed unrestricted U-boat war, peace movement will presumably come to an end. Nevertheless, it is possible on the other hand that Wilson will make redoubled efforts for peace, if a time-limit be allowed. I should like to leave no stone unturned in order to avert war with United States. As I understand the situation, our refusal to submit our peace terms arises out of the fear that they may appear too moderate to public opinion in Germany. Would it perhaps be possible, before opening the unrestricted U-boat war, to state the peace terms, which we should have submitted at the Peace Conference we proposed, and to add, that, in view of our enemies' insolent rejection of our scheme, we could no longer abide by these moderate terms? And then we might hint that, as victors, we should demand an independent Ireland. A declaration of this sort would win over public opinion on this side, as far as this is possible, and might perhaps also satisfy public opinion in Germany."

The day after the President had read his appeal to the Senate, I received a telegram inviting me to visit Mr. House in New York. During the interview the Colonel read me a memorandum of Mr. Wilson's, in which the President formally offered us to act as mediator, in order to bring about a peace by arrangement. The memorandum left me in no doubt whatever that Mr. Wilson was certain of being able to achieve this end. With the utmost possible speed I sent the following telegrams about my interview with Mr. House, by three different routes to Berlin, on the assumption that it was impossible for us to abide by our former resolve:

(1) CIPHER WIRELESS TELEGRAM

(Most urgent)

"Washington, 27th January, 1917.

"After having had very important conference request most urgently postponement till my next two messages received. Suggest reply by wireless."

(2) CIPHER TELEGRAM

"Washington, 26th January, 1917.

"Wilson offered officially, but in first place privately, to mediate for peace, on basis of his appeal to Senate, that means without interference with territorial terms of peace. Wilson's simultaneous request for communication of our peace terms not to be regarded as private.

"I am wiring with full particulars through State Department. To begin U-boat war without previous negotiations regarding above proposals would among *other things* put us seriously in the wrong, and owing to

Wilson's personal sensitiveness, would make prevention of rupture quite impossible."

(3) Cipher Telegram

"Washington, 27th January, 1917.

"House suddenly invited me to visit him on behalf of Wilson, and told me the following as an official message from President:

"First of all, Wilson offers privately to mediate for peace on basis of his appeal to Senate, i.e., therefore without interference in territorial terms of peace. Wilson's simultaneous request to us to submit our terms of peace is not to be regarded as private. House revealed to me following thoughts of the President. Our enemies had openly expressed their impossible peace terms. Thereupon President had, as a direct contrast to these, developed his programme. Now we are also morally bound to make our peace terms known, because our desire for peace would otherwise appear insincere. After Your Excellency had informed Mr. Wilson that our peace terms were moderate, and that we agreed to second Peace Conference, President thought he had given expression to our wishes in his appeal to the Senate.

"Wilson hopes that we shall communicate our peace terms to him, which might he published both in Germany and over here, so that they could become known immediately all over the world. If only we had confidence in him, President was convinced that he would be able to bring about both Peace Conferences. He would be particularly pleased if Your Excellency were at the same time to declare that we are prepared to enter the second Peace Conference on the basis of his appeal. Our declaration might be shown to have been actuated by Wilson's having sent us a direct request for our peace terms.

President is of opinion that Note sent to him by the Entente was a piece of bluff which need not be taken seriously. He hopes definitely to bring about Peace Conferences, and quickly too, so that the unnecessary bloodshed of the Spring Offensive may be averted.

"To what extent Your Excellency will and can meet Wilson, it is impossible to tell from this side. Meanwhile I urgently beg leave to submit the following remarks for your consideration. If the U-boat campaign is opened now without any further ado, the President will regard this as a smack in the face, and war with the United States will be inevitable. The war party here will gain the upper hand, and the end of the war will be quite out of sight, as, whatever people may say to the contrary, the resources of the United States are enormous. On the other hand, if we acquiesce in Wilson's proposal, but the scheme nevertheless comes to grief owing to the stubbornness of our enemies, it would be very hard for the President to come into the war against us, even if by that time we began our unrestricted U-boat war. At present, therefore it is only a matter of postponing the declaration for a little while so that we may improve our diplomatic position. For my own part, I confess that I am of opinion that we shall obtain a better peace now by means of conferences, than we should if the United States joined the ranks of our enemies.

"As cables always take several days, please send instructions by wireless, in case telegraphic privileges 157 cannot be used on February 1st."

I had hoped that the communication of the President's appeal through Mr. Gerard, would have led to a postponement of the unrestricted U-boat war. This, however, was not the case. I can pass over all that happened in Berlin at that time, and all the deliberations which led to the ultimate decision, for not only did I not take part in them, but they have also become general knowledge since the taking of the evidence before the Examination Committee of the National Assembly. I need only mention here that I received the following reply to my proposals, from the Imperial Chancellor :—

CIPHER TELEGRAM

"Berlin, 29th January, 1917.

"Please thank President on behalf of Imperial Government for his communication. We trust him completely, and beg· him to trust us likewise. Germany is ready to accept his secret offer· of mediation for the purpose of bringing about a direct Conference of the belligerents, and will recommend. similar course to her Allies. We wish our acceptance of offer, as well as offer itself, to be treated as quite secret.

"A public announcement of our peace terms is at present impossible, now that Entente has published their peace terms which aim at the degradation and annihilation of Germany and her Allies, and have been characterized by President himself as impossible. We cannot regard them as bluff, as they entirely agree with professed opinions of enemy Powers expressed not only before, but afterwards. They also correspond exactly with the objects for which Italy and Rumania entered the war, and as regards Turkey, with the assurances made on behalf of Russia by both England and France. So long as these war aims of our enemies are publicly maintained, it would be impossible to interpret public announcement of our own peace terms, as anything else than a sign of weakness which at present does not exist, and would only lead to a prolongation of the war. In order to give President Wilson a proof of our confidence, however, tell him just for his own private information the terms on which we should have been prepared to take part in peace negotiations, if the Entente had accepted our offer of peace on the 12th December, 1916.

"The restitution to France of that part of Upper Alsace occupied by her. The acquisition of a strategical and economic safety-frontier-zone, separating Germany and Poland from Russia.

"Colonial restitution in the form of an understanding which would secure Germany colonial possessions compatible with the size of her population and the importance of her economic interests.

"Restoration of those parts of France occupied by Germany, on condition that certain strategic and economic modifications of the frontier be allowed, as also financial compensation.

"Restitution of Belgium under definite guarantees for the safety of Germany, which would have to be determined by means of negotiations with the Belgian Government.

"Economic and financial settlement, on the basis of exchange, of the territory invaded by both sides, and to be restituted by the conclusion of peace.

"Compensation for German undertakings and private persons who have suffered damage through the war.

"Renunciation of all economic arrangements and measures, which after the peace would constitute an obstacle in the way of normal commerce and trade, with the conclusion of corresponding commercial treaties.

"The Freedom of the Seas to be placed on a secure basis.

"The peace terms of our Allies coincide with our own views, and observe the same limits.

"We are, moreover, prepared to enter the International Conference which he wishes to invoke after the war, on the basis of his communication to the Senate.

"Your Excellency will give President these details at the same time as you hand him Note relating unrestricted U-boat war, and will inform him as follows:

"If his offer had only reached us a few days earlier, we should have been able to postpone opening of the new U-boat war. Now, however, in spite of best will in the world, it is, owing to technical reasons, unfortunately too late, as far-reaching military preparations have already been made which cannot be undone, and U-boats have already sailed with new instructions. Form and content of enemy's reply to our offer of peace, and the Note of the President, were so abrupt and harsh, that, in view of the life and death struggle which has once again been proclaimed against us, we cannot any longer delay the use of those means which appear to us best calculated to end the war quickly, and for the relinquishment of which we could not have taken the responsibility in the face of our whole nation.

"As the order regarding the unrestricted U-boat war shows, we are prepared, at any moment, to make every possible allowances for America's needs. We would beg the President to prosecute—that is to say, pursue, his plan notwithstanding, and declare ourselves ready to discontinue the unrestricted U-boat war the moment we are completely assured that the President's efforts will lead to a peace that would be acceptable to us.

"BETHMANN-HOLLWEG."

I immediately communicated the peace terms contained in this telegram to Mr. House, and I still cherished a small hope that he would, after all, perhaps, be able to exercise a favorable influence over the President. Truth to tell, he actually went to Washington in order to take part in the deliberations which were to decide the attitude which America was henceforth to adopt towards us.

Apart from the fact that the secrecy covering the communication of our peace terms deprived them of all diplomatic value, the simultaneous declaration of the unrestricted U-boat war gave the death-blow to all hope of maintaining peace. As Herr von Bethmann-Hollweg declared before the Examination Committee of the National Assembly: "It was perfectly clear to the authorities in Germany, that the decision to prosecute the unrestricted U-boat war would destroy all chance of further efforts on the part of the President to bring about peace. The U-boat war meant rupture, and ultimately war with America. The discussions between General Head Quarters and the Political Leaders had turned upon this question for years. That which led to the decisive step being taken was, that General Headquarters was firmly resolved to face even the risk of America's entry into the war, and that it wished to use the circumstances as a trial of strength with the political leaders."

On January 31st, at 5 o'clock in the afternoon, I handed Mr. Lansing the official communication about the U-boat war. This was my last political interview in America. We both knew that the end had come, but we did not admit the fact to each other. The Secretary of State contented himself with replying that he would submit my communication to the President. I cherished no illusions regarding the expected outcome of this interview, for the Ultimatum of April 18th, 1916, no longer allowed of any chance of preventing the rupture of diplomatic relations. Consequently on the morning of the 31st January, I had already given the order that the engines of all ships lying in American harbors were to be destroyed. I had already been given instructions to this effect at the time of the *Sussex* crisis, and these instructions had now been repeated from Berlin. As a matter of fact it was dangerous to allow of any delay, for on the evening of January 31st our ships were already seized by the American police. As far as I know, however, all of them without exception were made unfit for use before this occurred.

On the 3rd February, at twelve midday, Mr. Wilson announced to a joint meeting of both Houses of Congress, the rupture of all diplomatic relations with Germany, and at the same time my pass was brought to me by a higher official of the Department of State.

Thus war was decided upon, even if it was not immediately declared. Everything that followed amounted only to preparation for war or war propaganda. Nothing except the abandonment of the U-boat campaign could have prevented war.

It has frequently been asserted that the notorious Mexico telegram led to the war with the United States. I do not believe this is correct. The telegram was used with great success as propaganda against us; but the rupture of diplomatic relations—as I have already pointed out—was, in view of the situation, equivalent in all circumstances to war. I had nothing to do with the Mexico telegram, which took me completely by surprise. It was addressed, in the usual way, direct to the legation in Mexico, and passed through the Embassy at Washington on the same day on which I received the notification that the unrestricted U-boat war was to be declared. I had neither the right, nor was it my duty, to hold up the telegram, although I disapproved of its contents. But even if I had held it up, I should have served no useful purpose. As I afterwards heard from a certain Englishman, there was an office in England which deciphered all the telegrams which we sent over the English cable, and this office placed all their intercepts at the disposal of the American Government after the rupture of diplomatic relations. There is nothing surprising in this, for we also deciphered all enemy telegrams which we were able to intercept. Nowadays there is no cipher which is absolutely safe, if it has been in use for some time. At that time, however, I did not know that all our cipher telegrams were being read by the English. If, therefore, I had held up the Mexico telegram in Washington, its contents would have been revealed to the American Government by the English, notwithstanding, and no one would have believed that the message had not been forwarded in some way to Mexico. Moreover the telegram, as is well-known, was only conditional; the instructions it contained were only to hold good if the United States came into the war. I strained every nerve, at that moment, to prevent this from taking place. If I had been successful, the Mexico telegram would have served no purpose. I am therefore able to say, with a clean conscience, that I did everything that stood in my power, to remedy the error committed in the dispatch of the telegram.

In Helfferich's account of these events, the author says:

"If Count Bernstorff was, and apparently is still, of the opinion, that Wilson was actually engaged in trying to bring about a peace which would have been acceptable and tolerable to us, and with a promise of success, this can only be explained as the result of the enduring effect of suggestion, which, acting upon him for two years, had had no really adequate knowledge of home opinion to counteract it. As the communication between Berlin and the German Embassy in Washington was completely cut off, it is not surprising that our representatives on the other side of the vast ocean should have lost touch with their fellow-countrymen struggling for their lives, and should have failed to retain the proper standpoint in regard to what was either necessary or tolerable.''

To this I should like to reply, in the first place, that the unrestricted U-boat war did not in the least bring the German people either what was necessary or tolerable. Furthermore, not only I myself, but almost all those gentlemen who returned with me to Germany, had the feeling, on reaching home, that we in America had formed a much clearer notion of the true state of Germany, than those of our fellow-countrymen who had been living at home; for they had been completely cut off from the world by the Blockade. After we had seen the conditions prevailing in Germany, we could understand even less than we had before, why the Imperial Government had not snatched with joy at the chance of making peace.

As to the question whether we should have obtained an acceptable and tolerable peace through Mr. Wilson's efforts, I am still firmly convinced to-day, that this would have been the case. The President would not have offered to mediate if he had not been able to reckon with certainty upon success, and he was better situated than any German, to know the attitude of the Entente. In his farewell letter to me, Mr. House wrote:

''It is too sad that your Government should have declared the unrestricted U-boat war at a moment when we were so near to peace. The day will come when people in Germany will see how much you have done for your country in America.''

Moreover, later on, Mr. Bonar Law publicly admitted in the English Parliament that Great Britain would have collapsed financially, if American help had not saved her. The war-spirit in France, during the year 1917, was simply upheld by the hope of American help, and finally, in March, the Russian Revolution broke out. If we had accepted Wilson's mediation, the whole of American influence in Russia would have been exercised in favor of peace, and not, as events ultimately proved, against ourselves. Out of Wilson's and Kerensky's Peace programme, we might, by means of diplomatic negotiations, easily have achieved all that we regarded as necessary. My conviction that we could in the year 1917 have obtained a peace which would have been acceptable to ourselves, is based not so much on Wilson's good will, as upon the fact that, without American help, the Entente could not possibly have achieved a victory.

Against this view, the argument is advanced that the United States would in any case have entered the war, in order to avoid a German victory. I have already pointed out, that according to my view, no "German Peace" was any longer possible after the first battle of the Marne. Besides, it was precisely the object of the policy which was directed at American mediation, to prevent the United States from entering the war.

At the present time, even Mr. Wilson himself is produced as crown-witness in support of the view that America would have entered the war against us whatever might have happened. In the discussions about the Peace Treaty, which the President held in the White House on the 19th August, 1919, much stress is laid upon a certain passage in particular, which gives the impression that Mr. Wilson would have wished America to enter the war, even if Germany had not declared the unrestricted U-boat campaign. Almost without exception, all the German national newspapers interpreted the short dialogue in question between the President and Senator McCumber in this way, and the *Deutsche Tageszeitung* even went so far as to regard it as a striking proof of what they called Wilson's "*a priori* resolve to have war with Germany."

I must most emphatically reject this interpretation of the passage under discussion, which was turned to account by some papers in America in the political fight.

In the first place I should like to point out that it is obviously inadmissible to take the above-mentioned passage out of the context, and to regard it in itself as an interchange of 'views between Mr. Wilson and Mr. McCumber. It ought, on the contrary, to be judged in conjunction with the passage that precedes it.

The proposition for discussion was the President's motion that the League of Nations made it obligatory upon all States united, under it, to take common action against any country guilty of a breach of international law. Senator Harding, one of the keenest opponents of the League of Nations, suggested the idea in the debate that it was impossible for a sovereign State like the United States of America to have her moral obligation in any international conflict dictated to her by an external body consisting of the Council of the League of Nations. Driven into a corner, Mr. Wilson had to acknowledge this fact; but he emphasized the point that in spite of this the value of the League of Nations was in no way impaired. He said:

"The American Republic is not in need of any advice from any quarter, in order to fulfil her moral duty; but she stabilizes the whole world by promising in advance that she will stand by other nations who regard matters in the same light as herself, in order to uphold Justice in the world."

Following upon this, Senator McCumber then tried to confute the President's theory, by applying it practically to the most recent events in the world's history. He referred to the last war, at the outbreak of which there was no League of Nations in existence, and the following discussion took place:

McCumber: Would our moral conviction of the injustice of the German war have drawn us into this war, if Germany had been guilty of no aggressive acts, and, what is more, without the League of Nations, for of course we had no League of Nations then?

Wilson: As things turned out, I hope that it would finally have done so, Mr. Senator.

McCumber: Do you believe that, if Germany had been guilty of no act of injustice against our own citizens, we should have come into this war?

Wilson: I believe it.

McCumber: You believe that we should have come in whatever happened?

Wilson: Yes.

It is abundantly clear that with his first answer, "as things turned out, I hope that it"—that is to say, America's moral conviction of the injustice of the German war—"would finally have drawn us into the war"— the President lays the emphasis on the words "as things turned out." There can be no doubt that he meant to say: "As things turned out in regard to his efforts for peace," the first ready concurrence of the Imperial Government, notwithstanding, was thwarted at the decisive moment. With such a Government, Mr. Wilson seems to imply, it was impossible in the long run for America to remain on terms of peace. From that time henceforward—there can be no question of any earlier period, because up to that moment he had been in constant negotiation with us —he regarded the Imperial Government as morally condemned. Then, however, he calls to mind very clearly the feeble war-spirit of the American people in the spring of 1917, which, as is well known, had to be whipped into the war by propaganda on a prodigious scale. That is why the President says he "hopes," that the moral conviction of the American people regarding the injustice of Germany's cause would finally have triumphed over his readiness for peace expressed so brilliantly as late as November, 1916. His words are, therefore, to be regarded as a reflection in retrospect, not as a proof of an *à priori* intention to urge the United States into the war in any circumstances.

Truth to tell, if Mr. Wilson had really been striving to declare war against us, he would, of course, only have needed to nod in order to induce his whole country to fight after the *Lusitania* incident, so great was the war feeling at that critical time. Later on, the President concentrated all his efforts upon the idea of being the Peacemaker of the world, and even made such prominent use of the motto, "He kept us out of the war," in the campaign for his re-election, that it is quite unthinkable that all this time he should have secretly cherished the intention, ultimately, to enter the war against Germany. In this matter, the fact that after the rupture of diplomatic relations between America and Germany, Mr. Wilson really did urge on the war by every means in his power, proves nothing. For, after January 31st, 1917, Wilson himself was a different man. Our rejection of his proposal to mediate, by our announcement of the unrestricted U-boat war, which was to him utterly incomprehensible, turned him into an embittered enemy of the Imperial Government. But this is by no means a proof of the contention that, before the date named, he was secretly watching for an opportunity to make war upon Germany. Neither does it excuse the President for having allowed himself at Versailles to be convinced of the alleged complicity of the German people in the general war-guilt. Theretofore he had certainly always differentiated between the autocracy, as also Militarism, on the one hand, and the German people on the other. At Versailles he suddenly advanced the theory that the Germans must be punished for their crimes, and not only those among them who were responsible, but also the innocent German people, who neither desired the breach of Belgium's neutrality, nor understood the moral consequences of the U-boat war, nor were aware of Mr. Wilson's mediation for peace.

The above dialogue is also interesting from the standpoint that the President is most clearly convinced that the Entente could not have conquered without American help. If to-day he concludes therefrom that America would have been obliged ultimately to join in the war, in order to punish Germany, in former days he concluded that his duty was to bring about a Peace without victory. If he had succeeded in doing this, all of us, friend and foe alike, would now be living in a better world than the present one. It would be the world as we had been shown it in a vision of the future on the 22nd January, 1917, and not the world of the Peace of Versailles, blooming with starvation, Bolshevism and nationalistic hatred.

In his Memoirs, Herr von Tirpitz says that of all the practical advantages which I declared would follow from a compliant attitude on our part, not one had fallen to our lot. But I must confess, I was not aware that the U-boat war had brought us any advantages either. Its results have been a heavy moral debt and a huge bill of costs that the German people must pay. And how could the policy which I recommended have yielded practical results, seeing that I was never able, or even allowed, to carry it through? Never at any time was the U-boat war really given up. Every time a diplomatic success was in view, an incident occurred which made it necessary to start one's labors all over again.

Other people have said that as I was not in agreement with the policy of the Imperial Government, I ought to have resigned my office. This view does not take into account all the facts of the case. As long as Herr von Jagow was Secretary of State for Foreign Affairs, I worked in complete harmony with him. We both worked together in trying to avert war with the United States. I knew as little as Herr von Jagow himself did, whether we should succeed in scoring every point in the policy we pursued, for the Secretary of State was in perpetual conflict with the Military and Naval Authorities. If I had heard in time that Herr von Jagow's resignation had occurred in connection with the question of the U-boat war, and was the result of it, I should have resigned at the same time as he did; because my name was identified with the idea of American mediation for peace. Moreover, up to the 9th, or rather the 19th, January, 1917, I was completely in accord with the Imperial Chancellor; for Herr von Bethmann-Hollweg declared before the Examination Committee of the National Assembly:

"The whole of my work in connection with Wilson's efforts for peace was, indeed, directed towards rendering the threat of a U-boat war unnecessary, by bringing about a peace movement which would, of course, have some promise of proving successful."

These words amount to a complete approval of the policy which I pursued in Washington. When, therefore, on the 19th January, I received the Note informing me of the intended opening of the unrestricted U-boat campaign, I could not tender my resignation, for I regarded it as my duty to the German people, to resist until the last the unrestricted U-boat war, and, if possible, to avert a breach·with the United States. When, on the 31st January, 1917, the U-boat policy had definitely triumphed, I had no further chance of resigning my office, seeing that owing to the immediate rupture of diplomatic relations it was lost to me.

The various reasons, for and against Mr. Wilson's mediation, were all thrashed out in great detail in this country, before the Examination Committee of the National Assembly, in the winter of 1916-17. And, according to the evidence given, the decisive cause of the failure of the scheme was the distrust which the most influential· statesmen felt towards the President. If any confidence had been felt in Mr. Wilson, Herr von Bethmann-Hollweg would have opposed the adoption of the U-boat war, and would have allowed the President's efforts for mediation to pursue their course. As a witness before the Committee, he himself said:

"There can be no doubt, now that we can look back upon events, that we should have done better had we placed our fate in President Wilson's hands, and had accepted his offers of mediation."

As I have already pointed out, the factor which in my opinion was largely responsible for determining the course we ultimately adopted was the under-estimation and ignorance of America which was so widespread in Germany. From the very first moment the problem was not properly understood by the German nation. The fact was overlooked that the most important battle of the war was taking place in Washington, and when the tragedy reached its climax, no one believed that, with all her political, military and economic power, the United States of America would ever enter into the war.

Finally, it has been pointed out as an objection to my view, that, after all, the Entente would have rejected Wilson's efforts at mediation. I am no longer in a position to prove the contrary to-day, and it is, of course, just possible, that the President· and Mr. House were mistaken in assuming as much as they did. If at that time, however, we expected the Entente to reject Mr. Wilson's offer of mediation, we should at all events have postponed the U-boat war, and accepted American intervention, in order to improve our diplomatic position in Washington, before having recourse to the *ultima ratio*. It seems to have been our destiny that all our most important decisions of the war were the outcome of military and not of political considerations. On the Entente side, the converse was always true, and that is why, though it suffered many military reverses, the Entente won the war.

In pursuing the policy I advocated, I was influenced by considerations, which now, in conclusion, I should like to sum up as follows:

(1) It was no longer possible to achieve a decisive German victory after the first Battle of the Marne, that is why German policy should have been directed towards obtaining "Peace without Victory"; and, as things turned out, such a victory was only to be obtained by means of American mediation.

(2) The personality of Mr. Wilson played no decisive part in determining my attitude. I never once reckoned upon his personal friendliness towards ourselves; for I knew him too well to suppose him capable of pro-German tendencies. I expected nothing more from him than that he would play America's game—America's and no other country's—supported by the public opinion of the United States. American policy, however, pursued the object

of a "Peace without Victory," from the standpoint of practical politics, in order that, neither Germany nor England should attain to a superlatively powerful position. A "Peace without Victory" of this sort, under American patronage, would have left the United States in the undisputed position of the first political power in the world. To this, there was added certain other reasons of an ideal political nature, owing to the fact that both Mr. Wilson and the great majority of the American people wished to put an end to all the bloodshed and misery.

(3) The beginning of the unrestricted U-boat war was bound, as things had developed, to lead automatically to the rupture of diplomatic relations with the United States.

(4) As matters stood in America, the rupture of diplomatic relations was equally bound automatically to bring about war with the United States.

(5) War with the United States had to be averted at all costs, because America's help meant giving our enemy such an overwhelming preponderance of power, that a German defeat became an absolute certainty.

(6) The political situation was such that, the acceptance of the American offer of mediation was the only means of preventing the United States from entering the war.

(7) If America did not enter the war, the Entente were not in a position to beat us.

(8) If Mr. Wilson had succeeded in bringing both belligerent parties to the conference table, a sort of Hubertsburg Peace* would have been concluded. In

*This refers to the Treaty of Hubertsburg, which was one of the treaties that put an end to the Seven Years War on the 15th February, 1763. It was concluded between the States of Prussia, Austria and Saxony. Nobody seems to have derived any advantage from the treaty, except perhaps Frederick II., on whose province of Silesia Marie-Thérèse renounced all further claim.

view of the situation, a peace unfavorable to ourselves was unthinkable. Who, at that time, could have compelled us to accept terms which we regarded as incompatible with Germany's position in the world? Herr Helfferich, before the Examination Committee of the National Assembly, expressed the view that in the end Mr. Wilson would have forced peace upon us with the butt-end of a rifle. But whence would he have obtained this butt-end? He had not one, and it took him a year to create an army. No one who is familiar with the United States can believe that it would ever have been possible to drive the Americans into the war, once a Peace Conference had assembled. For then it would only have been a matter of deciding the fate of one or two pieces of territory or colonies, in which the Americans would not have felt the slightest interest. Naturally, we should have had to restore Belgium and accept the disarmament programme, etc. But we had already declared ourselves ready to take these measures, and, as regards disarmament, etc., this reform was inevitable, in view of the economic position of all the countries concerned. If America had not entered the war, no one could have forced us to accept less advantageous terms than the *status quo ante*, with possibly some mutual compensation.

CHAPTER XII

THE RETURN HOME

AFTER the rupture of diplomatic relations, I entrusted the care of our interests to the Swiss Legation, and from that time I did not speak a word to any American official except to the Assistant Secretary of State, Breckenridge Long, who accompanied us as far as the boat at New York. From the majority of those gentlemen with whom I had official relations, however, I received very friendly letters of farewell.

The principal passage in the letter from Lansing, the Secretary of State, was as follows:

"I shall bear in mind all your earnest efforts in the cause of peace, and will gladly recall our personal relations, which, in spite of the difficulties of the situation, were always a pleasure to me."

In view of the conditions prevailing at the time, the preparations for our departure took a long time. It was only with difficulty that we were able to obtain the necessary accommodation for the large number of German officials and their families on the Danish ship *Friedrich VIII*. The business of getting the necessary papers—such, for instance, as the Entente's safe conduct—also necessitated lengthy negotiations, which were conducted by the Swiss Legation with the assistance of Prince Hatzfeldt, the Secretary of the Embassy. Our departure could only take place on the 14th February.

It was not pleasant to be obliged to remain eleven days longer in Washington. The moment the rupture of diplo-

matic relations occurred, the secret police took possession
of the Embassy, and shadowed every one of my movements. These precautionary measures were supposed to
guarantee my personal safety; but I should have been
quite safe without them, for all Americans behaved towards me with perfect propriety and courtesy. Our
personal friends did not allow the rupture of diplomatic
relations to make any difference in their attitude towards
us. Until the very day of our departure, my wife and I
were the daily guests of American friends. Even the
Press, with but a few exceptions, maintained a friendly
attitude; for all the journalists knew that I had worked
hard to maintain peace. As an example of this, I reproduce below an article from the *New York Tribune,* which
is one of the leading anti-German papers in America. I
give the article, somewhat abbreviated, in the original,
in order to preserve its American character:

"Diplomacy and Friendship twin arts of Bernstorff.

"Departing German Envoy, target of critics here and
at home, quits post with brilliant record and many personal friends.

"The sailing of *Friedrich VIII.* invites the cordial
obituary style, though diplomatic deaths are supposed to
warrant no sadness. And yet, curiously enough, Count
Bernstorff probably finds himself leaving when more
people are personally for him and fewer against him than
at any time in the last two years. A less distinguished
diplomat would not have had the art to stay so long.

"A letter from Washington, dated June, 1915, is in my
desk. It tells incidentally about the visit of a friend to
the Ambassador shortly after his interview with the
President. 'It's coming out all right,' the Count said
cheerfully, his melancholy eyes lighting up, and the
anxious lines etched in his face during the months past

lightening. 'No, they're not going to get rid of me yet for a while,' referring to the Press clamor for his dismissal.

" 'I'm glad of that,' answered the friend. 'Then you'll stay and get some more degrees.' (Eight American universities had honored him.) 'Oh,' he answered with a gesture, 'I may leave by degrees.' It is winning to catch an Excellency at puns.

"At his departure many persons—close friends of the last eight years and newspaper correspondents—are going to miss his amazing charm and the easy candor of his talk. He has had an intimate directness in his dealings with all sorts and conditions of people, that only a personage of magnetic personality can adopt.

"Sheer charm alone can forget caste consciousness. Count Bernstorff has had none of the patent heavy regard for himself that makes three-quarters of official Germany a chore to meet. 'I'll put you through,' the little telephone girl, at his favorite New York hotel, used to say promptly, when his Excellency was asked for, and knew that she was safe.

"Reporters will miss seeing him teeter informally by the Embassy fireplace as he interviewed them, or gave out a significant something from behind a hastily-raised newspaper.

"The insistent friends of Germany, heavily friendly and advisory, will miss his English, very soft with an attractive ghost, now and then, of a lisp. He learned it in London, his first language, for he was born there fifty-five years ago. His father, Count Albrecht, was on service as Ambassador to the Court of St. James'.

"Count Bernstorff came to America from his post as Consul-General in Cairo. He was stationed there in the trying diplomatic period of Anglo-French rapprochement and the rise of naval competition between the English and the German empires. By many, Count Bernstorff is credited with saving Turkish Egypt and most of the Moslem world to the German balance. They say he did it over coffee with Khedive Abbas Hilmy, who never, never was bored by his wit, nor failed to appreciate the graces bred down from thirteenth-century Mecklenburg of the tall Herr Consul-General. And in return from the Moslem Count Bernstorff may have caught some of his comforting regard for kismet.

"The man is more than a little fatalist. 'What happens must happen,' he was wont to say, as he sorted the threatening letters from his morning correspondence. And again: 'What difference does it make? They've killed so many that one more can make no difference.'

"He goes back to Berlin now, there as here different things to different people. A rank Social Democrat I have heard him called in drawing-rooms, where news of his earnest plea to his Government for a liberal *Lusitania* Note had leaked out.

"It has not been easy for him to construe and weigh the American situation for his Government, and have his judgment taken, any more than it has been easy for Mr. Gerard to convince the German Foreign Office that the American Notes were really meant. Often the same agent knocked both men and got in ahead of either as the authority on what America would do.

"A certain American Baroness, Egeria to the American journalists in Berlin, who has no use for Bernstorff or Gerard or Zimmermann, has been one of his many cockle burrs. Most of the German-Americans who chose to protest about the shipment of munitions and all of pro-submarine Germany plus an aspirant or two for his post—all of these have been busy against him. And the Americans are legion who have seconded the hate. He himself has been silent, with an occasional wry smile over it all. He has never excused himself when attacks on him, personally, followed German actions against which he had counselled.

"He has tried over and over again to explain to the German Foreign Office the temper of the American people, whose sentimentality is so different from that which prevails in the Hanover-Bremen-Leipzig breast. The *Hamburger-Nachrichten* has reviled him. It has been hard to see with Hamburg eyes what Count Bernstorff must know—that hardly a diplomat alive could have stayed so long on friendly terms with Washington, through these two years, or reaped so heavy a harvest of understanding from his study of poker and baseball as well as American commerce and institutions. People like to write—I, too—of his melancholy eyes, his gently cynical estimates of most dreamers' hopes. Over one circumstance he has been always hopeful. He has clung always to the hope that America neutral would be a leader in the erection of peace machinery, eager that every diplomatic transaction should perhaps have the possibility of an instrument. His real object in leaving, I am sure, is that not again will he turn over a communication from the American State Department to read a faint hope of peace between lines."

Apart from the measures taken for our security, our departure from Washington and New York was not very different from what it would have been in ordinary times, had I been moving to take up my duties in another country. Many friends came to the railway station at Washington, and on the boat at New York. Telegrams and letters of farewell came in hundreds, and our cabins were full of presents, consisting of baskets of fruit, flowers, cigars, books, beverages of all kinds, which are the custom at leavetakings in America. In these circumstances, and after all that I have described in the foregoing pages, I was not a little astonished when, about a year later, the American War-Propaganda Department began to hold me responsible for proceedings which were partly simply fiction, and for the rest of a kind that had occurred without any assistance from me whatever. I can understand perfectly the wish of the American Propaganda Department to create a war spirit, just as the same department in all belligerent countries strove to do; nevertheless, it was not necessary to adorn the war propaganda with unjustifiable personal attacks. Nothing happened after my departure from America to prompt such attacks. A few of my telegrams were, to be sure, deciphered and published in order to prove that I had hatched a conspiracy. When the Military and Naval Attachés were compelled to leave the United States, I could not very well avoid discharging the whole of the naval and military business myself. But this does not prove that I had previously had any dealings with these matters, even admitting that the Naval and Military Attachés had been guilty of illegal practices, which, despite all the uproar created by enemy propaganda, I do not believe to have been proved. Once the fever of war has died down, no one, presumably, will feel any interest in devoting any attention to such questions. If, however, later on, anyone should feel inclined to investigate the "German conspiracies," and "German propaganda," in the United States, in an impartial spirit, he will be astonished to find how many fantastic fictions were brought to the notice of the Investigation Committee of the Senate, and what small justification lay at the bottom of the charges made against the German Embassy.

When, on the afternoon of the 14th of February, we took to sea, we had no idea that we were to enjoy the hospitality of the gallant steamer *Friedrich VIII.*, and its amiable captain, for four long weeks. Ever since the establishment of regular lines of passenger steamers between America and Europe, we must certainly have broken all records in regard to the length of time we took to complete the journey. There were on board the *Friedrich VIII.*, in addition to the whole of the staff of the Embassy, together with their wives and children, the complete personnel of the consulates, as also a few native Germans, who for some reason or other, happened to be in America and had not yet had an opportunity of returning home. A few Scandinavians completed the list of the passengers. The total number of Germans was approximately two hundred. According to the wording of the Safe Conduct which we had been granted, we were allowed to take with us our personal belongings and "a reasonable amount of money." We were expressly forbidden to carry any papers.

The first twenty-four hours of the journey were the most pleasant. The sea was calm and the weather was not too cold, and on the following evening we reached Halifax, which was the port at which we were to be examined. It was selected in order that we might not have to enter the war zone. Here we had the first taste of the vexations of the journey. Our captain wanted to enter the port; but he was ordered to anchor outside. On the following morning the authorities allowed us to enter. We were placed under the supervision of the English cruiser *Devonshire*, and I cannot help admitting that the English naval officers discharged the undignified and distasteful duties imposed upon them with great courtesy. The Canadian officials, on the other hand, behaved with the utmost disrespect and boorishness. They appeared to be accustomed to dealing only with immigrants and stowaways.

I do not know to this day, why, in spite of our Safe

Conduct, we were held up twelve days in the Bedford Basin, which, with its encircling snow-clad hills, was completely shut off from the rest of the world. The examination in itself could not adequately account for this strange and uncustomary behavior, particularly towards an Ambassador: for although the ship's coal was ultimately sifted in the search for contraband goods, if any good-will had been shown, the examination could have been finished in three to four days at the outside. I suppose, however, that the delay was intended to serve political ends. The English probably wanted to keep us shut up in Halifax until the United States had entered into the war. They were perfectly well aware of my views, and feared that in Berlin I might after all succeed in effecting an understanding with the American Government. As, however, developments in the United States dragged on very slowly, and at first only an armed neutrality was contemplated, the English were ultimately obliged to allow us to continue our journey, because they could not very well keep us confined for weeks.

Personally, I cannot complain of the treatment to which I was subjected at Halifax, for I was the only one among all my fellow passengers of German nationality who had not to submit to having my person searched, and was only required to sign a declaration that I was carrying no papers. Everybody else—even my wife—had to consent to being searched, an operation which was performed in a humiliating manner, and which led to many an unpleasant scene. Even little Huberta Hatzfeldt, who was only three months old, was stripped of her swaddling clothes. The Canadian authorities assessed the "reasonable sum of money" allowed at ninety dollars a head, and confiscated all moneys above that sum as contraband. In this way, Countess Manfred Matuschka lost 25,000 dollars, which, in ignorance of the regulations, she had brought with her. The sum was to be deposited with a Canadian Bank, but has probably been lost forever by its owner. As I was forbidden to have any communication whatsoever with the outside world, I was not able to carry out my intention of lodging a complaint at Washington regarding this breach of the Safe Conduct that had been granted to us.

At last, however, our imprisonment came to an end, and we were allowed to pursue our journey. Amid the cheers of all on board, including particularly those of our excellent captain, who felt the affront we had received very deeply, we weighed anchor. Judge of the almost panic-stricken disappointment of all the passengers, therefore, when at the end of a few knots, the ship turned back on her course! To the great relief of all concerned, however, it appeared that we had only forgotten to take on board the wireless telegraphy apparatus which had been taken from us at Halifax. From that moment, apart from very bad and cold weather, we continued our journey without further incident. We took a sweeping curve northward, then sailed down the Norwegian coast without meeting either an enemy ship or a German submarine. Some of the neutral passengers were so much terrified of the latter, that they did not retire to their beds for many nights at a stretch.

At ten o'clock in the morning we landed in the snow in Christiania. Meanwhile the Mexico telegram had been published in Washington, and Michaelis, the German Ambassador, in accordance with instructions, came on board, in order to learn from me whether I could offer any explanation of the fact—that is to say, whether I suspected treachery on the part of any of my staff. It is indeed plain from the oft-quoted reports of the Committee of the Senate, that a host of underhand tricks must have been played, particularly in the Post Office;

nevertheless, I am of opinion that in this case the explanation which I gave above is the correct one. The telegram in question, like many others, was presumably deciphered by the English. From the experience gained during the war, we have learned that the diplomacy of the future will never be allowed to rely, for important matters, upon the secret of a cipher; for skilful experts are now able to discover the most complicated code, provided that they are able to intercept a sufficient number of telegrams. Over and above this, owing to our isolation in Washington, we were able to alter the cipher but very seldom. As to the suggestion of treachery on the part of any member of my staff—I never believed in this at the time, nor do I believe in it now. In very hard times they all proved themselves to be thoroughly loyal and efficient.

We had to remain in Christiania longer than we expected, because the route across the Sound to Copenhagen was entirely ice-bound. Finally, with the help of ice-breakers, even this obstacle was overcome, and after a day's halt at Copenhagen, we at last reached Berlin via Warnemünde. We had received an extremely hospitable and cordial welcome at Christiania and Copenhagen, at the hands of the Ambassadors, Michaelis and Count Brockdorff-Rantzau—we also had an opportunity of convincing ourselves that the feeling in Denmark and Norway had turned against us just as sharply as in America. The balance of power was, however, different. If our neutral neighbors had not been living in fear of German power, they would at this time have responded to Mr. Wilson's call, and would have broken off all diplomatic relations with us. I believe that the President was hoping that events might take this turn, and that he would thus be spared the need of waging war. If all the countries in the world were to declare war against Germany and her Allies—this is what was assumed in Washington

—the economic pressure would alone suffice to compel the Central Powers to yield. The policy proposed was similar to the one which, in the future, the League of Nations would pursue against any refractory member of its body, and which the Entente proposes to adopt to-day against Bolshevist Russia. The great length of time which it took the United States to enter the war is, in my opinion, to be explained in this way. The idea was to wait and see how things would develop. Meanwhile, thanks to the Mexico telegram, war-propaganda in America was being worked with great success, and the military preparations made such steady progress, that even if economic measures did not prove sufficient to end the war, the United States would have obtained the army they had longed for for so many years, as also the fleet of war and merchant ships, for which in times of peace Congress would never have voted the necessary funds.

On the evening of the day after our arrival in Berlin, I was received by the Imperial Chancellor, with whom I had a long interview. It was on this occasion that Herr von Bethmann-Hollweg informed me that he could not help consenting to the U-boat war, as the German people would never have understood it if we had concluded an unsatisfactory peace, without attempting to bring about a happy decision by means of the last and most effective weapon in which the nation felt any confidence. He also said that he would have been unable to go before the Reichstag with an offer of mediation from Mr. Wilson, because such intervention would not have been popular, public opinion would not have liked it, and it would only have been accepted by the Social Democrats. Herr von Bethmann-Hollweg declared that the Reichstag would have "thrown him out." This was the very expression he used. But this did not explain why, a few weeks previously, Mr. Wilson's mediation had seemed desirable, if, as a matter of fact, it was impossible to get the Reichstag to agree to it. Meanwhile, the political situation at that time has been completely elucidated by the evidence which Herr von Bethmann-Hollweg gave before the Examination Committee of the National Assembly. In his account of the interview he had with me, he spoke as follows:

"As regards my interview with Count Bernstorff, on his return from America, I should like to make the following remarks: I cannot recall all the details of the conversation I had with Count Bernstorff. Count Bernstorff has revealed in his evidence what I said to him, and I have no doubt that he has accurately reproduced my actual words. My duty was—and this is an idea I already touched upon earlier in the day—once the policy of an unrestricted U-boat war was resolved upon, never to reveal to anyone any doubts as to the efficacy of the scheme. In this case, too, I had to say, we shall achieve something by means of it. And that is why in my conversation with Count Bernstorff, I did not reveal my inmost feelings on the subject—there was no need for me to do so—but simply referred to the reasons which could be adduced in favor of the U-boat war."

The reception which I was given in Berlin, certainly at first left nothing to be desired. The Imperial Chancellor, on the occasion of our first meeting, had thanked me in a very hearty manner for my work in Washington, and a few days later, proposed that I should go on an extraordinary mission to Stockholm. On principle I was quite prepared to do this, seeing that the recent outbreak of revolution in Russia, and the prospective international Socialist conference in Stockholm, would offer fresh possibilities of peace, and an opportunity for useful work. From various things I had noticed in Berlin, I gathered that—as the evidence before the Examination Committee proved—the Imperial Chancellor would have preferred to give up the idea of the U-boat war, and to accept American intervention in favor of peace, but that he was compelled to give in, owing to the overwhelming advocacy of the U-boat campaign. It was to be hoped, therefore, that with the expected speedy failure of U-boat tactics, Herr von Bethmann-Hollweg would snatch at the next opportunity of making peace. As he remained in Office, in spite of the U-boat war, his chief motive for so doing must certainly have been that "after his departure the whole of the power, both of external and internal politics, would have gone over without resistance to the machinery of war-fever." I regarded any policy as the right one, which arrived at a prompt conclusion of peace, provided that we did not make any confession of weakness by ourselves initiating fresh offers of peace. We had already erred once in this way. But in Stockholm it seemed likely that opportunities might occur of winning either the Russians or the foreign Socialists over to a movement in favor of peace.

As I heard nothing, either about the Stockholm Mission, or about an audience with the Kaiser, which I was led to expect in connection with it, I went at the end of a few days to find out what had happened, and I was told that the Kaiser had declined to sanction my mission to Stockholm. Although I had a second interview with the Imperial Chancellor, I was never able to ascertain definitely the reason of the Kaiser's anger against me. Since, however, General Ludendorff, simply on the grounds of my particular views, made his "impassioned" attack on me before the Examination Committee of the National Assembly, I have no longer been in any doubt whatsoever as to the nature of the influence that was at work at General Headquarters. At the time, I only suspected the prevalence of some such feelings in that quarter, because I had heard it whispered that the Monarch did not like my "democratic views." The reasons for the Kaiser's anger, which were given me officially, were of too trivial a nature to be even plausible.

I must next refer to the dispatch box of the Swedish Legation in Washington. At New York Herr Ekengren had put on board the steamer *Friedrich VIII.* a box containing Swedish telegrams, which was to be forwarded to its destination.

This box, the very existence of which we Germans knew nothing about, was taken possession of by the British authorities in Halifax, and dispatched to England. The London newspapers then reported that a dispatch box, belonging to Count Bernstorff, and containing documents of the German Embassy, had been opened there. Although the mistake, whether intentional or the reverse, was very soon elucidated, someone had laid the matter before the Kaiser in a distorted light. Apparently the Kaiser was allowed to form the suspicion that the opening of the box had betrayed the secret of the Mexico telegram.

A further reason for his displeasure, at the time, was told me subsequently at Constantinople by the Kaiser himself. He said that I had "let him down most dreadfully," when I had recommended Mr. Gerard as American Ambassador to Berlin. I ought never to have supported the nomination of such a "Tammany Hall" creature. If he—the Kaiser—had only known at the time who Gerard was, and what Tammany Hall could be, he would never have accepted this Ambassador. In Constantinople I was able to reply to the Kaiser pretty fully, as the interview took place during a somewhat long journey on the Bosphorus. I certainly did recommend

Mr. Gerard in due course, but only after he had already been selected as Ambassador by Mr. Wilson. Before he had been chosen I was not asked. If at that time—in the year 1913—I had advised the rejection of Mr. Gerard, it would only have created a lot of unnecessary ill-feeling, as was the case at the nomination of Mr. Hill. It is the custom in America to select the Ambassadors from politically influential circles of the triumphant party; irrespective of whether Tammany Hall or any other organization is concerned.

Moreover, in 1903 I believed that Mr. Gerard would be welcome in Berlin, for social reasons alone. Everybody knew that the Kaiser liked to have Ambassadors who entertained on a lavish scale. Mr. Gerard was the only man, among all the candidates of that day, who seemed fitted for this and in a position to live up to it, while his rich and amiable wife was admirably suited to help him in his task. Before the war, an American Ambassador in Berlin really never had any political business to transact, for it was the tradition with the United States Government to conduct all negòtiations almost exclusively with the diplomatic corps in Washington. In 1913, therefore, I had no reason to advocate the rejection of Mr. Gerard in Berlin. Unfortunately, it was precisely in the social sphere that he had, before the war, experienced certain disappointments in Berlin, which, as far as we were concerned, might have been avoided, and it is possible that Mr. Gerard may have been influenced by these regrettable incidents. In any case, the Ambassador did not like Berlin, and he took too little pains to conceal the fact. Mr. Gerard was not the sort of man to be able to swim against the tide of anti-German feeling, once it had become the proper thing in America to be pro-Ally. As to whether any other United States Ambassador would have shown less hostility to us, however, may be

reasonably doubted. I have already singled out the
Adlon dinner as a proof of the fact that Mr. Gerard
could behave differently.

Be all this as it may, the reasons which were alleged
genuinely to justify the hostile attitude of General
Headquarters towards myself, struck me as not being
sufficiently weighty. I say "General Headquarters"
intentionally, for the Kaiser was manifestly only prejudiced against me by the usual whisperings that characterized the Wilhelminian epoch.

Nevertheless, I had conducted the most important
negotiations of the war, and the Monarch must, in any
case, have had the wish to hear the report of it all from
the person chiefly concerned. Besides, the Kaiser knew
as well as I did, that in Washington I had pursued the
policy of which he and the Chancellor were actually in
favor. Otherwise, the Imperial Memorandum, which was
sent to me about the U-boat war, and to which I have
already referred, would be inexplicable. Meanwhile,
however, this policy had not been able to prevail against
the preponderating influence of the military party, who
demanded the U-boat campaign. Now, of course, I have
no longer any doubt that the views which General Ludendorff expressed against me before the Examination Committee of the National Assembly, simply as his personal
opinion and without proof, constituted more or less what
was suggested to the Kaiser at this time. Briefly, they
wished to make me the scapegoat for the United States'
entry into the war, and this, despite the fact that all that
I had prophesied in regard to American policy had
proved correct, and all that my opponents had prophesied
had proved wrong. In their efforts to accomplish this
end, they found that a poisonous mixture could be brewed
out of my efforts for peace, and my well-known democratic views, which the Kaiser was not able to resist.

The unhappy Monarch unfortunately never once realized that the "Democrats" were his best friends. The Imperial power could, in the long run, only be upheld, if it found both its support and its counter-weight in a strong democracy. Like Friedrich Wilhelm IV., William II. was also unable to adapt himself to the changing circumstances of his time. The one-sided composition of his entourage, which was always recruited from among people who held his own views, was, at all events, chiefly to blame for this.

Although the Imperial Chancellor had told me that he would overcome the Kaiser's displeasure in regard to myself, almost two months elapsed before I was received at General Headquarters, and even then, it was only because a question had been asked about the matter in the Reichstag. When I saw the Kaiser, towards the beginning of May, in Kreuznach, the American question was of interest merely to historians, and no longer to politicians. Consequently, my interview with the Monarch, which took place on a walk, was not of very great moment. With his customary skill, the Kaiser steered clear of any attempt to enter deeply into the political problems of the hour, and behaved towards me, for the rest, just as affably as he had been wont to do in the past.

I had made the journey to Kreuznach in the company of my late friend, Ballin, whom I was never to see again. Whereas I was invited to lunch at the Imperial board, Herr Ballin was only asked to dinner.

Among the many and various charges which were brought against me in my Washington days, was the allegation that I was principally an agent of Ballin's. I had, in cordial agreement with Herr Ballin, always energetically supported the interests of German Shipping Companies; but even my most bitter enemies can only justify their charge against me for the period preceding the war. For, during the war, Herr Ballin had no influence at all, either in America or at home. He was, for instance, kept aloof from the Kaiser, because he was regarded as an "interested party" and as a pessimist. On the occasion in question, a high official of the Court said to me at the Imperial table that if I was seeing Ballin again before I left Kreuznach, would I please tell him that he was not to speak so pessimistically to the Emperor as he was wont to do. The Emperor ought not to be allowed to hear such stuff, otherwise he would lose nerve. This little passage of conversation is a proof of the carefully "insulated" position in which, as everyone knows, the Kaiser was kept.

After lunch I paid a visit to both of our great Army Commanders, whose acquaintance I made for the first time on this occasion.

"Bowing to necessity rather than to my own personal tastes," I must now, unfortunately, enter into personal matters, which hitherto I have diligently avoided in this book. I cannot, however, help referring here to the utterly unwarranted attacks made upon me by General Ludendorff, in his evidence before the Examination Committee of the National Assembly, with the view of refuting my own account of the interview which we had at G. H. Q. At all events, the General so completely lost control of himself before the Examination Committee, that this possibly explains his false interpretation of my evidence.

To deal first with the reason which actuated me in visiting General Ludendorff, I reproduce below the dialogue which took place thereanent before the Examination Committee:

Delegate Dr. Cohn: Was your interview with Field-Marshal Hindenburg and General Ludendorff brought about by any particular person or persons—either by yourself, by the Imperial Chancellor, or by the Foreign Office; or was it purely accidental?

Witness Count von Bernstorff: It was the outcome of the circumstances. I received a telegram which informed me, through the Foreign Office, that I was to report to the Kaiser at Kreuznach on the 4th of May. Now, Field-Marshal Hindenburg and General Ludendorff were also present at the lunch table, and I felt that I was bound in courtesy to pay a visit to the two gentlemen after the meal.

Delegate Dr. Cohn: Good. If I understand you correctly, my lord, G. H. Q. did not even feel the need of speaking with the Ambassador just recently returned from America?

Witness Count von Bernstorff: No. I never received any summons for that purpose.

I abide by these utterances to this day, because I actually remained seven weeks without being summoned to an interview with General Ludendorff, and then only visited him of my own free will, on the occasion when I reported to the Kaiser. In these circumstances, therefore, I was entirely justified in describing my visit as simply an act of courtesy. In view of the circumstances, I might perhaps say: an act of super-courtesy.

I do not dispute General Ludendorff's statement that I had expressed the wish to see him; for if I had not had the wish, I should have left Kreuznach without paying him a visit. As, however, General Ludendorff, in his evidence before the Examination Committee, allowed it to be plainly understood that, owing to the difference of our views, he did not like to have anything to do with me, I will at once emphasize the fact, that my wish to see him was actuated by purely official motives. In politics

I have at all times laid all personal feelings entirely aside, and have thought only of the business and the interests of my country. While I was kicking my heels in Berlin for all those weeks, waiting upon a summons to the Emperor, I was urged by many people to try and obtain an interview with General Ludendorff, in order to enlighten him regarding American affairs, as in this respect he was very badly informed. The latter fact, has, at all events, been substantiated by General Ludendorff himself, in his evidence before the Committee. The gentlemen who urged me to obtain this interview, themselves made efforts to bring it about. But these efforts were of no avail, and I therefore regarded them as too insignificant to be mentioned in my own evidence. In all my utterances before the Committee, I refrained from all allusion to personal and subjective matters.

General Ludendorff has further maintained that I impugned his honor by declaring that, generally speaking, he did not wish to conclude peace. I naturally never made such a nonsensical statement. Immediately after my visit to General Ludendorff at G. H. Q., I made notes of the essential passages of our interview; because I suspected, what in my opinion has since become a certainty, to wit, that the General wished to heap all the blame of the war with America upon my shoulders. Every impartial reader who examines the Notes given below, will be forced to admit, that they contain nothing whatsoever except assertions, which have been confirmed by all the evidence given before the Committee of the National Assembly; that is to say:

(1) That I wished to accept Mr. Wilson's offer of mediation.

(2) That the Imperial Government—that is to say, G. H. Q. or whoever was responsible for taking the final

decision—did not wish to accept Mr. Wilson's offer of mediation, in order to declare the unrestricted U-boat war instead.

(3) That the Naval Authorities had declared themselves in a position to bring about a desire for peace in England in five months from the 1st of February.

My notes about the interview I had with General Ludendorff ran as follows:

General Ludendorff received me with the following words:

"In America you wanted to make peace. You evidently thought we were at the end of our tether."

I replied:

"No, I did not think that; but I wanted to make peace before we came to the end of our tether."

Whereupon the General said:

"We, however, did not want to. Besides, it would not have been surprising if you had thought that we had come to the end of our resources. The communications you received, which I read from time to time, certainly led to that conclusion."

Later on in the conversation, General Ludendorff asked me when, in my opinion, the Americans would participate in the war with great force. I replied that in twelve months a large American army was to be expected in France, and that this army would be organized with comparative ease. To this the General rejoined that in that case we had ample time to end the war meanwhile; for the U-boats would force England to a peace in three months. He had received absolutely certain information on this point. When I was on the point of leaving, General Ludendorff repeated this remark very positively.

Though the sense was the same, the actual wording of my evidence before the Examination Committee differs somewhat from that of the notes given above. This is explained, however, by the fact that I spoke quite freely, and therefore prefaced my remarks with the words: "So far as I can remember, and so far as I am able to say, under oath, the conversation was more or less as follows," etc.

I did not enter into the personal views which General Ludendorff thought fit to express in his evidence before the Examination Committee; for I am of the opinion that the duty of the Committee was simply to establish the real truth by an inquiry into the facts. It is open to the Committee to put to me any questions they like concerning my activities in Washington, and I will answer them frankly; but I think that a quarrel between witnesses about their own personal opinions would have been an undignified spectacle, in which I distinctly refused to participate. I gladly leave it to the reader of the present volume to form his own ideas regarding my work in America.

In May, 1917, I left G. H. Q., feeling quite convinced that for the moment there was no room for me in German diplomacy; for the only policy which I regarded as right, had no prospect of being realized. After my return from America, I was placed on half-pay. I was therefore at liberty to return home, however unwilling I may have felt, at that moment of great tribulation for my country, to give myself up to a life of ease and idleness. During my period of rest, a Reichstag resolution was passed, and there was a change of Chancellors.

When Herr von Kühlmann, who is a friend of mine, took over the Foreign Office, he summoned me by telegram to Berlin, and told me that the Imperial Chancellor, Michaelis, was going to offer me the post of Ambassador in Constantinople. Some years previously Herr von Kühlmann and I had worked together in London. We had been on very good terms, and since then I had never lost touch with him. As he assured me very positively that he had taken over the Foreign Office in order to conclude peace, I felt no qualms about returning once more to diplomatic duties. I did not, however, conceal from Herr von Kühlmann, that I expected that there would be very strong opposition at G. H. Q. to my being employed again on Foreign Service. The Secretary of State was of the opinion that we might confidently leave this side of the question to the Imperial Chancellor, who at that moment was on his honeymoon, and was therefore admirably situated to carry things through. My interview with Herr Michaelis only made me more eager than ever to undertake the Mission to Constantinople. He said to me that he was offering me a very difficult and unpleasant billet, for I should have to wring concessions from the Turks with the object of bringing about peace. This view of the situation corresponded entirely with my own. Contrary to my expectations, the Imperial ratification of my appointment arrived; but the Monarch also seized the opportunity of making certain remarks about my democratic views, without, however, withholding his signature from my credentials.

In September I set out for Constantinople, where thirty years previously I had started my diplomatic career, and where I was now to end it.

INDEX

INDEX

Ackerman, Karl, 338

Albert, Privy Councillor, appointment of, 36; financial affairs of, 40, 42, 46; office of, 41; propaganda work of, 49; moving picture work•of, 56; shipping activities of, 80 ff., 85 ff.; hindrance of, 83 ff.; marine insurance and, 89, 92; "conspiracies" and, 119; duties of, 165; robbing of, 196 ff., 270

Albrecht, Count, 395

Algeciras Conference, 13 ff.

Alsace, 329, 376

America, see United States

American Criminal Court, 119
 Embassy in London, 316 ff.
 Institute in Berlin, 23
 Law Department, 44, 262, 274
 Peace League, 291
 Peace Note, 318-321
 Press, 49 ff., 57, 94, 316 ff., 326, 332 ff., 336 ff., 342 ff., 394
 Press Bureau, 47
 Secret Service, 47, 197
 War Propaganda Department, 398

Amsinck and Company, 261

Ancona, sinking of, 210, 214 ff.; Lansing and sinking of, 230

Andrew, 83

Anglo-Saxons, 21

Annie Larsen, 121

Appam, 265

Arabia, 303, 306, 342

Arabic, sinking of, 90, 144, 168, 173; effect of sinking of, 173 ff., 248; negotiations concerning, 176 ff., 180 ff., 187 ff., 191 ff.; defense of sinking of, 181 ff.; settlement of, 212, 217, 219, 227, 236

Arbitration Treaty, 24, 27

Archibald, James, 197 ff.

Armenian, sinking of, 163

Asquith, Herbert, 298

Associated Press, 32 ff., 51, 179, 221

Atlanta, 102, 124, 338

Atlantic, 87

Austria-Hungary, Germany allied with, 2, 5; Serbian threat to, 7; battle front of, 287; desire for peace in, 348

Bagdad, 20

Bakmetieff, 141

Balkans, 7

Ballin, 409 ff.

Baltimore, 266

Baltimore *Sun*, 38

Bartelli, 261

Baumgarten, Prof., 20

Beachy Head, 246

Beecher, Henry Ward, 43

Belgium, invasion of, 30, 59, 130, 387; atrocities in, 39, 53; atrocities of, 64; American aid to, 128, 267; proposed restoration of, 278, 287, 329, 377, 392; deportations from, 302, 305, 308 ff., 339 ff.

Berchtold, Count, 7

Berlin, 6, 36, 42, 46, 50, 53, 69, 71, 95, 98 ff., 145, 154, 162, 164, 167 ff. 173, 178 ff., 197, 214, 220 ff., 230 ff., 243 ff., 247, 250, 254 ff., 259, 262, 264, 283, 285 ff., 290, 292 ff., 307, 309 ff., 314 ff., 320, 322 ff., 325, 340, 351, 358, 368 ff., 371, 373, 375, 379, 400, 402, 407

Bern *Freie Zeitung*, 44

Bernstorff, Count, in London, 1, 16; pre-war policy of, 1 ff.; arbitration efforts of, 6 ff.; Amer-

419